AF262002

# Empowering IT and CAT Teachers

## SECOND EDITION

EDITOR
Elsa Mentz

# CONTENTS

# CHAPTER 1

# Introduction to IT and CAT education

**Betty Breed**

# OBJECTIVES

**After completing this chapter, you should be able to:**

- *demonstrate knowledge and understanding of IT/CAT as part of the school curriculum;*

- *demonstrate knowledge and understanding of the nature and purpose of IT/CAT;*

- *understand and know the important concepts pertaining to a school subject curriculum;*

- *demonstrate knowledge and understanding of the typical successful IT/CAT learner and teacher; and*

- *critically evaluate each of the above mentioned aspects and formulate your own opinion on each of them.*

## 1.1  INTRODUCTION

In this chapter, the nature of Information Technology (IT) and Computer Applications Technology (CAT), as well as the purpose and aims of these subjects as they are presented at school-level, are discussed. Since the purpose and aims serve as guidelines for teaching and learning of the subjects, it is essential that the IT/CAT teacher should have the necessary knowledge of the national curriculum regarding these subjects and a sound understanding of the teaching-learning that should take place in the IT/CAT classroom in order to ensure that these objectives can be attained.

## 1.2  THE NATURE OF IT AND CAT AS SCHOOL SUBJECTS

Computer-related disciplines, in general, can be divided into three main categories. While some disciplines are particularly concerned with the acquisition of programming skills, others are more concerned with using computer applications effectively, while the third group deals with more technical aspects, such as hardware and networks. Since IT and CAT differ a great deal in terms of their practical components, their nature as school subjects will be examined and discussed separately.

### 1.2.1  Information Technology

IT is described as originating from and being a subset of the broader knowledge domain of information and communication technologies (ICTs), which is "the combination of networks, hardware and software and the means of communication, collaboration and engagement that enable the processing, management and exchange of data, information and knowledge" (DOE 2008b). IT as a school subject consequently addresses a wide spectrum of knowledge and skills as it consists of a practical and a theoretical component, which require different approaches regarding the teaching-learning of each of these components. IT thus "involves the integration of theory and practice as well as structured experiential learning which affords learners the opportunity to exercise and reinforce computer skills and knowledge acquired in the school and to provide orientation to further study in this field" (DOE 2003b).

The scope of IT as a school subject goes beyond the mere transformation of learners into programmers or application users or even technicians. IT as a school subject "is the study of the various interrelated physical and non-physical technologies used for the capturing of data, the processing of data into useful information and the management, presentation and dissemination of data. IT studies the activities that deal with the solution of problems through logical and computational thinking. It includes the physical and non-physical components for the electronic transmission, access, and manipulation of data and information" (DBE 2011b).

In 21st century life, the great demand for information processing and information communication makes it necessary for learners to be equipped with the skills to convert data into information and to be able to manage information effectively. The value of these information management skills, combined with the skills in programming, problem-solving and algorithm design done in Information

Technology ultimately goes beyond the field of computers, in that learners are equipped to apply them in all areas of their lives. The degree of precision required for programming, the higher-order thinking skills and the creative work that is required, equip learners with skills that enable them to play a role in society as productive and competent human beings.

## 1.2.2  Computer Applications Technology

CAT as school subject is seen as a subset of the broader knowledge domain of information and communication technologies (ICTs). ICTs are "the combination of networks, hardware and software as well as the means of communication, collaboration and engagement that enable the processing, management and exchange of data, information and knowledge" (DBE 2011a).

Per definition CAT as a school subject is "the study of the integrated components of a computer system (hardware and software) and the practical techniques for their efficient use and application to solve everyday problems. The solutions to problems are designed, managed and processed via end-user applications and communicated using appropriate information and communication technologies (ICTs)" (DBE 2011a).

Computer Applications Technology is responsive to the developmental vision of the country, that all South Africans will be equipped with marketable skills to cope in an information society (DOE 2003a).

---

## ACTIVITY 1.1

**Debate the following statement with regard to either IT or CAT:**

**"At school level the subject focuses on activities that deal with the solution of problems through logical thinking, information management and communication."**

**Motivate your opinion of this statement.**

---

## 1.3  THE INCLUSION OF IT AND CAT IN THE CURRICULUM FOR SA SCHOOLS

An important aspect of studying IT and/or CAT, and especially being a teacher of IT and/or CAT, is a clear understanding of why the subject is part of the school curriculum at all. At this level IT focuses on activities that deal with the solution of problems through logical and critical thinking, information management and information communication. IT also focuses on the development of computer applications by employing current development tools (DOE 2003b). CAT, on the other hand, at this level focuses on the effective use of information and communication technologies in an end-user computer applications environment in different sectors of society (DOE 2003a). In addition, both subjects foster awareness and an understanding of the social, economic and other implications of using computers.

The distinctly technological era in which we live means that the computer plays an ever-increasing role in our daily lives. Computers can be found wherever you go – in our homes, schools, businesses, hospitals, workplaces, and even in our cars. People can communicate via computers and gain access to information from all over the world. Owing to the digital revolution, technology keeps improving and infiltrates virtually all aspects of our daily existence. The exponential rate of change brought about by digital technologies at all levels of our lives is one of the aspects that necessitate the teaching-learning of IT and CAT at school level.

Considering that the purpose of education is to equip and prepare the learner for life, and to shape and develop the learner in order for him/her to become an independent, balanced adult who can play a role in society, IT and CAT thus are of paramount importance at school level. The knowledge, insight, understanding and skills, especially problem-solving skills, acquired by the learner through IT and/or CAT, should contribute to the development of competent citizens who are effective at all levels of society. Teachers should not only prepare learners for their future. We are also obliged to equip them with the relevant knowledge and skills that they need NOW. IT as a school subject enables learners to use ICT in social and economic applications, systems analysis, problem-solving, logical thinking, information management and communication (DOE 2003b). CAT, however, ensures that learners are able to make informed decisions when assessing, capturing and analysing data, manipulate, interpret and process information, apply problem-solving skills, use critical and creative thinking within the context of end-user computer applications, communicate effectively using different communication modes and tools, demonstrate effective management of information and engage in lifelong learning, effective job performance capabilities and jobs (DOE 2003a).

The importance of the subjects IT and CAT does not merely reside in the general use of computers in everyday life and in being competent citizens, but also in the career possibilities created for each learner through the presentation of the subject. The importance of training high-level computer experts to meet the urgent, global demand in this regard cannot be denied. IT or CAT at school level is the first step in this training process. IT specifically forms the underpinning basis for studies in computer science, information systems, engineering and the business sciences (DOE 2003b), while CAT ensures that learners can enter different career paths in a number of fields or apply these and related skills to create employment for themselves and for others (DOE 2003a).

> # ACTIVITY 1.2
>
> **Many countries abroad do not teach IT or CAT as a school subject, but only concentrate on computer literacy at school level. Briefly formulate and motivate your own point of view on the necessity for IT or CAT as a school subject.**

## 1.4   DEPARTMENTAL POLICY DOCUMENTS

The implementation of IT and CAT as school subjects is guided by the national departmental policy documents concerning basic education. Since these documents may change from time to time it is of the utmost importance that IT/CAT teachers obtain the latest version of the policy documents regarding the subject they are teaching. Teachers should study the documents thoroughly to ensure that they are implemented in a valid and reliable manner.

### 1.4.1  Aims of the policy documents

The policy documents of the national department concerned with education in the schooling sector represent policy statements for teaching and learning in South African schools. These documents usually comprise policy statements with respect to the content and assessment for each approved school subject, programme and promotion requirements, and a national protocol for assessment. Included in the documents regarding the content and assessment for each school subject, for example IT and CAT, one may find an explanation of the purpose of the curriculum, the principles it is based on, and the envisaged abilities of the learners it aims to produce. For the IT/CAT teacher one of the important aspects addressed in these documents is the description of the specific aims of the particular subject, in other words, what has to be achieved with the teaching-learning of IT/CAT. This aspect will be addressed in more detail later. Therefore, the aim of these policy documents is to prepare IT/CAT teachers for their task of the teaching, learning and assessment of IT/CAT.

## ACTIVITY 1.3

**Obtain a copy of the policy documents that are currently implemented with regard to the teaching-learning of IT or CAT as a school subject and identify the following:**

- **Purpose of the curriculum**
- **Principles the curriculum is based on**
- **Abilities of the learners it aims to produce**

### 1.4.2 Achieving the purpose of IT and CAT

Achievement of the general aims of the curriculum necessitates contemplating how the teaching-learning of IT/CAT should be approached, while keeping in mind what the purpose of the specific subject is. The following sections provide some guidelines on how the purpose of IT/CAT can be achieved in light of the abilities that the curriculum aims to develop in learners.

#### *1.4.2.1 Information Technology*

IT as a school subject "will enable learners to understand the principles of computing through the use of current programming languages, hardware and software, and how these apply to their daily lives, to the world of work and to their communities" (DOE 2003b). The subject is designed to specifically develop learners' higher-order thinking skills, technology skills, information skills, problem-solving skills, creative skills, collaborative skills and lifelong learning skills (DOE 2008b). The specific topics can be viewed in the CAPS documents (DOE 2011b). According to the DOE (2011b:10), the objectives can be achieved by providing learners with opportunities to:

1. use appropriate techniques and procedures to plan solutions and devise algorithms to solve problems using suitable techniques and tools;
2. understand and use appropriate communication technologies for information dissemination;
3. appreciate and comprehend the various systems technologies used in the development of a computer-based system;
4. understand that all ICT systems are built upon software engineering principles;
5. understand and use internet technologies for various tasks;
6. comprehend and apply the concepts of data and information management to understand how a knowledge-driven society functions; and
7. understand the social implications of ICTs and how to use ICT technologies responsibly.

### 1.4.2.2  Computer Applications Technology

The aim of CAT is to develop digitally enabled learners, and to create the opportunity for learners to use ICTs in an end-user environment to solve problems that relate to the processing, presentation, and communication of information. In CAT learners are developing the following skills:

- **Technology skills:** the ability to use the facilities of technology in an end-user environment and operate it purposefully and effectively;
- **Information skills:** the ability to access, retrieve, store, organise, manipulate, evaluate, maintain, analyse, interpret, present and communicate information, as well as use ICTs to process information;
- **Problem-solving skills:** the application of an authentic methodology for solving problems in an irregular range of cases;
- **Creative skills:** the ability to design, develop and produce creative and elegant solutions;
- **Collaborative skills:** the ability to develop multifaceted and multi-levelled systems through collaborative teamwork; and
- **Lifelong learning skills:** the ability to achieve and maintain the knowledge, skills, values and attitudes required in a dynamic knowledge domain (DOE 2008a).

The specific topics and subtopics of CAT can be viewed in the CAPS documents (DOE 2011a).

According to the DOE (2011b:10), CAT learners must be provided with opportunities that allow them to:

- use end-user software applications proficiently to produce solutions to problems within a defined scenario;
- understand the concepts of ICTs with regard to the technologies that make up a computing system;
- understand the various technologies, standards and protocols involved in the electronic transmission of data via a computer-based network;
- use the internet and the WWW and understand the role that the internet plays as part of the global information superhighway;
- find authentic and relevant information, process the information to draw conclusions, make decisions and communicate the findings in appropriate presentation media; and
- recognise the legal, ethical, environmental, social, security and health issues related to the use of ICTs and learn how to use ICTs responsibly.

## 1.4.3  Concluding remarks: Specific aims and content of IT and CAT as school subjects

As mentioned in 1.4.1 and 1.4.2, the policy documents regarding IT/CAT stipulate specific aims to be achieved with the teaching-learning thereof. These are meant to direct the teaching-learning of IT/CAT and ground the choice of content to be included in the subject. IT/CAT teachers should be familiar with these aims and how they relate to the prescribed content of the subject, as these have a direct influence on how the IT/CAT teacher plans work schedules and lessons. The compilation of work schedules will be outlined in 1.4.4, while lesson planning will be addressed in Chapter 2.

The policy documents also provide the weighting of the main topic areas of the content to be mastered in IT/CAT, as well as guidelines regarding time allocation to each of the topics per grade. IT/CAT teachers have to adhere to these guidelines when compiling work schedules.

## ACTIVITY 1.4

**Obtain a copy of the policy documents that are currently implemented with regard to the teaching-learning of IT or CAT as a school subject and make a summary of the following:**

**(a)  the general aims of the curriculum, and the skills envisaged for learners**

**(b)  the specific aims of IT/CAT**

**(c)  the main topic areas and subtopics for IT/CAT**

**(d)  the weighting of the main topic areas for IT/CAT**

**(e)  the approximate time allocation to the main topic areas for IT/CAT**

### 1.4.4  Important concepts pertaining to the teaching-learning of IT and CAT

In this textbook there are numerous definitions and descriptions of various concepts regarding the curriculum and the implementation of the curriculum and the teaching-learning of IT/CAT. Some of them are relevant now, while the others will be studied in detail in later chapters. For the meaningful use of this book, it is important to take notice of the following concepts:

### Teaching plan

A teaching plan indicates the minimum content to be covered per term. The sequence of the content or topics listed per term is usually not prescribed, but it serves as an aid to help teachers to design their own work schedules. Suggested teaching plans might sometimes be provided in the policy documents regarding the teaching-learning of IT/CAT. Lately, there is a tendency to combine the teaching plan and work schedule.

### Work schedule

A work schedule for IT/CAT refers to the specific planning of teaching the content in appropriate sequence and pace per grade for a period of one year. Suggested work schedules might sometimes be provided by the Department of Basic Education, but as the lengths of school quarters vary from year to year, and schools' programmes differ from one another and from one year to the next, work schedules should be adapted accordingly on a year-to-year basis. The compilation of the work schedules for Grades 10 to 12 remains the responsibility of the IT/CAT teacher(s) involved.

## Lesson plan

A lesson plan for IT/CAT comprises daily, weekly, monthly or thematic planning. Therefore, a lesson plan should not necessarily be conducted per period, since the same theme or topic might be dealt with over a number of periods. The compilation of a lesson plan is the responsibility of the teacher(s) involved.

## Lesson objectives

Lesson objectives for IT/CAT are statements which indicate what should be achieved as far as the teaching and learning of IT/CAT for the specific lesson is concerned. These outcomes describe the knowledge, skills and values that learners should have acquired upon completion of the lesson.

## Assessment

Assessment is a continuous planned process of identifying, gathering and interpreting information on the performance of learners. Assessment will be examined and explained in further detail in Chapter 4.

### 1.4.4.1  Suggested format of IT/CAT work schedules

Work schedules differ from teaching plans in that work schedules are specific in terms of assessment and learning and teaching support materials (LTSMs). Grades 10, 11 and 12 each require their own IT/CAT work schedule. The purpose of such a schedule for a particular grade is to indicate the sequence of and pace at which the subject's content and contexts will be presented in that grade. A thoroughly compiled work schedule ensures that the intended learning objectives would have been achieved at the end of the year. It is the responsibility of the IT/CAT teachers for a specific grade to develop the year-long IT/CAT work schedule for that grade.

An IT/CAT work schedule should be a carefully prepared document that reflects what teaching, learning and assessment will take place in the 36 to 40 weeks of the school year. Serfontein (2009) suggested the following approach to develop a work schedule for a particular grade:

**STEP 1**  **Package the content:** Study the prescribed content for the grade and the suggested teaching plan for the grade, and package it into topics according to natural and authentic links. It is possible to package the content into such a level of detail that it could become the lesson topics for lesson planning.

**STEP 2**  **Sequence the content:** Determine the sequence in which you want to present the topics you have identified.

**STEP 3**  **Pace the content:** Determine how much time will be spent on each topic in accordance with the time allocation and weighting provided in the policy documents.

**STEP 4**  **Determine forms of assessment:** Identify the forms of assessment that will appropriately address each of the identified topics.

**STEP 5**    **Identify appropriate LTSMs:** Consider the LTSMs (resources) available to you and your learners, and identify the LTSMs for each topic that will appropriately address and support it.

Based on the above development process it is recommended that an IT/CAT work schedule should include the following:

- Available weeks in the school calendar for IT/CAT teaching, learning and assessment – numbered with starting dates. This will be used to sequence the presentation of the lesson topics.
- Time allocation for every lesson topic.
- Lesson topics – these are the result of packaging the content of the subject into topics according to natural and authentic links. It is recommended that the content is packaged into such a level of detail that the topics could become lesson topics.
- LTSM – this refers to the printed, internet and other resources that will be used for every lesson topic. The textbook sections and other resources that will be used for each lesson topic must be indicated specifically.
- Assessment – the forms of assessment that will be used for every lesson topics. Also indicate where and when the specific assessment tasks are scheduled. It is important to provide for time that will be used for examinations.

## 1.5    PROFILE OF THE SUCCESSFUL IT/CAT LEARNER

In this section, some of the most common qualities and characteristics that can be identified in successful IT/CAT learners are summarised. However, we do acknowledge that there are other determinants, such as the knowledge, skills, strategies and teaching-learning approach of the teacher, which contribute to learners' success. Self-directed learning as a teaching-learning approach has proved to be invaluable with regard to learners' success. Self-directed learning goes hand in hand with the quality of lifelong learning, which is intended to be one of the skills developed by both IT and CAT. Self-directed learners take responsibility for their own learning by diagnosing what they want to learn, setting learning goals, identifying appropriate resources, implementing appropriate strategies to achieve their goals, and evaluating if they have achieved their goals (Knowles 1975). Self-directed learners who also display most the qualities and characteristic listed below will most probably succeed in IT and/or CAT.

Furthermore, because of the difference in the nature of IT and CAT, it is obvious that there will be a difference in the profiles of the successful IT learner and the successful CAT learner.

### 1.5.1  The successful IT learner

The comprehensiveness of IT as a subject calls for rather a wide variety of abilities, skills and characteristics to ensure a successful learner in IT. These include:

- a preference for working with symbols (Wu, Dale, and Bethel 1998);
- a preference for structured and precise work (Teague 1998);

- the ability to think logically (Chmura 1998);
- the ability to arrange steps in the correct order (Chmura 1998);
- the ability to remember detail (Chmura 1998);
- the ability to visualise information (Chmura 1998);
- the ability to verbalise own thoughts (Chmura 1998);
- good abstract reasoning skills (Chmura 1998);
- good decision-making skills (Byrne and Lyons 2001);
- the ability to make conceptual presentations (Robins, Rountree, and Rountree 2003);
- the ability to analyse, synthesise and evaluate (Deek 1999);
- a well-structured domain knowledge (Deek 1999);
- syntactic, semantic and practical knowledge of the programming relevant language (Deek 1999);
- patience (Chmura 1998);
- determination (Chmura 1998);
- motivation (Chmura 1998);
- good working and study habits (Chmura 1998);
- the ability to plan, monitor and evaluate own progress (Gourgey 2001); and
- continuous reflection on both process and product (Fekete *et al.* 2000).

In an extensive study on the characteristics of successful programmers, Sterling and Brinthaupt (2003) identified criteria for individual and group programming settings. Shared criteria for both individual and group programming settings included being creative, conscientious and enjoys solving problems. Interpersonal cooperation skills were also important for group settings. Thus, having the ability to cooperate effectively is important for any successful programmer.

## 1.5.2   The successful CAT learner

In accordance with the nature of CAT (see 1.2.2) and with the aims of CAT as a school subject (see 1.4.2) in mind, the learner that will most likely succeed in CAT will be the one who, according to DOE (2008a), shows evidence of:

- sound communication skills;
- language proficiency;
- fine motor skills;
- logical and practical thinking skills;
- creativity;
- problem-solving skills;
- visual literacy;
- a willingness to learn and apply skills in different situations;

- an ability to communicate and collaborate with others; and

- a willingness to engage in lifelong learning.

Learners' performance and success in IT/CAT is not determined only by their knowledge, cognitive and meta-cognitive skills. Some other determinants that may to some extent contribute to their performance and success include aspects such as personality traits, as well as their interests, beliefs and attitudes.

## ACTIVITY 1.5

**Use the internet, electronic databases and/or the library to find three articles or books on the characteristics, skills and abilities of the successful IT/CAT learner. Write a report of approximately 300 words on your findings from the literature.**

## 1.6 PROFILE OF THE SUCCESSFUL IT/CAT TEACHER

Just as there are no hard and fast qualities and characteristics for being a successful IT/CAT learner, there are no specific rules and qualities for being a successful IT/CAT teacher. However, if you become aware that learners are keen to come to the IT/CAT class, that they are excited about what they learn, and that they are willing to try to master the learning content by themselves, it might be an indication that you are doing something right!

Stephenson (2007) mentions five qualities of exemplary teachers that fit well into our current approach to education. According to Stephenson (2007) these teachers:

- *use a problem-solving approach*: learners are allowed to examine problems from different angles and perspectives and formulate solutions;

- *focus on the real world*: learners are motivated by having them create real-world artefacts and encouraging them to understand the essential link between the problem, the user, and the solution;

- *explicitly emphasise design*: the design process is taught and used, ensuring that learners master the steps involved in designing, creating, testing, and debugging software in the case of IT, or the steps involved in designing a database or a website in CAT;

- *create a welcoming environment*: classrooms are made welcoming environments for all learners, and creative ways are found to engage all learners with relevant examples and exercises; and

- *model lifelong learning*: the teachers serve as role models for their learners by continuing to enhance their own teaching and technology skills and by exploring new ideas and new technologies.

Although not all successful teachers display exactly the same characteristics, qualities, skills and competencies, most of the following in the more detailed list should be true regarding the successful IT/CAT teacher. The successful teacher:

- has adequate academic and professional training;
- displays a sound knowledge of and interest in IT/CAT and related subjects;
- has a disposition to lifelong learning and the ability to do original, scientific research on the subject;
- is enthusiastic about his/her subject and stays up to date with developments in computer and information technology (SACTE 1995);
- ensures that every learner is aware of the value of the subject, whether for personal, occupational or further training purposes;
- is aware of the demands on and standards required of novices in IT/CAT;
- is able to identify the needs of different learners based on their abilities and methods of learning, and differentiates accordingly (SACTE 1995);
- is well organised and has clear ideas about his/her daily teaching plans, assignments, and grading policies (Tolani 2007);
- links to the experience and level of development of the learner and then moves from the known to the unknown;
- uses real-world problems or scenarios to guide teaching-learning activities;
- confronts learners with problems and situations that they will encounter in practice;
- formulates objectives clearly so that learners know what has to be achieved and what is required of them (SACTE 1995);
- uses a variety of teaching and learning strategies to prevent boredom (SACTE 1995);
- uses a variety of learning aids effectively (SACTE 1995);
- encourages learners to probe topics further, to analyse matters more critically, and to look beyond the obvious (Tolani 2007);
- motivates learners to trust their own abilities, to take chances, and to experiment with different approaches (Tolani 2007);
- has the ability to assess learners' performance and abilities by setting realistic and accountable tasks;
- sees to it that every learner in class is actively involved and works according to his/her optimal tempo (SACTE 1995);
- creates opportunities for the more advanced learners to express their knowledge and skills, thus preventing them from becoming bored (SACTE 1995);
- is kind, yet firm;
- takes an interest in all learners and treats everyone with respect; and
- has the ability to win the trust of every learner by being honest and fair.

## 1.7 CONCLUSION

In this chapter, IT/CAT as part of the school curriculum, its nature and purpose, the national policy documents, the aims of IT/CAT as school subjects, and the typical successful IT/CAT learner and teacher were discussed. The information gained in this chapter can be used as a framework to position the building blocks (knowledge and skills) of the next chapters in the appropriate place in your conceptualisation framework of IT/CAT as school subjects.

# ASSIGNMENT 1

**1.1** Formulate and motivate your opinion on the view that the purpose and aims of IT/CAT will equip the learner to fulfill his/her role in the community as an independent and competent citizen.

**1.2** Critically evaluate the possibility of making IT/CAT a compulsory school subject for all learners from Grade 10 to Grade 12.

**1.3** Study the specific aims provided in the policy documents for IT/CAT, as well as the main topic areas of the content of IT/CAT. Critically discuss whether the main topic areas satisfy the specific aims set for the subject. Motivate your answer by providing examples from the content prescribed for IT/CAT.

**1.4** Design a presentation of approximately 10 slides that you can use to promote IT/CAT as a subject. Your presentation must be aimed at convincing learners and parents of the advantages and value of the subject.

**1.5** Write a report of approximately 300 words to explain what you, as a practising teacher, will do to ensure you "stay up-to-date with developments in ICTs" and comply with the requirement of "lifelong learning and the ability to do original, scientific research on the subject".

## REFERENCES

Byrne, P. and Lyons, G. 2001. The effect of student attributes on success in programming. *ACM SIGCSE Bulletin*, 33(3):49-52. https://doi.org/10.1145/507758.377467

Chmura, G.A. 1998. What abilities are necessary for success in computer science? *ACM SIGCSE Bulletin*, 30(4):55a-58a. https://doi.org/10.1145/306286.306316

Deek, F.P. 1999. A framework for an automated problem solving and program development environment. *Transactions of the Society for Design and Process Science*, 3(3):1-13.

DBE (Department of Basic Education) see South Africa. Department of Basic Education.

DOE (Department of Education) see South Africa. Department of Education.

Fekete, A., Kay, J., Kingston, J. and Wimalaratne, K. 2000. Supporting reflection in introductory computer science. *ACM SIGCSE Bulletin*, 32(1):144-148. https://doi.org/10.1145/331795.331844

Gourgey, A.F. 2001. Metacognition in basic skills instruction. (In H.J. Hartman, ed. *Metacognition in Learning and Instruction: Theory, research and practice*. Dordrecht: Kluwer, pp. 17-32.) https://doi.org/10.1007/978-94-017-2243-8_2

Knowles, M.S. 1975. *Self-directed learning: A guide for learners and teachers*. Englewood Cliffs, NJ: Prentice Hall.

Robins, A., Rountree, J. and Rountree, N. 2003. Learning and teaching programming: A review and discussion. *Computer Science Education*, 13(2):137-172. https://doi.org/10.1076/csed.13.2.137.14200

SACTE (South African College for Teacher Education). 1995. *Study Manual Teaching Method of Computer Science: Theoretical work*. Pretoria: College of Education of South Africa.

Serfontein, C.P. 2009. Information Technology learning programmes. (In E. Mentz, E.A. Breed, L. Goosen, J.H. Hahn, M.H. Havenga, C.P. Serfontein and U. Wassermann. *How to do IT: Teaching and learning Information Technology*. Orkney: EFJS Printers, pp. 18-37.)

South Africa. Department of Basic Education. 2011a. *Curriculum and assessment policy statement: Computer Applications Technology*. Pretoria: DBE.

South Africa. Department of Basic Education. 2011b. *Curriculum and assessment policy statement: Information Technology*. Pretoria: DBE.

South Africa. Department of Education. 2003a. *National curriculum statement. Grades 10-12 (General)*. Computer Applications Technology. Pretoria.

South Africa. Department of Education. 2003b. *National curriculum statement. Grades 10-12 (General)*. Information Technology. Pretoria.

South Africa. Department of Education. 2008a. *National curriculum statement. Grades 10-12 (General). Learning programme guidelines*. Computer Applications Technology. Pretoria.

South Africa. Department of Education. 2008b. *National curriculum statement. Grades 10-12 (General). Learning programme guidelines*. Information Technology. Pretoria.

Stephenson, C. 2007. *Computer science in the classroom: challenges and opportunities*. http://www.csta.acm.org/Publications/UCIPres.pdf

Sterling, G.D. and Brinthaupt, T.M. 2003. Faculty and industry conceptions of successful computer programmers. *Journal of information systems education*, 14(4):417-424.

Tolani, R. 2007. *Characteristics of great teachers*. http://www.educationcrossing. com/article/index.php?id=470011

Teague, J. 1998. Personality type, career preference and implications for computer science recruitment and teaching. (In *Association for computing machinery*. Paper read at the 3rd Australasian conference on computer science education held in Brisbane, Australia, pp. 155-163.) https://doi.org/10.1145/289393.289416

Wu, C.C., Dale, N.B. and Bethel, L.J.. 1998. Conceptual models and cognitive learning styles in teaching recursion. *Special Interest Group on Computer Science Education bulletin*, 30(1):292-296. https://doi.org/10.1145/273133.274315

# Lesson planning

## Carl Serfontein & Betty Breed

# OBJECTIVES

**After completing this chapter, you should be able to:**

- *explain the instructional principles for IT/CAT teaching and learning;*

- *discuss and apply the fundamentals of lesson planning;*

- *develop a balanced set of IT/CAT lesson objectives;*

- *investigate the applicability of different teaching strategies and methods for IT/CAT; and*

- *prepare a lesson for IT/CAT.*

## 2.1 INTRODUCTION

A school curriculum, as prescribed by the country's educational authorities, expresses the knowledge, skills and values to be learned at school level (DBE 2011) and aims to provide guidance for teachers in facilitating the learning of the specific subject. The curriculum of each school subject prescribes the content that has to be covered for that subject in each grade. It is the task of teachers to use the prescribed content and design their own work schedules and lesson plans. The design and implementation of work schedules were discussed in Chapter 1. The aim of this chapter is to introduce you to teaching and learning principles for IT/CAT, and the fundamentals and process of lesson planning.

## 2.2 TEACHING AND LEARNING PRINCIPLES FOR IT/CAT

Teaching and learning principles provide fundamental guidelines for approaches in teaching and learning. It means that the teaching and learning activities we plan and the intended objectives of a lesson must be based on and comply with one or more such principles. The following four principles provide a theoretical foundation for IT/CAT teachers in planning and conducting student-centred lessons:

### 2.2.1 Principle of knowledge construction

This principle assumes that knowledge cannot simply be transmitted by the teacher or an instructional system to learners. It proclaims that learners construct their own knowledge, that is, they make their own meaning (Jonassen, Peck and Wilson 1999). In the context of an IT/CAT lesson it means that learners should be given opportunities to construct their own knowledge. This can be achieved through learning activities in which learners interact, investigate, explore, experiment, experience and apply the IT/CAT learning content themselves. Through such interactions and experiences with the IT/CAT learning content they will be able to make their own meanings of the concepts involved. The role of the IT/CAT teacher is to design and develop opportunities for learners to construct their own knowledge and meaning, and to help them by guiding, supporting and coaching them in this meaning-making process.

### 2.2.2 Principle of active learning

This principle argues that the knowledge we construct (or the meaning we make) emerges from activities, interactions and experiences we have with phenomena in the world (the learning content). In other words, knowledge is embedded in activity (Jonassen, Peck and Wilson 1999). The emphasis here is on activity, which is the active involvement of learners. This is made possible by creating and providing learning opportunities in which learners are actively examining, exploring, experimenting and interacting with learning content. The role of the IT/CAT teacher is to create and provide learning opportunities that actively involve learners. There is a very close relationship between this principle and the principle of knowledge construction – they go hand in hand. One cannot have one's own knowledge construction of a concept without directly and interactively experiencing that concept.

### 2.2.3  Principle of social interaction

Knowledge construction does not only occur individually, but also in interactions with fellow learners and teachers in a process that is described as a social negotiation of meaning. Humans are social creatures who rely on feedback from fellow humans to determine the validity of their own beliefs (Jonassen, Hernandez-Serrano and Choi 2000). This principle emphasises IT/CAT learners working together in discussing, debating, discoursing and reaching consensus on the meaning of things. The IT/CAT teacher's responsibility in this regard is to arrange collaborative learning opportunities in which learners perform learning activities together, share and discuss experiences, understandings and meanings, and reach consensus on the meaning of things through dialogue.

### 2.2.4  Principle of situated learning

This principle proclaims that part of the meaning of a concept is embedded in the real-life context from which it originates. The knowledge of phenomena that learners construct and the associated skills they develop include information about the context in which they experience those phenomena. The knowledge that learners construct consists of not only the ideas (content), but also of the context in which it was acquired. So, the more directly and interactively learners experience phenomena in meaningful real-life contexts, the more meaning about it they are likely to construct (Jonassen, Peck and Wilson 1999). For IT/CAT learners to perceive and experience learning as meaningful and relevant, it must occur in contexts that are grounded in reality. Such contexts must engage them in real-life problems that foster and encourage them to make direct connections between the new learning content being taught and their existing prior knowledge. The basic message of this principle is that new learning content should be presented to learners in real-life and meaningful contexts that bring the real world into the classroom. By interacting with and experiencing the learning content in real-life and meaningful contexts, the meaning that learners make of the concepts involved will not only include understanding of the concepts, but also of the contexts from which it originates. The challenge for the IT/CAT teacher is to plan and create authentic (real-life related) and meaningful contexts and scenarios that involve real-world problems and tasks which will allow IT/CAT learners to explore, discuss and meaningfully construct their own understanding of concepts and relationships.

These four teaching and learning principles provide guidelines and a basis for planning student-centred teaching, learning and assessment activities in IT/CAT. While complying to these educational principles, self-directed learning can be promoted by allowing learners more control over learning situations (Merriam, Caffarella and Baumgartner 2007). Teaching-learning strategies that allow for more learner control include, amongst others, cooperative learning and problem-based learning. The teacher then facilitates the learners' personal goalsetting, identification and implementation of appropriate resources and learning activities, monitoring of their progress, and evaluation of the product and process (Bosch, Mentz and Goede 2019). In a formal educational setting it is generally not possible to give learners full control of the learning objectives and activities, but they can be guided to take control of certain aspects of their own learning, such as setting personal learning goals within the parameters of the formal set objectives, and implementation of alternative resources and learning strategies.

## 2.3 FUNDAMENTALS OF LESSON PLANNING

Lesson planning is a highly professional activity and one of the most important skills that you will have to acquire in order to become an effective IT/CAT teacher. It is a multifaceted activity that requires sound knowledge of and skills in aspects such as the content of the subject, how learners learn (i.e. learning theories such as behaviourist and constructivist learning), teaching and learning principles, teaching-learning strategies and assessment strategies. You will be required to plan lessons many times throughout your professional career as an IT/CAT teacher. So, lesson planning is a very important part of being an IT/CAT teacher. The following is a brief introduction to and an overview of lesson planning:

### 2.3.1 The meaning of a lesson

A lesson can be described as a unit of teaching and learning around a particular topic (or theme) in which a coherent series of teaching and learning activities are performed in order to reach specific learning objectives. Its duration is not necessarily equivalent to a period in the school timetable, but is determined by how long it takes to complete the activities planned for the lesson topic – it might require one or several periods.

### 2.3.2 The necessity of lesson planning

As with any task, you cannot expect your lessons to succeed without proper planning. As a professional teacher you should be able to plan, develop, facilitate learning and evaluate your professional practice (teaching-learning events). You need to know beforehand what a lesson's intended objectives are, what the content is, how the lesson will be sequenced, what teaching-learning strategy you will use, what your role should be, what activities your learners should do, and how they will be assessed. On completion of a lesson, you should also reflect on ways of improving your teaching practice.

### 2.3.3 The advantages of lesson planning

Lesson planning:

- ensures familiarity with the intended learning objectives and lesson content;
- gives you confidence that comes from knowing what you are doing;
- shows learners that the teacher is prepared;

- gives structure and direction to a lesson;
- helps to ensure optimum time management; and
- ensures that teaching and learning activities are based on fundamental principles and not planned haphazardly.

The less experienced teacher obviously needs more detailed lesson planning. As you gain experience the need to plan in detail will lessen, but even the most experienced teachers must still give careful thought to their lesson plans if they are to be successful in the long run.

## 2.3.4  The basic ingredients of a lesson plan

Simply put, a lesson plan is a document that explains how a lesson will progress. A lesson plan has three essential ingredients:

- **Lesson objectives:** In every lesson a teacher expects learners to have learned something at the end of the lesson. This expectation is described in terms of one or more objectives. Lesson objectives are knowledge, skills and values about the subject content of the lesson (or lesson topic) that learners are expected to achieve.

- **Activities:** On the one hand, there are learning activities – learners learn by doing. On the other hand, there are teaching activities – it is the activities of the teacher that prompt learners to do certain activities. Teaching and learning activities are planned to be performed in a certain way – not haphazardly. In other words, there is a specific methodology involved that is based on aspects such as official policy, teaching and learning principles, and teaching and learning strategies and methods.

- **Assessment:** Lastly, a lesson plan should include activities that will determine whether the objectives of the lesson have been reached.

Therefore, a lesson plan can also be described as a document that explains the learning objectives that learners are expected to reach in the lesson, the teaching-learning approach that will be followed, the teaching and learning strategies and the activities that are planned for the lesson, and how the achievement of the expected objectives will be assessed.

## 2.3.5  The process of lesson planning

The process of planning a lesson includes the following:

- **Decide on a lesson topic:** If the IT/CAT work schedule is developed to such a level of detail that the IT/CAT content is already packaged into lesson topics, then they are ready for development into lesson plans. If not, then the content topics of the IT/CAT work schedule must be divided into topics that represent units of deliverable learning events.

- **Do a content analysis of the topic:** A lesson topic is normally made up of a number of different components, facts, concepts, parts and/or elements. Content analysis of the lesson topic means that you have to investigate and identify the essential components (i.e. facts, concepts, parts and/or elements) of the lesson topic. The reason we do this is that every one of these essential components provides us with a basis for writing a lesson objective. Not everybody will identify the same set of essential components, but that is not really a problem. If done properly, the content analysis of different teachers will in most cases be similar.

- ▸ **Develop expected objectives for the lesson:** At this stage the IT/CAT teacher is expected to identify and develop the specific knowledge, skills and values that he or she expects the learners to have achieved at the end of the lesson. These are described as lesson objectives. The development of lesson objectives will be discussed in detail in 2.4.

- ▸ **Decide on the teaching-learning strategies to be employed:** During this step, the teacher needs to decide upon a teaching-learning strategy, like cooperative learning, problem-based learning, pair programming or whatever strategy appropriate to achieve the lesson objectives. This will directly determine the type of teaching and learning activities planned for the lesson.

- ▸ **Describe the teaching and learning activities:** Here the IT/CAT teacher will describe the teaching and learning activities that he or she plans, based on the chosen teaching-learning strategy. Teaching and learning activities have a very close relationship – it is the activities of the teacher that prompt learners to perform certain activities. The teacher, on the other hand, observes and monitors the learning activities and, based on his or her professional insight, will respond to them in order to ensure that lesson progress is in the required direction.

- ▸ **Identify and describe the form(s) of assessment:** The purpose of this is to determine whether the learners have achieved the lesson objectives, and whether the teaching was effective.

In the next sections, you will be introduced to the various aspects of lesson planning. Here the focus is specifically on teaching and learning of IT/CAT. Only principles, processes, strategies and models that are relevant to IT/CAT teaching and learning are introduced.

## 2.4 DEVELOPMENT OF IT/CAT LESSON OBJECTIVES

Setting lesson objectives is an important aspect of lesson planning. In every lesson a teacher expects learners to achieve something at the end of the lesson. This expectation is described in terms of one or more lesson objectives. It describes the knowledge, skills and values that a learner should know and be able to demonstrate at the end of an IT/CAT lesson. These objectives are not specified or described in the IT/CAT curriculum documents. It is the responsibility of every IT/CAT teacher to develop lesson objectives for every lesson that he or she plans, because these objectives give direction and purpose to the lesson. IT/CAT lessons should be built on and be developed around lesson objectives. The following is a brief introduction to and an overview of the development of IT/CAT lesson objectives:

### 2.4.1 The meaning of an IT/CAT lesson objective

It describes the knowledge, skills and values that a learner should know and be able to demonstrate at the end of an IT/CAT lesson.

### 2.4.2 The importance of IT/CAT lesson objectives

The following are some reasons why it is important to formulate lesson objectives:

- IT/CAT lesson objectives enable you as an IT/CAT teacher to know in advance what learners are expected to know and be able to do at the end of an IT/CAT lesson;

- It provides direction and purpose to an IT/CAT lesson that is essential for lesson planning; and

- It also enables IT/CAT learners to know in advance what they will be expected to know and be able to do at the end of a lesson.

### 2.4.3   The responsibility for developing IT/CAT lesson objectives

Every individual IT/CAT teacher is responsible for developing lesson objectives for every IT/CAT lesson.

### 2.4.4   The difficulty of developing IT/CAT lesson objectives

Once an IT/CAT teacher is skilled and experienced in lesson objective development as part of IT/CAT lesson planning, he or she will be able to do it in a matter of minutes.

### 2.4.5   An appropriate number of lesson objectives for an IT/CAT lesson

The number of lesson objectives depends on the complexity of the lesson topic, but on average three to six lesson outcomes should suffice for most IT/CAT lessons.

### 2.4.6   The format of IT/CAT lesson objectives

Lesson objectives should be written in the following format:

---

**"At the end of the lesson the learner should be able to [...A ...] [... B ...]."**

**A = an action verb that introduces an action that a learner should be able to perform, for example recall, give, name, describe, explain, apply, use, develop, compare, distinguish, propose, evaluate, criticise, judge, and so on. The action verb indicates at what cognitive (intellectual) level the learner should be able to perform that action.**

**B = the aspect with which the learner should be able to perform an action at the end of the lesson.**

**Example: At the end of the lesson the learner should be able to describe the economic reasons for using computers. In this example the action verb A = "describe", and the aspect B = "the economic reasons for using computers".**

---

### 2.4.7   The cognitive levels that could be used in developing IT/CAT lesson objectives

We use taxonomy of cognitive levels for this purpose. Taxonomy of cognitive levels provides us with a number of categories (or levels) into which you can classify cognitive activities. One of the taxonomies of cognitive levels that is often used for the development of lesson objectives is Bloom's taxonomy with knowledge, comprehension, application, analysis, synthesis and evaluation as its six cognitive levels. The Revised Bloom's taxonomy also has six stages, namely remember, understand, apply, analyse, evaluate and create, but these are viewed as a cognitive processing dimension instead of a cumulative hierarchy (Pickard 2007). Another known taxonomy is that of Marzano (Intel 2012) with knowledge retrieval, comprehension, analysis and knowledge utilisation as its components, where each process is composed of all the previous processes.

When developing IT/CAT lesson objectives the objective is to develop a balanced set of lesson objectives that cover the whole spectrum of cognitive levels of the taxonomy. For example, it is no good developing a number of IT/CAT lesson objectives that only deal with "knowledge" and none that deal with the other levels. Remember that in traditional teaching, the focus tended to be more on content knowledge, but in the information age and student-centred approach we consider it important that learners should not only have knowledge, but they should also be able to use and apply skills and do so in responsible ways that benefit society (values).

The process of developing lesson objectives for a specific IT/CAT lesson topic is explained in more detail in a later section. Let us explore the use of the Revised Bloom's taxonomy in this process first.

### 2.4.7.1 *Revised Bloom's taxonomy of learning outcomes*

The taxonomy we will illustrate is the Revised Bloom's taxonomy, which is a highly-regarded and proven taxonomy that is used extensively worldwide. Benjamin Bloom originally identified three domains of learning objectives, namely the cognitive, affective and psychomotor domains. However, instead of considering all three in the same taxonomy, he developed one for the cognitive domain only. The original taxonomy of cognitive levels was revised and the six cognitive levels of this taxonomy are described below from the simplest to the most complex (Pickard 2007), each with appropriate action verbs and an example of a lesson objective on that cognitive level. You will find that some verbs appear in more than one level, which is possible depending on how it is used in a question.

**LEVEL 1**   **Remember (knowledge):** This level involves shallow processing like the act of remembering and recalling specific facts and other information without necessarily understanding it.

      **Action verbs for remember:** arrange, choose, collect, define, describe, duplicate, explain, label, locate, list, match, memorise, name, omit, order, quote, recall, recite, recognise, relate, repeat, reproduce, select, show, state, tabulate, and tell.

      **Example of a lesson objective (not limited to only IT or only CAT):**

      **For IT:** The learner should be able to *name* the various steps in problem-solving (or program development) in IT, for example: (1) define the problem, (2) outline the solution, (3) develop the outline into an algorithm, (4) code the algorithm into a program, (5) test the program on a computer, and (6) document the program.

      **For CAT:** The learner should be able to *list* three functions of an operating system.

**LEVEL 2**    **Understand (comprehension):** This category of cognitive activities represents the first level of understanding and learners must not only be able to recall facts and other information, but must understand the information and be able to describe its meaning.

**Action verbs for understand:** associate, classify, contrast, defend, describe, differentiate, discuss, distinguish, estimate, extend, explain, express, give example, identify, illustrate, indicate, infer, interpret, judge, locate, match, paraphrase, predict, recognise, report, represent, restate, review, rewrite, select, show, summarise, and translate.

**Example of a lesson objective:**

**For IT:** The learner should be able to *explain* the steps in the IT problem-solving process.

**For CAT:** The learner should be able to *discuss* the functions of an operating system.

**LEVEL 3**    **Apply:** This refers to the ability to use (or apply) information (e.g. rules, processes, methods, principles or theories) in new situations.

**Action verbs for apply:** apply, calculate, change, choose, classify, complete, construct, demonstrate, dramatise, employ, examine, explain, generalise, illustrate, interpret, judge, manipulate, modify, operate, organise, practise, produce, propose, relate, schedule, select, show, sketch, solve, use, and write.

**Example of a lesson objective:**

**For IT:** The learner should be able to *apply* a problem-solving methodology to solve a programming problem.

**For CAT:** The learner should be able to *calculate* values using standard spreadsheet functions.

**LEVEL 4**    **Analyse:** A learning objective on this level refers to the ability to break down a whole into its component parts. In this way the elements embedded in a whole are identified and the relations amongst the elements are recognised.

**Action verbs for analyse:** analyse, appraise, arrange, categorise, classify, compare, contrast, criticise, differentiate, discriminate, distinguish, divide, examine, formulate, identify, infer, investigate, order, propose, select, separate, and test.

**Example of a lesson objective:**

**For IT:** The learner should be able to *distinguish* the critical stages of a process in a flow chart.

**For CAT:** The learner should be able to *identify* the different fields that were inserted during the design of a given form and explain why the different fields in the form are appropriate or not appropriate.

**LEVEL 5**    **Evaluate:** At this level, judgements are made and explained, based on certain criteria.

       **Action verbs for evaluate:** appraise, argue, assess, attach, choose, compare, convince, conclude, contrast, criticise, defend, decide, discriminate, estimate, grade, interpret, judge, justify, measure, predict, prove, rank, rate, recommend, score, select, support, test, value.

       **Example of a lesson objective:**

       **For IT:** The learner should be able to *criticise* a graphical user interface designed by a fellow learner, based on criteria applicable to good interface design.

       **For CAT:** The learner should be able to *criticise* an existing application form, based on criteria applicable to good form design.

**LEVEL 6**    **Create (synthesis):** This category refers to the ability to put elements together to form a new whole.

       **Action verbs for synthesis:** arrange, assemble, collect, combine, compile, compose, construct, create, design, develop, formulate, generalise, hypothesise, integrate, invent, manage, modify, organise, plan, prepare, produce, propose, rearrange, rewrite, reconstruct, set up, substitute, write.

       **Example of a lesson objective:**

       **FOR IT:** The learner should be able to *design* an algorithm using the variables and processing steps.

       **For CAT:** The learner should be able to *design* a new application form by taking into considerations the purpose of the form, professional layout of forms, similar forms in praxis and suitable word processing functions to use during the design of forms.

When applying the Revised Bloom's taxonomy for the cognitive domain, it is easy to see that it is well suited for teaching problem-solving in IT and CAT. This is because there is an almost direct relationship between the steps in the problem-solving process and the levels of the taxonomy.

The use of taxonomy of cognitive levels in developing IT/CAT lesson objectives is explained and demonstrated in the next section. Taxonomies are also used in developing assessment instruments (refer to the chapter on assessment).

# ACTIVITY 2.1

**Classify the lesson objectives in the following groups according to the Revised Bloom's taxonomy. IT students will do Groups A and B, while CAT students will do Groups C and D.**

| GROUP A: The learner should be able to: | Revised Bloom level |
|---|---|
| list data validation techniques | |
| explain a data validation technique | |
| employ a data validation technique in a program | |
| choose a data validation technique for a specific problem | |
| examine the data validation technique used in an existing program | |
| judge the effectiveness of a data validation technique used in a computer program | |
| GROUP B: The learner should be able to: | |
| list three types of user interfaces | |
| distinguish between a good and poor user interface from a visual perspective | |
| describe a graphical user interface | |
| classify a given group of user interfaces | |
| criticise a given user interface | |
| design and develop a user interface | |
| identify the shortcomings of a given user interface | |
| GROUP C: The learner should be able to: | |
| list the factors affecting the overall performance of a computer system | |
| explain how the technique of pipelining improves the performance of a computer system | |
| propose how the performance of a given computer configuration can be improved | |
| GROUP D: The learner should be able to: | |
| list the number formats that can be used in a spreadsheet | |
| explain the difference between the number formats General, Number and Currency | |
| employ the number formats General, Number, Currency, Date and Time in a spreadsheet | |
| choose appropriate number formats for specific data in a spreadsheet | |
| examine the number formats used in an existing spreadsheet | |
| judge the appropriateness of the number formats used in a spreadsheet | |

In answering the following questions, assume that Groups A and B (IT) or C and D (CAT) are proposed sets of lesson objectives for IT or CAT lessons:

1.  Are the lesson objectives presented in the correct format? If not, describe the shortcoming(s).

2.  Is the number of lesson objectives in each group sufficient for an IT/CAT lesson?

3.  What does it mean for a set of lesson objectives to be "balanced"?

4.  Are the groups of lesson objectives "balanced"? Motivate your answers.

### 2.4.7.2  The process of developing IT/CAT lesson objectives

The process of developing IT/CAT lesson objectives is described in three steps below. The IT/CAT lesson topic "Economic reasons for using computers" in Grade 10 is used for this purpose, and the Revised Bloom's taxonomy is used to develop the lesson objectives.

**STEP 1**  **Identify the lesson topic:** Normally you would choose the lesson topic as indicated in your IT/CAT work schedule for the particular grade.

**Example of a lesson topic:** Economic reasons for using computers

**STEP 2**  **Do a content analysis of the lesson topic:** Refer to 2.3.5 regarding the content analysis of the topic.

**Examples of essential components of the lesson topic:**
- Modern society that includes the economic world of business and work
- Information needs of modern society
- Uses of computers in modern society
- Advantages of using computers in modern society
- Reasons for using computers in the world of business and work
- Dangers of using computers in modern society

Note that these essential components identified in the content analysis are not written in lesson objective format.

**STEP 3**  **Formulate a set of provisional lesson objectives:** Write at least one IT/CAT lesson objective for every essential component identified in the previous step. You do this by rewriting the essential component in the following format:

At the end of the lesson the learner should be able to [...action verb...] [...aspect with which learner should perform an action...].

Not everybody will formulate the same set and number of IT/CAT lesson objectives. That is not a problem, as long as the lesson objectives collectively contribute and lead learners towards the required knowledge, skills and values that learners should know and be able to demonstrate at the end of that lesson.

**Example of a set of provisional lesson objectives:** At the end of the lesson the learner should be able to:

- describe modern society that includes the economic world of business and work (remember);
- explain the information needs of modern society (remember);
- list the uses of computers in modern society (remember);
- name the advantages of using computers in modern society (remember);
- define a danger of using computers in modern society (remember); and
- discuss the reasons for using computers in modern society (remember).

**STEP 4**  **Balance the set of provisional lesson objectives in terms of the cognitive levels of a taxonomy:** Balancing a set of lesson objectives in terms of taxonomy means that they should evenly cover (a) the whole spectrum of the cognitive levels of the taxonomy, and (b) all the essential components of the lesson topic. In the Revised Bloom's taxonomy learning objectives it means that if a lesson has six outcomes, then ideally for Grade 10 two or three should be levelled at the "remember" level, one or two at the "understand" level, and the rest at higher levels, and that they should cover all essential components of the lesson topic.

The principle of progression should also be kept in mind. This implies that IT/CAT lesson objectives in Grade 10 should progress from a larger number on lower cognitive levels towards a larger number on higher levels in Grade 12.

If we analyse the action verbs of the set of lesson objectives of the example in Step 3 above, we find that all six of them relate to the "remember" level of the Revised Bloom's taxonomy. This is clearly not a balanced set of lesson objectives. In the example below they were reformulated so that they now form a balanced set of objectives – three outcomes are "remember"-related, two are "understand"-related, and one is "apply/analyse"-related.

**Example of a set of balanced lesson outcomes:** At the end of the lesson the learner should be able to:

- describe the information needs of modern society that include the economic world of business and work (remember);
- list the advantages of using computers in modern society (remember);
- discuss the reasons for using computers in modern society (remember);
- identify the reasons for using computers in a comprehensive human resources system at a university (understand);
- classify the individual computer uses in a list of such uses in modern society according to the reasons for using computers in modern society (understand); and
- examine and motivate why a particular computer use is not to society's advantage (apply/analyse).

In the next example, the Grade 10 lesson topic is "The concept of a path (location of and access to a file on a mass storage device)", and the Revised Bloom's taxonomy is used to develop the lesson objectives.

| PROCESS | EXAMPLE |
| --- | --- |
| **STEP 1: Identify the lesson topic** | **STEP 1: Lesson topic** |
| Normally you would choose the lesson topic as indicated in your IT/CAT work schedule for the particular grade. | The concept of a path (location of and access to a file on a mass storage device) |
| **STEP 2: Do a content analysis of the lesson topic** | **STEP 2: Essential components of the lesson topic** |
| A lesson topic is normally made up of a number of different components, facts, concepts, parts and/or elements. Content analysis of the lesson topic means that you have to investigate and identify the essential components (i.e. facts, concepts, parts and/or elements) of the lesson topic. The reason we do this is that every one of these essential components provides us with a basis for writing a lesson outcome.<br><br>Not everybody will identify the same set of essential components, but that is not really a problem. If done properly, the content analysis of different teachers will in most cases be similar. | • Mass storage drive<br>• Directories (folders) and subdirectories (subfolders)<br>• File name and extension<br>• Format and components of a path<br>• Creating directories and subdirectories<br>• Copying and moving files from one path (location) to another<br>• Legal aspects of copying files<br><br>Note that these essential components are not written in lesson outcome format |
| **STEP 3: Formulate provisional lesson objectives** | **STEP 3: Provisional lesson objectives** |
| As a first effort, write one or more IT/CAT lesson objective(s) for every essential component identified in the previous step. You do this by rewriting the essential component in the following format:<br><br>At the end of the lesson the learner should be able to [...action verb...] [...aspect with which learner should perform an action...].<br><br>Not everybody will formulate the same set and number of lesson objectives. That is not a problem, as long as the lesson objectives collectively contribute and lead learners towards the required knowledge, skills and values that a learner should know and be able to demonstrate at the end of that lesson. | At the end of the lesson the learner should be able to:<br>• describe the concept of a path (remember);<br>• create a directory and subdirectory on a particular drive (apply);<br>• use file management software (apply);<br>• copy a file from one path to another (apply);<br>• name the components of a path (remember); and<br>• identify the file type from a file name (understand). |

| STEP 4: Balance the set of provisional lesson objectives in terms of the cognitive levels of a taxonomy | STEP 4: Balanced set of lesson objectives (Revised Bloom's taxonomy) |
|---|---|
| Balancing a set of lesson objectives in terms of a taxonomy means that they should evenly cover:<br>1. the whole spectrum of the cognitive levels of the taxonomy, and<br>2. all the essential components of the lesson topic.<br><br>In the Revised Bloom's taxonomy it means that if a lesson has six objectives, then ideally one lesson objective should be levelled at each of the six cognitive levels of the taxonomy, but for Grade 10 more can be on the lower levels.<br><br>If we analyse the action verbs of the set of lesson objectives in Step 3 above, we find that all of them are in the lower three cognitive levels of the taxonomy. Therefore, they are not balanced. The objective now is to reformulate them so that there is at least one lesson objective for every cognitive level. | At the end of the lesson the learner should be able to:<br>• name the components of a path (remember);<br>• describe the concept of a path (understand);<br>• create a directory and subdirectory on a particular drive (apply);<br>• examine and criticise the existing directory structure of a hard disk (analyse);<br>• argue the legality of making copies of programmes (evaluate); and<br>• propose a directory file structure according to the storage needs of a user (create). |

Balancing a set of lesson objectives in terms of the cognitive levels of taxonomy is an important aspect of developing IT/CAT lesson objectives. It means that you should ensure that your IT/CAT lesson objectives should evenly cover (a) the whole spectrum of the cognitive levels of the taxonomy, and (b) all the essential components of the lesson topics.

# ACTIVITY 2.2

**The topic of a Grade 10 IT/CAT lesson is "Functions of an operating system". Your task is to eventually develop a set of balanced lesson objectives for this lesson topic, using the Revised Bloom's taxonomy. Do the following:**

**(a) Do a content analysis of the lesson topic.**

**(b) Formulate a set of provisional lesson objectives based on the Revised Bloom's taxonomy.**

**(c) Balance the set of lesson objectives based on the Revised Bloom's taxonomy.**

## 2.5 TEACHING-LEARNING STRATEGIES FOR IT/CAT

Success in teaching and learning does not happen by chance – it only comes through careful planning. One of the aspects that need careful planning is the approach that an IT/CAT teacher wants to take to ensure that the expected objectives of a lesson are achieved. A teaching approach refers to a particular way of doing things (teaching and learning activities). In other words, there is a methodological aspect involved in lessons. This methodological aspect is described in terms of the concepts of teaching-learning strategies and teaching-learning methods. "Teaching strategies" and "teaching methods" in this section, refer to the strategies and methods that teachers use to facilitate learning.

A teaching-learning strategy is defined as a broad plan of action for teaching-learning activities in order to achieve teaching-learning outcomes. It is a blueprint or cohesive plan that outlines the approach a teacher intends to take in order for learners to achieve the intended objectives of a lesson (Van der Horst and McDonald 2001). It is the particular way or manner in which a teacher directs and guides his or her teaching activities and the learners' learning activities to ensure that the lesson objectives are achieved optimally. Examples include inductive and deductive teaching, inquiry learning, discovery learning, simulations, cooperative learning, problem-based learning, game-based learning, etc. Generally, teaching-learning strategies could be, and would be, integrated to achieve the objectives of lessons.

A teaching-learning method, on the other hand, is seen as the technique and/or tool that is used to carry out a teaching-learning strategy. A teaching-learning strategy is only a broad plan of action and is as such not directly implementable. Teaching-learning  methods are required as tools and techniques to put teaching-learning strategies into action during learning events (Van der Horst and McDonald 2001). Examples include review, questioning, application, demonstration, discussion, explanation, etc. These will be discussed in more detail in a next section.

In the next sections, teaching-learning strategies that are particularly relevant and appropriate for a student-centred and active learning approach to IT/CAT teaching and learning are briefly introduced and discussed: cooperative learning, problem-based learning, discovery learning, and game-based learning.. These and other appropriate teaching-learning strategies are examined and discussed in more detail in some of the further chapters. Blended learning as an approach to teaching and learning is then briefly explained. A short discussion of direct instruction as a teaching strategy also follows, *but it is recommended that direct instruction as a teaching strategy is avoided as far as possible, since direct instruction is a teacher-centred strategy that requires no or very little activity and involvement of the learners.*

### 2.5.1 Cooperative learning

Cooperative learning is a teaching-learning strategy that is specifically designed to encourage learners to work together, drawing on their individual experiences, skills and levels of motivation to help achieve a desired result. The emphasis in cooperative learning is on learners working together to learn collaborative and apply social skills while working towards a common academic goal. The group should be small enough so that everyone is responsible and accountable for a specific aspect of a clearly defined collective task (Newby *et al.* 2006). Cooperative learning as a teaching-learning strategy is discussed in more detail in Chapter 6.

Cooperative learning as a teaching-learning strategy complies with all four of the teaching and learning principles (presented in section 2.3), but it is especially focused on the principle of *social interaction*.

An example of an outline of an IT/CAT lesson that uses cooperative learning as a teaching-learning strategy:

---

## EXAMPLE OF AN IT/CAT LESSON THAT EMPLOYS COOPERATIVE LEARNING AS A TEACHING-LEARNING STRATEGY

In this lesson, the IT/CAT teacher introduces Grade 12 IT/CAT learners to a practical task that is in the form of a group programming project for IT learners or a practical task that integrates different application packages for CAT learners. The teacher plans the following teaching and learning activities based on a cooperative teaching-learning strategy:

▸ The teacher develops the requirements for the group practical project beforehand (see examples in boxes below).

▸ Next,the teacher introduces the learners to the practical project and its requirements.

▸ This is followed by an explanation of the basis for group forming, announcement of the project teams, discussion of social skills, and how the team members are expected to work together.

▸ The project teams start working on designing, developing and testing the projects.

▸ The teacher monitors progress and provides guidance and support to the project teams.

▸ Finally, the teacher (with/without the input of the learners)  designs and uses assessment instruments for assessing group functioning and the group-developed projects. The teacher also plans a demonstration of the developed projects created by learners to fellow learners and to parents during an open day at the school.

---

# REQUIREMENTS FOR A GRADE 12 DATABASE PROJECT

The project teams are required to develop a functional database that complies with the following requirements for a small business:

**<u>System requirements:</u>** The system must:

- operate with a user interface to allow user navigation within the system;
- display a welcoming form at the beginning;
- display the name of the business at the top and the name of the system at the bottom on all forms and reports;
- provide for client, product and transaction tables;
- provide for add, edit and delete record transaction types; and
- provide for sorted-client lists; product and transaction reports; daily, monthly and annual transaction reports; low product stock reports; and transactions-per-customer reports.

**<u>Project requirements:</u>**

- A proper project management plan based on a system analysis must be compiled and submitted. It should include at least a list of team members, subtasks, responsibilities, and a schedule.
- Interim progress reports must be submitted regularly.
- Technical and user manuals must be compiled and submitted.
- Team members must assess themselves and other team members individually on their achievements.
- On completion, team members must demonstrate the system to the teacher and be able to describe the purpose and functioning of all database objects.

## CAT: REQUIREMENTS FOR A GRADE 12 GROUP PROJECT

The project teams are required to compile the presentation of a comprehensive report. The report requires learners to advise the school management team on how to use an integrated package such as MS Office to administer a school's tuck shop.

**<u>Report requirements</u>:** The report must:

- be compiled using four application programs (a word processor, spreadsheet, database program and a fourth program such as a presentation program) in an integrated manner;
- communicate a solution to the school management team; and
- include examples/evidence that will explain and demonstrate **how** the application programs would facilitate the planning/administration/reporting of the activities of the tuck shop.

**<u>Project requirements</u>:**

- A project management plan must be compiled and submitted. It should include at least a list of team members, subtasks, responsibilities, and a schedule.
- It should include a list of the questions that the learners will have to ask to determine the type of information that is needed.
- It should also have a list of the sources that will be used to collect information.
- A completed report in which the use of a word processor, database and a fourth application software, e.g. publishing software, were integrated.
- On completion, team members must present the report to the teacher and be able to describe the purpose of all components included.
- Team members must assess themselves and other team members individually on their achievements.

## 2.5.2 Problem-based learning

Problem-based learning is a teaching-learning strategy that is defined as an approach in which learners are given opportunities to solve problems by applying their knowledge and skills in a systematic problem-solving process. The usual steps of such a problem-solving process are (Shelly *et al.* 2004; Breed 2006):

1. Define the problem.
2. Outline the solution.
3. Develop the solution.
4. Implement the solution.
5. Test the solution.
6. Document the process.

An IT/CAT teacher's responsibilities in designing, developing and implementing learning events that employ *problem-based learning* as a teaching-learning strategy include activities such as the following:

▸ Develop an appropriate and meaningful context for the problem in conjunction with the learners, and make available to the class the information resources that make up the context.

▸ Present and discuss the problem with the class and explain the problem-solving process.

▸ Monitor, facilitate, assist and guide the learners in the process of solving the problem.

▸ Design (with/without the input of the learners) and use assessment tools for assessing the achievement of the lesson's intended objectives.

Problem-based learning is especially focused on the principle of *situated learning*. It also complies with the other teaching and learning principles.

An example of a lesson outline using problem-based learning as a teaching-learning strategy:

---

## EXAMPLE OF AN IT/CAT LESSON WITH PROBLEM-BASED LEARNING AS A TEACHING-LEARNING STRATEGY

After completing a number of lessons about databases, the IT/CAT teacher of a Grade 11 class decides to do a practical task about databases. The teacher discusses possible scenarios in which learners can apply their newly learned database knowledge and skills. They decide on a scenario that involves the school's tuck shop. Many learners complain that some of their favourite sweets are not sold by the tuck shop or are often sold out. In an impromptu survey amongst themselves, the learners compile a list of 15 possible sweet lines that they would like to see available in sufficient stock at the tuck shop. The Grade 11 class agrees that they would like to investigate if and how this problem can be solved. In cooperation with their teacher they formulate the problem as follows:

> *"The tuck shop's line of sweets and their availability does not satisfy the majority of learners. Determine a line of sweets that is preferred by the majority of learners, and ratios in which they should be ordered."*

In planning and executing the lesson, the IT/CAT teacher does the following:

▸ Develops an assessment rubric.

▸ Uses a word processor to prepare a worksheet for the problem-solving task that contains the following background information (as context): the description of the problem; the list of 15 possible lines of sweets; the list of lines of sweets that the tuck shop currently stocks (obtained from the teacher responsible for the tuck shop); and the quantity of stock ordered by the tuck shop for their list of sweets over the last six months.

▸ Presents and analyses the collectively agreed problem to be solved.

▸ Discusses and shares the problem-solving process with his/her learners.

▸ Provides an example of a simple questionnaire that learners can use to design their own questionnaire for surveying 20 learners each about their sweets preferences.

▸ Provides guidance and support to learners in their attempts to solve the problem.

▸ Assesses the learners' solutions using the assessment rubric.

---

### 2.5.3  Discovery learning

Discovery learning is a teaching-learning strategy that is based on the assumption that learners are more likely to understand and remember concepts they had discovered themselves in the course of their own exploration of and interaction with the environment (Roblyer 2006). The role of the teacher is to provide learners with opportunities to interact with the environment by exploring and manipulating objects, investigating and solving problems through inquiry, or performing hands-on exercises and experiments. It is a non-linear process of learning in which you investigate and explore related topics as you encounter them. The Web with its hyperlinks and non-linear nature makes it a valuable and powerful tool to support discovery learning (Shelly *et al.* 2006).

Teachers' responsibilities in designing, developing and implementing learning events that employ discovery learning as a teaching-learning strategy include activities such as the following:

- Identifying and preparing an appropriate real-world context for the lesson in which discovery learning is going to be used.
- Formulating the theme for the discovery and exploration activities, taking care to not make it too unstructured.
- Facilitating learners' discovery and exploration activities, and providing guidance and support where necessary.
- Designing and using assessment tools for assessing the achievement of the lesson's intended outcomes.

Discovery learning as a teaching-learning strategy focuses in particular on the principles of *knowledge construction* and *active learning*, although it also complies with the principle of situated learning.

An example of a lesson outline using discovery learning as a teaching-learning strategy is demonstrated below. Note that this example uses discovery learning as a teaching-learning strategy combined with cooperative learning, which is completely acceptable. It happens quite often in practice that teachers combine cooperative learning with other teaching-learning strategies if they feel that group work (principle of social interaction) is important in the context of a lesson.

**EXAMPLE OF AN IT/CAT LESSON THAT USES DISCOVERY LEARNING AS A TEACHING-LEARNING STRATEGY**

After teaching his Grade 10 IT/CAT class the basics of the internet and the functions, features and facilities of a web browser, the IT teacher plans a research project in which he wants his learners to achieve the following objective:

Learners must be able to navigate the internet in order to retrieve information.

The Olympic Games are taking place and the IT/CAT teacher wants his learners to learn more about the national symbols of South Africa. He decides to let the learners discover for themselves what the national symbols are, and plans the following activities for the lesson:

- Conducts a general discussion on national symbols, examples of famous and/or notorious national symbols of countries all over the world and the value of national symbols during national and international events in order to create a real-life and meaningful context for the lesson.
- Reviews the features, facilities and functions of a web browser, and the value of a search engine in searching for information on the internet.
- Pairs learners and allocates the following tasks:
    - Explore the national symbols of South Africa in sources of information of yourchoice.
    - Create a database of the national symbols of South Africa – the records of the national symbols in the database must have at least six fields, including a graphic image.
    - Prepare and print a database report of the national symbols.
- Provides guidance and support to the research teams in creating a database table and report.
- Assesses learners' skills in searching for information on the internet by using an observation checklist specially prepared for this purpose.

## 2.5.4  Game-based learning

Game-based learning uses game elements to facilitate the learning of a specific skill or achievement of a specific learning outcome (Findlay 2016). The game should be embedded in the learning activities and relate directly to the learning objective. Although digital games are very popular, games do not always have to be digital. Boardgames and real-life games can also be used with great success. The game that is implemented in the learning situation depends on the specific learning objective, learner characteristics, and educational setting (Plass, Homer and Kinzer 2015). The game should have the capability to engage each learner in ways that are related to, amongst other, the learner's current level of knowledge, cognitive abilities and emotions (Plass, Homer and Kinzer 2015).

A game-based learning approach not only motivates learners to engage in class activities (Hartt, Hosseini and Mustafapour 2020), but also increases their learning motivation, involvement and enjoyment of learning (Gee 2003). The main aim should still remain to achieve the learning outcomes.

Closely related to game-based learning is the notion of gamification in learning. Gamification in learning is the application of game-based elements in a non-game context to promote learner behaviour and enjoyment (Findlay 2016). Game-based elements can include point scoring, competition between peers, teamwork and score tables (True Education Partnerships 2020). Learners may be motivated through incentive structures, such as points, stars, leaderboards, badges and trophies for completion of learning activities (Plass, Homer and Kinzer 2015).

The main difference between game-based learning and gamification in learning is related to the integration of game elements with learning content. Game-based learning fully integrates game elements and the learning content, so the game is the learning. On the other hand, gamification uses game elements as a reward for completing existing learning activities (Findlay 2016).

### 2.5.5 Blended learning

Blended learning as an approach to teaching and learning entails having learners engaged in both online and face-to-face learning environments – the balance between online and face-to-face engagement can be guided by the teacher and/or the topic at hand. Although several blended learning strategies exist, one of the most useful, and easily implemented in the IT/CAT class is the flipped classroom approach.

The flipped classroom approach addresses modern-day learners' need for engagement and active learning (Gillispie 2016). In the flipped classroom approach learners are exposed to the learning material prior to and outside of the classroom, usually in the form of written material, voice-over lectures, online videos (Gillispie 2016), curating online videos from various sources (Maher *et al.* 2015), or through online learning management systems. Learners have the advantage of reading prescribed material or watching the online videos as many times as necessary to be prepared for the formal class meeting (Mok 2014). Formal class time is then used to facilitate learner-centred activities to engage learners in higher levels of learning and critical thinking through, for example, discussions, case studies and complex problem-solving. Advantages of the flipped classroom also include opportunities for individualised education and real-time feedback (Gillispie 2016).

### 2.5.6 Direct instruction

Direct instruction (also known as expository teaching, explicit teaching, transmissive instruction and tutorial) is the teaching strategy that was commonly used in the traditional classroom. However, it is not considered as a teaching strategy that complies with the requirements of student-centred instruction and active learning. Direct instruction is a teacher-centred approach in which the teacher presents lesson content in a structured format, while maintaining control over what, when and how learners learn. Learners are mostly passive and submissively assimilating the new content and its meaning as presented by the teacher, an approach that is simply not suitable for modern-day learners. Modern-day learners prefer more engagement with and control over the learning situation..

## 2.6 A LESSON TEMPLATE FOR IT/CAT TEACHING AND LEARNING

After analysing all the essential components and ingredients of IT/CAT lessons, we are now ready to examine how such lessons are designed and developed. This is done by means of a lesson model or template. Many such templates exist and it is not particularly important which one IT/CAT teachers use, as long as it is done properly according to sound principles. As you become more experienced you will probably develop your own lesson template that you feel comfortable with. However, the example of a lesson template proposed below is particularly appropriate and relevant for IT/CAT lessons, yet simple enough to be used by a novice IT/CAT teacher. The sections of the lesson template are elaborated on in subsequent sections.

| Subject: (a) | | | | |
|---|---|---|---|---|
| Grade: (b) | Date(s): (b) | | Time allocation: (b) | |
| Lesson topic | (c) | | | |
| Lesson objectives | (d) | | | |
| LTSM(s) | (e) | | | |
| Lesson phases (f) | Teaching-learning strategy (g) | Teacher activities (h) | Learner activities (i) | Assessment activities (j) |
| Introduction Establish context Review prior knowledge State problem | | | | |
| Development Introduce new content Apply new content | | | | |
| Consolidation Review new content Assess achievements | | | | |
| Expanded opportunities Enrichment Remedial | (k) | | | |
| Homework | (l) | | | |
| Reflection | (m) | | | |

Figure 3.1   *An example of a lesson template for designing and developing IT/CAT lessons*

Sections (a) to (e) are concerned with the curriculum aspects and intended objectives of the lesson. These aspects provide the background and are the ingredients for planning the teaching, learning and assessment activities in the actual lesson that follow in sections (f) to (l). Section (m) provides the teacher with an opportunity to reflect on the success of his or her lesson planning and presentation.

## (a)    Subject

Usually this will be Information Technology (IT) or Computer Applications Technology (CAT), but a combination of two or more subjects is also possible if teachers want to do a cross-curriculum project.

## (b)    Grade, date(s) and time allocation

State the grade for which this lesson is intended, the date(s) when it is to start or to be continued, the length of each period and the number of periods allocated for the lesson.

## (c)    Lesson topic

If the IT/CAT work schedule was developed to such a level of detail that the IT/CAT content is already packaged into lesson topics, then they are ready to be developed into lesson plans. If not, then the content topics of the IT/CAT work schedule must be divided into topics that represent units of deliverable learning events. Select a topic for the lesson and indicate it in this section.

## (d)    Lesson objectives

The importance of lesson objectives cannot be emphasised enough because it determines the whole purpose of a lesson and what should be focused on in assessment. Indicate the specific IT/CAT lesson objectives that you want your learners to have achieved at the end of the lesson. The process of developing lesson objectives has been described extensively in section 2.4.

## (e)    LTSM(s)

Once you have indicated the lesson topic and lesson objectives, you need to decide on the learning and teaching support materials (LTSMs), which can be technology tools and/or other resources that will be required for the lesson. If appropriate, list the hardware (number of computers, printers, data projector and any other equipment) and software (specific application software) that are required for this particular lesson. Also, add any other resources such as websites and URLs, newspaper or journal articles, textbooks, etc. that will be used in the lesson.

## (f)    Lesson phases

Three broad phases can be distinguished in any lesson, namely an introductory phase, a development phase in which learners develop the intended new knowledge, skills and values under guidance of the teacher, and a consolidation and assessment phase. Let us examine these phases in more detail.

▶ **Introduction:** The introductory phase creates a learning need and sets the stage for the activities to follow in the development phase. Its function is to indicate clearly where we are, where we want to go, why we want to go there and how to get there. Its aim is to prepare and provide learners with a framework for engaging in the subject matter through various learning activities. In particular, the introduction aims to:

  – **Setting the context:** In this part of the lesson the IT/CAT teacher establishes a real-life context (or scenario) in which the new lesson topic can be embedded and that will make the lesson meaningful for learners as it provides an anchor for their learning activities. Such a context will also provide a setting for introducing a challenging and authentic real-life problem that will create a learning need and enhance learner interest and motivation. A class will consist of a diverse group of learners. Teachers should know their learners and understand their contexts in order to relate to the learners' cultural background and experiences.

  – **Review prior knowledge:** It is essential to review and refresh any prior knowledge, skills and/or values that are relevant to and provide a basis for the new lesson topic.

  – **State the problem:** Here the IT/CAT teacher's responsibility is to introduce a meaningful and authentic real-life problem to which learners can relate. A requirement for the lesson to succeed is that learners should be motivated to take ownership of the problem. This is only possible if learners experience the problem as meaningful and relevant to the world in which they live.

▶ **Development:** The aim of this phase is to facilitate activities where learners can construct their own knowledge in order to develop the new lesson content. This is where learners develop the new knowledge, skills and values required to achieve as indicated in the lesson's intended objectives. Two aspects , which can quite often not be separated from each other, are included in the development phase:

  – **Construct knowledge/develop understanding:** Here the IT/CAT teacher's responsibility is to guide learners in actively exploring, researching and discovering the new content. The aim is for learners to come to a complete understanding and mastery of the new content, and to integrate it into their existing knowledge structures.

  – **Apply new content:** Teachers should create opportunities for learners to apply and transfer their new knowledge, skills and values in similar and in new situations. These could range from simple drill-and-practice exercises to tasks that will require learners to fully apply their new knowledge, skills and values in solving problems.

▶ **Consolidation:** The consolidation phase of a lesson has two objectives:

  – **Review new content:** The knowledge, skills and values that have been learned in the lesson are now summarised. This includes clarifying relationships of the new content with other concepts, and guiding learners to regroup and reorganise their knowledge structures after learning the new concepts.

  – **Assess achievements:** In the final part of the lesson, it is necessary to assess whether learners have achieved the intended objectives of the lesson. The feedback from this assessment will tell the IT/CAT teacher a number of things, for example which knowledge, skills and/or values need to be revisited, whether the learners are ready to progress to the next lesson topic, and how effective his or her own teaching practice was.

## (g)   Teaching-learning strategy

In this part of the lesson plan, the IT/CAT teacher is required to indicate the teaching-learning strategy (or strategies) he or she intends to use in the different phases of the lesson. Depending on the nature and content of a lesson, it may be possible to employ only one teaching strategy throughout the entire lesson, which then represents a broad plan of action or approach for teaching and learning activities in the lesson.

## (h)   Teacher activities

Describe for every lesson phase the activities that you as IT/CAT teacher are going to perform and the methods that you are going to apply in accordance with your chosen teaching strategy. If technology is involved in some of the activities, indicate the technology tool (software package) and application clearly. Do not include the activities that have to do with planning and preparing the lesson. The teacher activities should focus on the attainment of the intended lesson objectives. Remember to synchronise the teacher activities with the learner activities because they go hand in hand.

## (i)   Learner activities

Describe for every lesson phase the activities that you want your learners to perform in accordance with your chosen teaching strategy. If technology is involved in some of the learning activities, indicate the technology tool (software package) and application clearly. Keep in mind the close relationship between teaching and learning activities – they go hand in hand and respond to and complement each other. The learning activities should also focus on and reflect the lesson objectives that you want your learners to achieve.

## (j)   Assessment activities

Assessment is an integral part of teaching and learning and should not be neglected and seen as a less important part of the activities or the lesson plan. IT/CAT teachers should plan assessment activities to complement teaching and learning activities throughout all lesson phases. This informal daily monitoring of learning progress can be done through question-and-answer sessions or short assessment tasks, completed during the lesson by individuals or small groups, or can even be done through homework exercises. Self-assessment or peer-assessment can be used to mark these assessment tasks, to allow learners to learn from and reflect on their performance. The results of the informal daily assessment tasks need not be formally recorded. Refer to the chapter on assessment for further guidance.

## (k)   Expanded opportunities and enrichment

In this section of the lesson plan, an IT/CAT teacher should plan expanded (optional/additional) opportunities in the form of enrichment activities for learners who would like more challenging activities, and remedial or other relevant activities for learners who need additional support.

## (l)    Homework

The activities and/or work that the learners are required to do at home should be indicated.

## (m)    Reflection

Finally, after facilitating the lesson, the IT/CAT teacher should reflect on how well the lesson plan worked, and on what could be improved. Teachers need to note these as soon as possible while the experience is still fresh in their minds, and write down suggestions to adapt and change the lesson plan for future implementation. Keep a printed lesson plan in your teacher file and write down the reflection and suggestions on the lesson plan sheet.

**NOTE: Integration of the components of the lesson plan:** The above sections describe the various components of the lesson plan. It is only when an IT/CAT teacher plans these components with imagination, flair and creativity that the lesson becomes exciting and enhances learner motivation. That is why many educationists consider lesson planning an art. It is crucial that the subject, lesson topic, lesson objectives, LTSM(s), teaching-learning strategies, and teacher and learner activities form an integrated whole in which each part synchronises with and complements the other. Care should be taken to ensure that all the lesson objectives are covered and reflected in all of the phases and planned activities. It is often found in proposed lesson plans that the various phases do not all focus on attaining the lesson objectives (it is, for example, a simple fact that assessment should focus on the achievement of lesson objectives). Putting together all the parts of a lesson plan should result in an integrated and vibrant whole that is greater than the sum of the individual parts.

Study the following example of a lesson plan for the lesson that was outlined in section 2.5.3 – it is a Grade 10 IT/CAT lesson in which learners have to use their web browser skills to search for information on the national symbols of South Africa. Discovery learning is used as the teaching strategy.

| EXAMPLE: | | |
|---|---|---|
| **Subject** | Information Technology/ Computer Applications Technology | |
| **Grade 10** | **Date: 2 February 20XX** | **Time allocation: 2 periods of 35 minutes each** |
| **Lesson topic** | Search the internet for information on the national symbols of South Africa. | |
| **Lesson objectives** | At the end of the lesson, the learner should be able to (Bloom):<br>• explain the meaning and value of a search engine (understand);<br>• formulate a search string for effective information searches on the internet (analyse);<br>• compare two search strings to find the best one for searching for information on a topic (evaluate);<br>• list the national symbols of South Africa (remember);<br>• propose a database design for the national symbols of South Africa (analysis);<br>• create a database table to record the national symbols of South Africa (create);<br>• produce a database report about the national symbols of South Africa (apply); and<br>• criticise a given database design (evaluate). | |
| **LTSM(s)** | A work station with an internet connection and web browser for every pair of learners, and a curriculum page (or hot list) of teacher-selected and evaluated websites for searching information on national symbols | |

| Lesson phases | Teaching-learning strategy | Teacher activities | Learner activities | Assessment activities |
|---|---|---|---|---|
| **Introduction**<br>• Establish context.<br>• Review prior knowledge.<br>• State problem. | Discovery learning/ discussion<br>Discovery learning/ review<br>Discovery learning/ discussion | Initiate a discussion about SA's participation in a world event such as the Olympic Games, leading to the role of national symbols in it.<br>Ask review questions about:<br>• how to search for information on the internet;<br>• the basic features, facilities and functions of a web browser;<br>• the process of designing and developing a database table and report.<br>Pose questions about:<br>• possible ways of using technology to find information about a topic (e.g. search engines and curriculum pages);<br>• the specific national symbols of SA and how to make and keep a record of it. | • Contribute personal views on the value of participation in such events, and the role and value of our national symbols.<br>• Recall and regenerate existing knowledge, skills and values.<br>• Participate in discussions and share ideas about possible ways to solve these two problems. | Observe if all learners are participating Q&A session. |
| **Development**<br>Introduce new content. | Discovery learning/ discussion | Introduce the concepts of search engines and search strategies, and prompt learners to explain and share their understanding of it. | Explain the concepts (from own experiences) and demonstrate how they are used. | Q&A session to assess if all learners understand search engines and search strategies |

| Lesson phases | Teaching-learning strategy | Teacher activities | Learner activities | Assessment activities |
|---|---|---|---|---|
| **Apply new content** | Discovery learning/ guidance | Group learners randomly in pairs and task them to:<br>• search for information on South Africa's national symbols on websites by using a search engine and the supplied curriculum page;<br>• design and develop a database for recording the national symbols;<br>• print a database report about SA's national symbols. | Perform the following tasks, seeking guidance from the teacher when necessary:<br>• Search the internet for information on SA's national symbols.<br>• Create a database for recording the national symbols.<br>• Create and print a database report about SA's national symbols. | Observe and assess learners' skills in searching for information on the internet, creating a database, and printing a database report. |
| **Consolidation**<br>• Review new content.<br>• Assess achieve-ments. | Discovery learning/ review<br>Discovery learning/ questioning | Review and summarise:<br>• Internet search facilities and strategies;<br>• Designing and developing a database;<br>• Printing a database report.<br>Divide class in two groups for a class quiz on internet search facilities and strategies. | • Participate in reviewing and summarising activities.<br>• The two groups compete against each other by formulating questions for the other group, and answering questions from the other group. | Q&A session: Teacher acts as moderator. |
| **Expanded opportunities**<br>Enrichment and remedial | Random pairing of learners creates opportunities for guiding and supporting fellow leaners, as well as to learn from fellow learners. | | | |
| **Reflection** | Reflect on: aspects that were successful; problems that occurred with technology, learners, and/or learning content; to what level the lesson objectives were achieved; and aspects that can be improved. | | | |

## 2.7 PREPARING FOR FACILITATING THE LESSON

Once the IT/CAT teacher has planned what teaching and learning is intended to take place and how it is going to happen, the teacher has to think about what else needs to be done before the lesson is facilitated. The following may serve as guidelines in preparing for an IT/CAT lesson, but they may differ from lesson to lesson and from class to class:

- Ensure that you have personally mastered the content and/or skills: For the teaching and learning of theoretical content and/or practical skills to be effective, it is essential that the IT/CAT teacher should have mastered the specific content and/or practical skills personally. All examples and exercises that will be used in a lesson must be completed by the teacher beforehand. This ensures that the IT/CAT teacher can facilitate the teaching and learning activities with confidence and earn the trust and respect of the learners. Learners quickly realise when a teacher is unprepared and that can result in a negative perception of the teacher and the subject.

- Have additional resources available: Additional resources like other textbooks, magazines, videos and applicable website and their URLs can contribute to enhance learner interest.

- Ensure that computers and other devices are in working order. Printers, for example, should have sufficient paper and toner.

- Test other available technology such as overhead projectors and videos beforehand. Always have a backup of alternative activities should the equipment or power fail unexpectedly.

- Have a sufficient number of hard copies ready: If extra notes, handouts, activity sheets, additional exercises, etc. are required, ensure that the number of copies are sufficient for the number of learners in the class and that these copies are ready before the lesson commences.

- Have physical examples at hand and ready to use: If physical examples of items, such as network cables, network cards, mother boards, etc. are to be used during a lesson, it is important to place these examples within reach so that you do not have to walk around in the classroom to collect them. This also applies to items that you may have created yourself, e.g. posters, quiz cards, etc. Having the items within reach saves time and prevents possible loss of learners' attention.

- Prepare a well-designed PowerPoint. The purpose of the PowerPoint should not be to repeat the content in the textbook and to be a script for the teacher, but to highlight important aspects and guide learners through the activities. Find tips for effective PowerPoints online to enhance your PowerPoint skills and to not practise "death by PowerPoint" principles.

## 2.8 CONCLUSION

In this chapter, you were introduced to the science and art of IT/CAT lesson planning. The ingredients of IT/CAT lesson planning included teaching and learning principles for IT/CAT, the development of IT/CAT lesson objectives, teaching strategies and methods, and a lesson template for IT/CAT teaching and learning. In your professional life as an IT/CAT teacher, the daily planning of your lessons will probably be the most demanding yet satisfying and creative part. We have also shared some ideas on preparation that needs to be done before the lesson can be facilitated. At first, this planning of and preparation for a lesson may seem to be a demanding task, but as you gain experience it will become a lot less so.

# ASSIGNMENT 2

**2.1**  Grade 10 learners have to master the basic concepts of networks.

Do the following for this lesson:

a)  Do a content analysis of the lesson topic.                                         (6)

b)  Develop a balanced set of six lesson objectives – one each for the
six cognitive levels of the Revised Bloom's taxonomy (write down
the taxonomy level next to each lesson outcome in brackets).       (12)

c)  Identify the teaching-learning strategy/strategies that you are going to use
in this lesson, and summarise its/their meaning in your own words in five
or six full descriptive sentences.                                             (5)

d)  Identify the resources that you are going to use in the lesson.        (2)

e)  Describe the teaching and learning activities for each of the lesson phases,
and assessment activities.                                                    (15)

f)  Plan expanded opportunities for learners.                                (5)

[45]

**2.2** Design and develop a complete lesson for an IT/CAT lesson in solution development. You may not use any topic that is used in the study material or IT/CAT curriculum documents as examples. Marks will be allocated as follows:

- Grade level (1)

- Lesson topic (2)

- Content analysis (6)

- A balanced set of at least six lesson objectives – one each for the six cognitive levels of the Revised Bloom's taxonomy (indicate the taxonomy levels) (12)

- Teaching-learning strategy/strategies (2)

- Resources (2)

- Introduction and setting context (3)

- Teacher activities (at least two for every lesson phase) (6)

- Learner activities (at least two for every lesson phase) (6)

- Assessment activities (5)

- Expanded opportunities (2)

- Integration of lesson components (3)

[50]

Integration of lesson components refer to the lesson plan requirement that the subject, lesson topic, lesson objectives, LTSM(s), teaching-learning strategy/strategies, and teacher, learner and assessment activities form an integrated whole in which each part synchronises with and complements the other. To qualify for this:

- the lesson objectives must clearly relate to the lesson topic;

- all the lesson objectives must be covered and reflected in the teacher and learner activities; and

- the assessment activities must clearly reflect its focus on the achievement of the lesson objectives.

## REFERENCES

Bosch, C., Mentz, E. and Goede, R. 2019 Self-directed learning: A conceptual overview. (In E. Mentz, J. de Beer and R. Bailey, eds. *Self-directed learning for the 21st century: Implications for Higher Education*. Cape Town: Aosis, pp. 1-36.) https://doi.org/10.4102/aosis.2019.BK134.01

Breed, E.A. 2006. 'n Analise van die reflektiewe vermoëns van effektiewe en oneffektiewe leerders in rekenaarprogrammering. M.Ed. dissertation, North West University, Potchefstroom.

DBE (Department of Basic Education) see South Africa. Department of Basic Education.

Findlay, J. 2016. *Game-based learning vs, Gamification: Do you know the difference?* https://trainingindustry.com (Accessed: 28 October 2021).

Gee, J.P. 2003. *What video games have to teach us about learning and literacy*. New York, NY: Palgrave Macmillan. https://doi.org/10.1145/950566.950595

Gillispie, V. 2016. Using the flipped classroom to bridge the gap to generation Y. *Ochsner Journal*, 16:32-36.

Hartt, M., Hosseini, H. and Mostafapour, M. 2020. Game on: Exploring the effectiveness of game-based learning. *Planning Practice & Research*. https://doi.org/10.1080/02697459.2020.1778859

INTEL. 2012. Designing effective projects: Thinking skills frameworks. Marzano's new taxonomy. https://intel.ly/37CCc24

Jonassen, D.H., Hernandez-Serrano, J. and Choi, I. 2000. Integrating constructivism and learning technologies. (In J.M. Spector and T.M. Anderson, eds. *Integrated and holistic perspectives on learning, instruction and technology: Understanding complexity*. Dordrecht, The Netherlands: Kluwer Academic Publishers.)

Jonassen, D.H., Peck, K.L. and Wilson, B.G. 1999. *Learning with technology: A constructivist perspective*. Upper Saddle River, NJ: Prentice Hall.

Maher, M.L., Latulipe, C., Lipford, H. and Rorrer, A. 2015. *Flipped classroom strategies for CS education*. Paper delivered at SIGCSE '15 held in Kansas City, MO, USA, on 4-7 March.

Merriam, S.B., Caffarella, R.S. and Baumgartner, L.M. 2007. *Learning in adulthood: A comprehensive guide*, 3rd ed. San Francisco, CA: John Wiley & Sons.

Mok, H.N. 2014. Teaching tip: The flipped classroom. *Journal of Information Systems Education*, 25(1):7-11.

Newby, T.J., Stepich, D.A., Lehman, J.D. and Russel, J.D. 2006. *Educational technology for teaching and learning*, 3rd ed. Upper Saddle River, NJ: Pearson Education.

Pickard, M.J. 2007. The new Bloom's taxonomy: An overview for family and consumer sciences. *Journal of family and consumer sciences education*, 25(1):45-55.

Plass, J.L., Homer, B.D. and Kinzer, C.K. 2015. Foundations of game-based learning. *Educational Psychologist*, 50(4):258-283. https://doi.org/10.1080/00461520.2015.1122533

Roblyer, M.D. 2006. *Integrating educational technology into teaching*, 4th ed. Upper Saddle River, NJ: Pearson Education.

Shelly, G.B., Cashman, T.J. and Vermaat, M.E. 2004. *Discovering computers 2005: A gateway to information*. Boston, MA: Thomson Course Technology.

Shelly, G.B., Cashman, T.J.,Gunter, R.E. and Gunter, G.A. 2006. *Teachers discovering computers: Integrating technology and digital media in the classroom*, 4th ed. Boston, MA: Thomson Course Technology.

South Africa. Department of Basic Education. 2011. *Curriculum and assessment policy statement: Information Technology*. Pretoria: DBE.

True Education Partnerships. 2021. *Gamification in education: What is it & how can you use it?* https://bit.ly/36E7rt2 (Accessed: 28 October 2021).

Van der Horst, H. and McDonald, R. 2001. *Outcomes-based education: Theory and practice*. Pretoria: Kagiso.

# CHAPTER 3

# Facilitation of an IT/CAT lesson

## Betty Breed

# OBJECTIVES

**After completing this chapter, you should be able to:**

- ⊃ *discuss and apply the factors that contribute towards the successful facilitation of an IT/CAT lesson in practice;*

- ⊃ *discuss and apply your role as facilitator of teaching and learning through all the phases of a lesson, discipline and management of learners, the use of textbooks, worksheets and questions in a lesson, and also the handling of practical lessons; and*

- ⊃ *demonstrate knowledge regarding the teaching of groups or individual learners, as well as the handling of advanced learners or learners with disabilities in the IT/CAT class.*

## 3.1    INTRODUCTION

Although a lesson cannot be successful without proper planning and preparation, as discussed in Chapter 2, the facilitation of the lesson is of paramount importance to determine the eventual success of the lesson. Clear exposition of the lesson, purposeful guidance, enthusiasm, good communication skills, discipline, knowledge of the subject and motivation are some of the essential constituents of the facilitation process. In the following sections, important aspects regarding effective lesson facilitation will be addressed.

## 3.2    THE TEACHER AS FACILITATOR OF LEARNING

Probably the most important task of the teacher of IT/CAT is to stimulate learners' interest in the subject and get them actively involved in every lesson. In addition to involvement in research, group work, demonstrations, etc., learners should be encouraged to discuss and listen attentively, to make sense of the points of views of others, and to compare their ideas to their peers' ideas (Fraser 2006). The teacher must motivate the learners to provide solutions for problems and to acquire new knowledge. A teacher who is enthusiastic about his/her subject also imprints this enthusiasm on his/her learners.

Furthermore the teacher should display characteristics such as being sensitive to learners' differences regarding learning styles, pace of learning, levels of achievement, gender and culture (Department of Education 2008). Understanding how learning takes place and the importance of existing knowledge, taking context into account, encouraging an enquiring attitude in learners, and making learning interesting and enjoyable are important for a successful lesson (Fraser 2006).

Dismiss the old-fashioned idea that the teacher is a lecturer, and place the teacher on a new stage as a facilitator of learning. This role expects of the teacher to assist learners to bridge the gap between what they cannot do on their own at a given time to what they can do with a little assistance from someone else (Fraser 2006). As the facilitator (or what Fraser (2006) refers to as "mediator") of learning, the IT/CAT teacher should create learning opportunities such as:

▶ discussions, for example the ethical aspects regarding computer software;

▶ problem-solving exercises, for example during programming in IT or during database processing in CAT;

▶ true-to-life problems, such as what a user must consider before buying a computer;

▶ case studies, for example the establishment of a new computer room at the school;

▶ explanations, for example how the performance of a computer is influenced by the capacity of the primary memory; and

▶ videos on different computer-related topics.

When creating these types of opportunities the teacher must indicate to the learners what they must be able to do or know, monitor the learners' progress and give regular feedback (Fraser 2006).

# ACTIVITY 3.1

**Write an essay of approximately 300 words to explain the most important features of the IT/CAT teacher as facilitator of learning in the IT/CAT class.**

**Refer to the following:**

**(a)  what knowledge and skills the teacher should have;**

**(b)  what characteristics the teacher should have; and**

**(c)  different types of learning opportunities the teacher should create for learners to be able to take responsibility for their own learning.**

## 3.3    LESSON PHASES

In Chapter 2 it was mentioned that a lesson plan does not have to adhere to fixed lesson phases. However, a lesson should have three main phases, namely the introductory phase, the teaching-learning phase (also known as the development phase), and the consolidation phase. In the following sections, we will consider some general issues regarding these phases of the lesson.

### 3.3.1  Introductory phase

This phase normally includes aspects such as *setting of the context* for the lesson, *determination of previous knowledge* and the *problem statement* of the lesson. Getting the learners' full attention thus is of utmost importance. In a formal classroom setting, ensure that the entire class is quiet before you start. Keep the lesson introduction short, scan the entire class regularly, and make eye contact with as many individuals as possible (Banks 2000). In an online situation, it is just as important to get the learners involved. Make the first learner activities clear and straightforward and be clear about the sequence of activities – "what happens next" (Banks 2000:164).

An important feature of the introductory phase is the objectives of the specific lesson, which should be clearly linked to the problem statement In a self-directed learning approach, learners will also be allowed to set personal learning goals within the framework of the problem statement. Learners should know exactly what you want to achieve and what you want them to achieve. This motivates them to cooperate to solve the problem and to eventually achieve the objectives set for the lesson. If possible, provide the problem statement in a visual format, for example, by using PowerPoint, an overhead projector or the writing board.

Since the nature of IT/CAT involves problem-solving to a high degree, the problem statement of the lesson should be a main point of focus and it should never be gabbled through. It is important that the problem is clearly formulated and that it is both interesting and stimulating in order for learners to be eager to solve the problem. It is possible that a lesson may not feature only one problem, but that the teacher guides the learners through questions in order for them to fully understand the problem.

### 3.3.2  Teaching-learning phase

This phase focuses on the *teaching and learning of new content and/or skills* and *application of this new knowledge and/or skills*. The teacher should ensure that lessons are learner-centred and activity-based. The teaching-learning principles that were examined and discussed in Chapter 2 (knowledge construction, active learning, social interaction and situated learning) must be applied in this phase. The phase can comprise of a number of teaching and learning interactions and activities. It should not be a mere lecture where the teacher talks and the learners just listen. The teaching and learning activities in this phase must offer leaners the opportunity to be actively involved and socially inter-acting, constructing their own knowledge in contexts that engage them in real-life problems. Involving learners in the identification and implementation of teaching-learning strategies and appropriate resources contributes to promoting self-directed learning.

It is especially in this phase that the teacher's role as facilitator of learning is of importance. Irrespective of the teaching-learning strategies planned for the lesson, the teacher must stay actively involved and exercise control throughout the lesson through questions, by observing learners, testing reactions, etc., to ensure that all learners are involved and active, and that they are developing towards achieving the objectives. The teacher must see to it that learners are given the opportunity to apply what they have learned (SACTE 1995:30). The teacher must pace the progress of the teaching-learning phase to allow for sufficient time to do consolidation of the lesson.

### 3.3.3  Consolidation phase

This phase is aimed mainly at *reviewing the new content* and *assessing achievements* and can be handled in various ways (SACTE 1995). In this phase, the teacher, with the assistance of the learners:

▶ makes a summary of the main points or concepts of the lesson; it is advisable that the summary should be visual, once again by using PowerPoint, an overhead projector or the writing board;

▶ revises the objectives of the lesson to enable learners to determine for themselves whether they have achieved the objectives; and

▶ can do the daily assessment, using a short class test or homework to determine if the objectives have been achieved. Furthermore, evaluation of own learning promotes self-directed learning.

It is essential that you leave enough time at the end of a lesson to do consolidation. Get everyone's attention before the summary is done, the objectives revised, and/or homework given. Also plan for time to end off other activities, for example, if a demonstration of hardware was done by either the teacher or the learners during the lesson, time should be allowed to put away the examples. If something took longer than expected, do not try to rush through everything that was planned (Banks 2000).

## ACTIVITY 3.2

**Make a summary of the most important aspects that should be kept in mind during each of the three main phases of an IT/CAT lesson. The summary can be in the form of a mind map (diagram), table or sections with clear headings.**

## 3.4    DISCIPLINE AND MANAGEMENT OF LEARNERS IN THE CLASSROOM

Thorough planning, and even facilitation of a lesson according to all written and unwritten rules, cannot guarantee a lesson's success if a teacher cannot maintain discipline. This can be highly detrimental to the teaching-learning situation. Ensuring order and discipline in a classroom is regarded as a management function and a responsibility of the teacher (Pienaar 2006). However, the way you manage the learners in your classroom must be in accordance with the ethos prevalent in the school in general (Banks 2000:163). Totally different expectations in your class may lead to uncertainty amongst the learners on how to behave or interact in your class.

The facilitation of a skills-based subject such as IT/CAT specifically requires the maintenance of discipline, as well as thorough planning. Equipment could be seriously damaged if the IT/CAT teacher is not strict as far as the application of certain rules and regulations in the computer classroom are concerned. General guidelines to take note of are briefly listed below:

- In cooperation with the learners, compile a code of conduct (Pienaar 2006). This code of conduct must then be signed by all learners of IT/CAT.

- Be consistent and strict as far as adherence to the code of conduct is concerned.

- Do not be unapproachable or overly strict, seeing as this will result in learners not having the confidence to ask or answer questions.

- Treat all learners equally and with respect.

- It is not necessary to forbid discussions amongst learners, as long as they are discussing the problem at hand. Learners often learn more from each other than they would learn by themselves.

- See to it that the learners know what is expected of them at all times.

- Do not allow learners to be passive; instead, see to it that additional or enriching work is always readily available in order to keep learners occupied.

- Never leave learners unattended.

- As facilitator, always be actively involved in the lesson.
- Do not threaten learners if you never act on the threat.
- See to it that learners are motivated to complete their assignments, rather than having to threaten them before they do it. Award learners who cooperate.

To reduce the probability of misbehaviour it is necessary that you, as the teacher, control learners while they enter or exit the computer room. It is important that you are at or in the room when they arrive, that they are quiet and are not fiddling in their bags when the lesson starts, and that you do not allow latecomers (if permitted at your school!) to interrupt your flow (Banks 2000). Maintain discipline at the end of a lesson as well by not allowing learners to leave the room without your permission.

The discipline in an IT/CAT class can also be influenced when it is necessary to move learners from one place to another, for example to watch a video or demonstration (Banks 2000). Carefully plan the moving between activities and make sure that learners know exactly what is expected of them before they are allowed to move. Effective use of your voice, appropriate non-verbal communication and clever positioning of yourself in the classroom may help you to maintain good behaviour (Banks 2000).

## ACTIVITY 3.3

**Formulate your own opinion on how to manage the learners in your IT/CAT class to ensure a disciplined, yet motivational teaching-learning environment. Supply practical examples of ways you plan to maintain discipline, reward good behaviour and address unacceptable behaviour.**

## 3.5 USE OF TEXTBOOKS IN IT/CAT

Although you will study the use and evaluation of learning and teaching support material (LTSM) in detail in Chapter 9, it is necessary at this stage to consider a few guidelines regarding the use of textbooks during a lesson. The textbook must never replace the teacher, and should serve as an aid and a source of reference for learners. The teacher should never read from the textbook during a lesson. If necessary, the teacher may refer to the textbook for assignments, additional exercises, or other examples of a particular concept which learners are supposed to review on their own.

## 3.6 USING QUESTIONS IN A LESSON

Questions asked during a lesson, whether in class or online, stimulate learners' thoughts. The type of questions that you ask during a lesson depends on what the purpose of a specific question is. Questions can prompt learners to simply repeat what they have previously memorised, or encourage them to think for themselves and acquire their own insights in an exciting, learning environment (Monyai 2006). A question such as *"What is a computer network?"* is merely aimed at recalling knowledge, while a question such as *"Why will the use of a computer network be more effective than using stand-alone computers in a school environment?"* will elicit an argument or reasoning. Thus, questions should be asked to stimulate different cognitive processes (Monyai 2006:131). Where applicable, learners should be asked to explain their answers. Therefore, the posing of questions during a lesson should be thoroughly planned, and questions should not merely be posed for the purpose of gaining a learner's attention, but rather to aid the learner in achieving the objectives.

Always direct a question at the entire class, afford everyone the opportunity to think about it, and then ask a specific learner to provide the answer. Do not always select the same learner, and try to involve learners who tend to be passive. Learners should be confident to answer even though their answers might be wrong. Do not denigrate any answer, but guide the learner who supplied an incorrect answer by means of posing additional questions until he/she discovers the correct answer on his/her own, or with the aid of other learners. Try not to answer your own questions. Answer your own question only after learners have been given enough time to think about it and are still not able to provide a correct answer (Monyai 2006).

Keep questions as clear and unambiguous as possible. Ask only one question at a time and try to avoid situations where learners answer a question in unison (Monyai 2006). Encourage learners who do answer questions so that they will have the confidence to do so again. Use previous answers in the formulation of new questions. If learners cannot answer a question, the teacher may supply clues in such a way as to lead the learners in thinking that they have supplied the answer themselves.

According to Monyai (2006:132-133), the following different types of questions can be asked, depending on the objectives of the lesson and the abilities of your learners:

- Open questions, e.g. *"What can be done to improve the performance of your personal computer?".* This type of question does not have only one correct answer and it stimulates thinking and reasoning.

- Follow-up questions, e.g. *"Explain why you have made that suggestion."* This type of question requires extra explanation and rethinking of a previous answer.

- Closed questions, e.g. *"Name the three standard network topologies."* Only one correct answer can be given.

- Empowering questions, e.g. *"I'm sure you are able to design a network that meets the requirements of the scenario. Why don't you first revise the factors that affect a network design before working on your design?"* This is meant to give learners confidence to continue with a task they feel unsure about.

- Confrontational questions, e.g. *"Why do you think you need to plan a solution of a problem properly before implementing it?"* Learners have to address an issue that they are trying to avoid or that they find difficult.

## ACTIVITY 3.4

**Use your own examples of a lesson and relevant questions to debate the effective use of questions to help learners to achieve objectives in an IT/CAT lesson.**

### 3.7  USING ACTIVITY SHEETS

Often activity sheets are referred to as worksheets. Activity sheets may serve as a very effective aid in IT/CAT, especially when differentiating between learners. Activity sheets may be used during various phases of the lesson, but should always contribute towards learners' achievement of objectives.

General guidelines for the compilation of activity sheets comprise the following:

▶ Instructions should be clear and learners should know exactly what to do.

▶ Graphic layout of the activity sheet should motivate the learner to complete it.

▶ Activity sheets should be prepared neatly and preferably should not be handwritten.

▶ If learners are required to fill in their answers, sufficient space should be provided for this purpose.

▶ Activity sheets are not supposed to merely keep the learner occupied, but to support the achievement of a particular objective.

Examples of activity sheets:

▶ A schematic representation of the motherboard with numbered components may be provided, and the learners have to provide the name of each component next to the number of each component.

▶ The schematic representation of different types of ports may be provided and learners could, for example, answer the following questions regarding each port:
  - Identify the type of port.
  - What is the function of the port?
  - How is data transferred through the port?
  - Provide examples of where the port may be used.

## ACTIVITY 3.5

**Prepare an activity sheet that can be used in a Grade 11 IT/CAT class to master any of the theoretical topics. Start by clearly stating the objectives you want the learners to achieve with the use of the activity sheet.**

## 3.8 FACILITATING LEARNING

The conduct of the teacher during a lesson is to a large extent dependent on whether he/she is working with the entire class, with small groups or with individuals. In the following sections, we will discuss some general issues to be considered when working with the entire class, small groups or individuals in a formal classroom setting.

### 3.8.1 The entire class

As soon as you have to facilitate learning with an entire class, the range of aptitudes, different levels of understanding, and differences in motivation of the learners have to be considered (Banks 2000). Based on these aspects and depending on the objectives of the lesson, appropriate teaching-learning strategies must be selected. In a learner-centred and self-directed learning environment, cooperative learning, problem-based learning, discovery learning, and game-based learning are the preferred strategies to implement. Chapters 5 to 8 provide more detailed guidelines on these and other learner-centred teaching-learning strategies. From time to time, the IT/CAT teacher may find it necessary to address an entire class through exposition or by means of demonstrations.

### Exposition

Exposition refers to the situation where the teacher or learner stands in front of the class and talks to the entire group (Banks 2000). In an environment where activity-based and learner-centred learning is encouraged, this method should be carefully considered in order to keep all learners involved. Based on Banks' (2000) list, exposition in the IT/CAT class can probably be used in the following circumstances:

- at the beginning of the lesson when setting the objectives for the lesson;
- when giving a stimulus or setting the context for a topic, for example when you are using a video on different storage media as an introduction to the lesson on this topic;
- when demonstrating a technique or process;
- when using a question-and-answer session or allowing groups to inform one aother;
- when discussing general conduct in the class or points of safety;
- when preparing for a field trip or the reception of a visitor;
- when learners need to provide feedback from their group work;
- at the end of the lesson when consolidating the lesson and reviewing the lesson outcomes; and
- when providing assessment feedback.

### Demonstrations

Demonstrations could be used in the IT/CAT class, for example, when discussing hardware components or when investigating different types of network media. It is important, however, that you first practise the demonstration before doing it in class. This will leave you with more confidence to carry out the demonstration, it will help you to determine which points to stress during the demonstration, and it will also give you an idea of how long the demonstration will take (Banks 2000).

The following guidelines could be helpful when you carry out a demonstration:

- Make sure that everything you need is organised in advance.
- If you use physical items, place them in a logical order close to you.
- The demonstration must be clearly visible to everyone, otherwise it must be done in smaller groups.
- Ensure that the demonstration is competently performed and explained so that all learners understand why they are being shown the items or technique and how to carry it out themselves (Banks 2000).
- Involve all learners as far as possible, either by asking for their help to pass items around, to take readings (if appropriate), or to repeat certain tasks or techniques (Banks 2000).
- The demonstration must be carried out in a way that keeps everyone's attention (Banks 2000).
- Ask questions to check for understanding (Gunter, Estes and Schwab 2010).
- Summarise the main concepts and connect them to the next phase of the lesson (Gunter, Estes and Schwab 2010).

## 3.8.2 Groups

Research has shown the incredible value of group work in the IT/CAT class, either through cooperative or collaborative learning techniques. The need for learners to be able to work in groups originates from the group nature of projects in the industry. Thus, it has become essential that learners develop the appropriate skills at school level. In Chapter 6, the implementation of cooperative learning in the IT/CAT class is discussed in detail.

## 3.8.3 Individuals

The main purpose of teaching and learning is to ensure that each and every learner achieves the required objectives. Thus, although you mostly handle the class as a whole or in groups, it must be recognised that learning is a personal and individual process. From time to time, the IT/CAT teacher may find it necessary to facilitate learning with learners as individuals, especially when they experience problems. The teacher must ensure that every learner has the necessary skills and knowledge to carry out what he/she wants to do (Banks 2000), whether to make recommendations on how to enhance the performance of a personal computer, or to solve a problem using a computer program.

Using Banks' (2000) strategies, the following recommendations can be made for working with individuals in the IT/CAT class:

- When learners work individually, especially while doing practical work, visit each learner and ensure that they have planned their work properly and that they are making progress.
- Encourage learners to think for themselves and to be critical and creative. Do not give in to the urge to do their work for them, but rather guide them with hints and ideas and lead them to make their own decisions.

- When learners are stuck with a problem, lead them to reflect on previous actions and tasks to see if they can use their previous knowledge and/or experiences to solve the current problem.

- Treat all learners equally, and acknowledge and respect the diversity in terms of race, gender and culture.

- Motivate learners to persevere with their efforts and do not forget the value of appraisal of successful efforts and good work.

- Link to the level and experience of the specific individual when explaining work to an individual learner. It is usually the learner who struggles or the very advanced learner who needs individual attention from the teacher.

## ACTIVITY 3.6

**Write a report with recommendations to IT/CAT teachers on general guidelines for facilitating teaching and learning with the entire class, small groups or individual learners. Illustrate your recommendations by providing an example of a teaching-learning activity for each of these three situations (entire class, small groups, individuals) and explain how you will facilitate learning in each situation.**

## 3.9    HOW TO MANAGE PRACTICAL WORK IN CLASS

At this stage, we will only consider some general issues regarding the management of lessons on practical work.

During a practical work session the teacher should continuously act as facilitator, while still participating in the act of learning. Individual learners may require a lot of the teacher's time, yet this is the best time for addressing individual problems. Learners often tend to expect the teacher to correct errors in their practical work. Motivate and guide the learners to think independently and to try to solve the problem on their own, as this is the best way of learning. Be very careful not to solve learners' problems for them; instead, guide and stimulate learners by means of questions to solve the problems on their own.

If you are comfortable with it and are in control, you may allow learners to walk around during practical work sessions to discuss their problems with one another. However, these discussions should occur in accordance with set rules in order to prevent disorder. It is more valuable to discuss practical work in class and to indicate typical problems immediately. In addition, learners should be given the opportunity to explain their own practical work in class. In this way, learners realise that all solutions to practical problems do not have to be similar in order to be correct. If a learner has solved a problem in an original manner, he/she should be allowed to demonstrate it in class.

## ACTIVITY 3.7

**Discuss the general problems that the IT/CAT teacher may experience during a practical lesson. Give advice on how to handle these problems and what can be done to prevent them.**

### 3.10  DEALING WITH HIGH ACHIEVERS

An IT/CAT teacher should always account for learners who have already achieved the intended objectives. When an advanced learner has achieved an objective, the teacher often presumes that all the other learners have also achieved the objectives. Teachers then continue without taking the slower learners into consideration. Rather see to it that enriching activities are readily available to advanced learners and provide them with opportunities to broaden and deepen their knowledge of the subject (Hugo 2006). The advanced learner may, for example, be required to gather additional information him/herself, such as on specific new computer technology, and then convey this information in class. In the IT/CAT class it is also possible to involve advanced learners in the support of slow learners during practical sessions, but ensure that they do not do the other learners' work for them. See to it that advanced learners are constantly stimulated. These learners' nature should be taken into account before additional assignments are issued.

Learners who have already achieved the set objectives have the tendency to make teachers feel nervous since some teachers feel threatened by the knowledge these learners possess. However, these learners may be employed to the benefit of the entire class. The advanced learner should realise that the teacher does not have infinite knowledge and that you would like him/her to share his/her knowledge or skills with you. This may motivate and inspire learners to reach even greater heights, and if the situation is dealt with properly, it may motivate other learners as well.

## ACTIVITY 3.8

**Explain what you would do in the IT/CAT class to prevent advanced learners from becoming bored (and eventually deciding to quit this subject and take another subject because they have lost interest), or to prevent them from causing disciplinary problems.**

## 3.11  LEARNERS WITH PHYSICAL DISABILITIES

One of the core principles of IT/CAT is the provision of equal opportunities in terms of access to computers for all learners, even those with particular learning problems and physical handicaps. Inclusive education is promoted by the provision of opportunities, alternative teaching and learning methods and flexible assessment for learners experiencing barriers to learning (DOE 2008).

The adaptations which possibly may be made to a computer in order to accommodate learners with physical disabilities depend upon the type of computer, as well as the specific operating system. A few examples of adaptations that might be made in order to accommodate learners who experience problems in terms of sight, hearing and mobility include (DOE 2008):

- enlargement of information and icons on screen, as well as the provision of sound for learners who have poor eyesight;
- alteration of the way in which the mouse and keyboard operate;
- the use of voice recognition for the purpose of data input, as well as the output of sound;
- word or phrase prediction software that allows users to type more quickly by using fewer keystrokes;
- alternative input devices, such as a touch screen; and
- output by means of Braille printers.

In addition to the accessibility tools provided with operating systems, a variety of hardware and software exist and constantly are being developed to promote accessibility. IT/CAT teachers can use articles in magazines and on the internet to ensure that they stay up to date on these types of developments, since specific disabled learners may well need specific hardware or software with more advanced functionalities.

## ACTIVITY 3.9

**Use the internet, electronic databases and/or the library to find at least three articles on ways to make the computer more accessible to learners who experience barriers related to visual ability, hearing ability, and motor skills respectively. Write a report of approximately 300 words on your findings from the literature.**

## 3.12 CONCLUSION

In this chapter, a number of the factors that contribute towards the successful facilitation of an IT/CAT lesson in practice were discussed. These included the role of the teacher as facilitator of teaching and learning through all the phases of a lesson, discipline and management of learners, the use of textbooks, worksheets and questions in a lesson, and the handling of practical lessons. In addition, important issues regarding the facilitating of learning with groups or individual learners, as well as the handling of advanced learners or learners with disabilities in the IT/CAT class were discussed.

# ASSIGNMENT 3

**3.1** Formulate your **own opinion** on the practical implications and desirability of having learners with physical disabilities, such as those with poor eyesight, weak hearing or weak motor skills, in the same IT/CAT class as learners who do not have physical disabilities. Motivate your argument(s) with appropriate examples.

**3.2** The effectiveness of teaching and learning in the IT/CAT class is to a large extent influenced by the discipline in the class. Give your own opinion on:

a) what you consider to be "discipline" in the IT/CAT class;

b) how the discipline is influenced by advanced learners, group work and practical work; and

c) what precautions you will take to prevent teaching and learning in the IT/CAT class being negatively influenced by disciplinary problems.

**3.3** Create an activity sheet to be used in a Grade 10 IT/CAT practical class on a topic of your own choice. Clearly indicate what part of the worksheet should be completed by all learners, and what part contains enrichment activities for advanced achievers.

## REFERENCES

Banks, F. 2000. Teaching design and technology. (In G. Owen-Jackson, ed. *Learning to teach design and technology in the secondary school: A companion to school experience.* London: Routledge Falmer, pp. 151-169.)

DOE (Department of Education) see South Africa. Department of Education.

Fraser, J.D.C. 2006. Mediation of learning. (In M.M. Nieman and R.B. Monyai, eds. *The educator as mediator of learning.* Pretoria: Van Schaik, pp. 1-21.)

Gunter, M.A., Estes, T.H. and Schwab, J. 2010. *Instruction: A models approach*, 5th ed. Boston, MA: Pearson.

Hugo, A.J. 2006. Overcoming barriers to learning through mediation. (In M.M. Nieman and R.B. Monyai, eds. *The educator as mediator of learning.* Pretoria: Van Schaik, pp. 43-71.)

Monyai, R.B. 2006. Teaching strategies. (In M.M. Nieman and R.B. Monyai, eds. *The educator as mediator of learning.* Pretoria: Van Schaik, pp. 104-135.)

Pienaar, G.E. 2006. Creating a learning environment conducive to the effective mediation of learning. (In M.M. Nieman and R.B. Monyai, eds. *The educator as mediator of learning.* Pretoria: Van Schaik, pp. 159-173.)

SACTE (South African College for Teacher Education). 1995. *Study Manual Teaching Method of Computer Science: theoretical work* (CSCM11). Pretoria.

South Africa. Department of Education. 2008. *National curriculum statement. Grades 10-12* (General). Learning programme guidelines. Information Technology. Pretoria: Department of Education.

# CHAPTER 4

# Assessment in IT and CAT

Ulza Wassermann & Sukie van Zyl

## OBJECTIVES

**After completing this chapter, you should be able to:**

- distinguish between different types of assessment;

- describe the types of assessment in the national curriculum;

- apply the information gained from the policy documents to conduct and record assessment in IT or CAT for Grades 10 to 12;

- explain which steps to follow to increase validity and reliability of a test or examination; and

- analyse an assessment to ensure quality.

## TERMS YOU SHOULD BE FAMILIAR WITH

Assessment is the process of "gathering information" on how learning goals have been reached (Lubbe and Mentz 2021:22).

### Formative assessment

The purpose of formative assessment is to assess students' progress. Formative assessments are done while a specific topic is being studied or a specific skill is being learned. Formative assessment gives educators the opportunity to adapt their teaching and gives students the opportunity to reflect on their learning to improve teaching and learning. We can therefore say that formative assessment forms learning.

### Summative assessment

Summative assessments are done after a specific topic or section of the curriculum had been completed. Summative assessment aims to give a final mark to report on student achievement of a specific topic or attainment of a specific skill. Examples are tests, projects and final examinations (Airasian 2005:151).

### Informal/daily assessment

Assessment to determine if lesson aims have been reached. Informal assessment is carried out as part of normal classroom teaching (Siebörger and Macintosh 2004:20). Assessment which is done as part of the facilitation of a lesson to assess students' prior knowledge or to determine if lesson aims have been reached.

## 4.1    INTRODUCTION

As you have seen in Chapter 1, the Department of Basic Education is responsible for all policy documents with regards to the curriculum in South Africa. The specific content and/or titles of these policy documents may change from time to time, but these documents always contain policy statements relating to assessment. In this chapter, we are going to provide guidelines for you to be able to find and apply information relating to assessment in IT and CAT.

## 4.2    OFFICIAL DOCUMENTS RELATING TO ASSESSMENT

Policy documents are legal documents. They contain, for instance, the requirements for a learner to pass, guidelines on what assessments should be done and the weighting of assessments. If a learner fails to submit all the relevant assessments as stipulated in the assessment policy documents, such a learner may have to repeat the grade. Teachers also need to provide evidence that they have adhered to the assessment guidelines. As indicated before, assessment requirements may change, therefore you need to access the website of the Department of Basic Education and ensure you obtain the latest policy documents relating to assessment in IT and/or CAT. The following activity provides a structure to summarise the information regarding policy documents relating to assessment.

## ACTIVITY 4.1

**Complete the following table:**

| Name of official policy document relating to assessment | Is it a generic or an IT/CAT specific document? | Brief summary of the purpose and content of the document | Where can document be obtained? |
|---|---|---|---|
|  |  |  |  |

## 4.3 TYPES OF ASSESSMENT

The type of assessment is determined by the purpose of assessment. Assessment can test knowledge, but assessment is also used to promote learning (Lubbe and Mentz 2021). We can broadly classify assessment as assessment of learning, assessment for learning and assessment as learning (Manitoba Education 2006). Assessment of learning is summative and is mostly done at the end of a section or topic. Assessment for learning, which is connected to formative assessment, is designed to assist learners to identify their learning needs, to set learning goals and to evaluate their learning. Assessment as learning refers to learning-oriented assessment, where learners are engaging and collaborating, self-assessing, analysing and discussing (Lubbe and Mentz 2021). As a result, learners receive feedback, which provides them with ideas for "adjusting, rethinking, and articulating their understanding" (Manitoba Education 2006:48).

In Chapter 2, you learned that a lesson consists of different phases. These phases are introduction, development and consolidation.

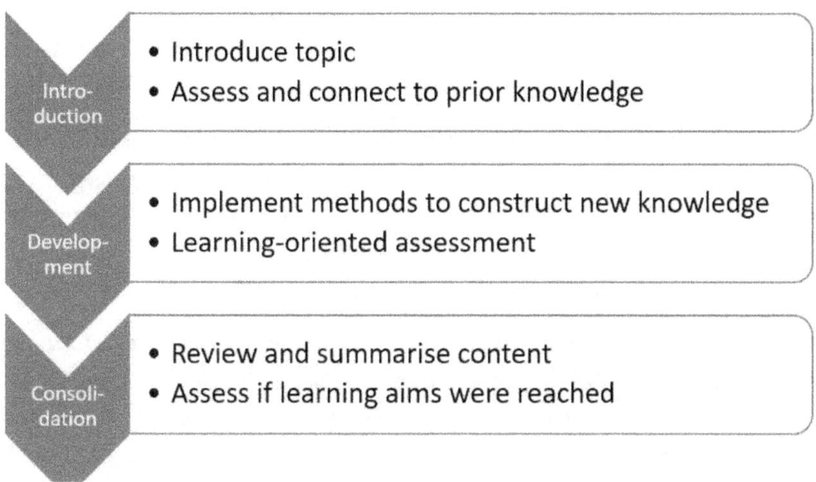


*Figure 4.1    Diagram of lesson phases to indicate assessment*

All phases include an aspect of assessment, as indicated in Figure 4.1. In the introduction phase, learners' prior knowledge is assessed. In the development phase, the principle of active learning is applied when learners are engaged in activities to bring forth their understanding of the lesson content and to construct their own knowledge. Robert Gagné, an educational psychologist, referred to this type of assessment as "eliciting the performance".

In the consolidation phase, assessment is done to determine whether learners have achieved the intended objectives or aims of the lesson (assess performance).

## 4.3.1  Elicit performance

Gagné motivated the need to elicit performance as follows: "Once the content is presented and hopefully understood, learners need an opportunity to practice. Often, the same examples that have previously been presented are used and new ones are introduced to see if the learner truly understands or is just repeating what was done before" (Gagné's Nine Events of Instruction n.d.:1). According to the International Board of Standards for Training, the purpose of eliciting performance is to verify that something has been learned. The Board also emphasises that students need to participate by showing what they have learned (International Board of Standards for Training, Performance and Instruction 2010).

Teachers should take care to ensure the activities they use to elicit performance comply with the following:

▶ The instructions to the learners should be very clear so that they know exactly what to do and what is expected of them.

▶ The activities should relate to the learning objectives and assess the skills and/or knowledge that were specified in the objectives.

▸ The activities should be provided as soon as possible after the new content was facilitated. The activities can also be part of the facilitation process, as in learner-centred teaching and learning strategies such as cooperative learning, where learners need to construct their own meaning of new content.

Activities can be practical or written, such as a PowerPoint presentation or a small, informal class test. Even if marks are assigned to these activities, the marks need not be recorded as part of the promotion marks of a learner. The results of these assessments can be used by the teacher to make decisions about learners' understanding and problems that learners may experience, to make informed decisions about what should be done in the next lesson.

Feedback is part of the learning process and should not be excluded, as it provides "powerful support" to learners and, if done appropriately, has "a positive effect on learning" (Mentz and Lubbe 2021:143). There are furthermore two sides to feedback as described by Boud and Molloy (2013). Feedback is firstly provided by the teacher to the student. Secondly, students need to be able to reflect on their assignments and provide feedback on their own tasks.

### 4.3.2  Assess performance

It may be necessary to repeat the steps of eliciting performance and providing feedback a number of times before a teacher is satisfied that learners have mastered the new knowledge or skills. Then, as stated in Chapter 2, in the final part of the lesson the IT/CAT teacher assesses whether learners have achieved the intended objectives of the lesson. One way in which assessment can be done in a structured way during a lesson while learners are actively participating, is to apply the GIG cooperative learning assessment method.

### 4.3.3  Group-individual-group (GIG) cooperative learning assessment

The focus of formative assessment should be to enhance learning. A method that can be applied to elicit performance and to assess performance is the Group-Individual-Group (GIG) cooperative learning method. With this method, students have to prepare for a test at home, but when entering the class, the students have to divide in groups (maximum four students) and receive the opportunity to prepare for the test together, discussing the important matters and explaining to each other possible difficult concepts. In the next phase, they have to take the test individually and submit their answers. In the last phase, they have to write the same test again, but this time as the group who prepared together. They have to discuss and debate what the best answer to each question is. After submitting the group test, the group reflects on the way in which they worked together on the assignment and the teacher concludes by facilitating a class discussion about the assignment. The main advantage of the GIG method is that students receive immediate feedback on assessment – first from their peers and then from the teacher.

# ACTIVITY 4.2

(a) Discuss the type of assessments that are mentioned in the CAPS document for CAT/IT.

(b) What type of assessments mentioned in the policy document for IT/CAT correspond with "eliciting performance" and to "assess performance"?

(c) Provide an example of a new concept to be facilitated in the IT/CAT class, and activities that can then be used to elicit and to assess performance.

(d) Design a diagram to portray the various aspects involved in the GIG cooperative learning method, that you can use for compiling lessons based on this method. Compile a lesson plan that incorporates GIG cooperative learning method of assessment on a topic in CAT/IT. Include a test that is focused on the lesson aims. Take into account the time available for one school period. Learners should be able to write the individual test in approximately 10 minutes. Indicate the various phases of the lesson and the GIG assessment in your lesson plan, as well as the time that you will allocate to each phase. (It might be a good idea to consult other sources on the GIG method before starting this activity.)

## 4.4 RECORDING AND REPORTING ASSESSMENT

### 4.4.1 Evidence of assessment

Teachers must provide evidence in the form of an assessment file and learner portfolio's to see whether they adhered to the assessment guidelines. Assessment policy documents contain specifications regarding the way evidence of assessment should be managed. It usually refers to:

▶ The teacher's evidence which will be an assessment file and electronic folder containing:
  - each formal assessment's specifications (the assignment, test or question paper);
  - the assessment instrument (a mark sheet , rubric or memorandum) for each assessment;
  - evidence of moderation of the question paper and of marked assessments; and
  - copies of a few learners' answer sheets, assignments or marked rubrics .

▸ The learners' evidence which will be a file and folder for each learner containing all their answer sheets and marked rubrics. The learners' files and folders should be in the same order as the teacher's file.

The format of the evidence of assessment will be communicated to you by the district office. The subject advisor or other representative will make an appointment to moderate your assessment file. As a teacher, you have to ensure you are familiar with the requirements before you start teaching, so that you can keep the relevant evidence from the beginning of the term. Do not wait for instructions from the Department of Basic Education, but put all your evidence of assessments in your assessment file as you are compiling the assessments, so that you are prepared and ready when you have to submit the evidence of assessment. It is a daunting task to compile an assessment file and collect all the evidence at a later stage. The same applies to learner evidence. Require of each learner to compile a neat portfolio file with their marked assessments.

## ACTIVITY 4.3

**During work-integrated learning (WIL), review the assessment policy documents you collected in activity 4.1, and have a discussion with the IT/CAT teacher to write a short summary indicating the following:**

(a) **the type and format of assessment evidence that should be kept by a teacher;**

(b) **the type and format of evidence that should be kept by a learner;**

(c) **the number of years the evidence should be kept; and**

(d) **the moderation procedures that should be followed for each grade.**

### 4.4.2 Record sheets

The format of record sheets containing learner marks is usually prescribed by each school. Schools use the software SAMS and/or other software where marks must be entered for each learner. You also need to compile an Excel spreadsheet where you record all marks and calculate percentages according to the weightings indicated in the policy documents. Marks are sensitive data and should be recorded meticulously. Always verify the marks that you enter in the spreadsheet with the learners (for example, read out loud with their permission), to make sure that you did not make a mistake when calculating or capturing the marks.

# ACTIVITY 4.4

**Study the policy documents containing the specifications for assessment for IT and CAT. Create an Excel spreadsheet with formulas that can be used to calculate the final mark of an IT/CAT learner in Grade 10 to 12. Test the formulas by adding full marks for all assessments for a dummy learner, to verify that the percentages are calculated correctly.**

## 4.5 ASSESSMENT PRINCIPLES

### 4.5.1 Validity and reliability

In all assessment, whether it is a test, examination or other task, you should ensure that the assessment is valid and reliable. According to Kubiszyn and Borich (2000), a test is valid if it measures what it is supposed to measure, and a test is reliable if the test yields the same or similar score rankings consistently. We are going to discuss how this can be applied in IT and CAT.

One way to determine if a test is valid, is to determine if it has sufficient validity evidence. The type of evidence that is the easiest to obtain is content validity evidence. "In the context of classroom testing, content validity evidence answers the question 'Does the test measure the instructional objectives?'" (Kubiszyn and Borich 2000). Practically, this means that you should look at each question and decide if it really corresponds to what you decided to assess (the lesson aim). For example, if you want to assess if a learner can apply basic formatting to a document, but the learner first has to type two pages of text, you are actually assessing typing skills, not formatting skills. Most learners may spend so much time on entering the text, that they do not have time left to do the formatting. Such a test will not be valid, since it assesses keyboarding skills more than formatting skills. In the IT class, a test will not be valid if a learner spends a lot of time on entering data, so that less time is available for the programming concept that you want to assess.

Therefore, to determine if an assessment is valid you need to:

▸ decide what the aim of the assessment is, and what learning objectives, skills or knowledge you want to assess;

▸ review each question and ask yourself if the question matches or measures the learning objectives, skills or knowledge you intended it to; and

▸ Work out the memo as soon as you have set the test, before handing out the test to learners, to see if the answer to each question is what you intended it to be.

"Reliability implies consistency in terms of how far the same test would give the same results if done by the same children under the same conditions" (Maree and Fraser 2004:35). Reliability is difficult to achieve, but there are a number of steps you can take to ensure that reliability is as high as possible:

- When creating a memorandum, ensure that the criteria for assigning marks are as clear as possible (more information and examples will be provided in section 4.7).

- If possible, mark a few tasks, and discuss variations in the memorandum with a colleague who has knowledge of IT or CAT. Adjust the memorandum if necessary. Ask yourself if learners understood the question as you intended it, or could they have interpreted the question differently. Adjust the memo if necessary.

- Have the assessment moderated by a colleague.

## 4.5.2  Quality assurance

Most assessment tasks focus on assessing knowledge and skills (Bloom's revised taxonomy levels 1 and 2). The six cognitive levels of Bloom's revised taxonomy are described using specific verbs or nouns (revise the action verbs in Chapter 2 of this book). It can assist you in the classification of learning objectives and questions. Especially as a beginner teacher, you should analyse your assessment tasks to ensure that you include questions on all relevant levels of Bloom's taxonomy. In IT/CAT, assessment tasks in the topic Solution Development (software applications or programming) tend to be on higher cognitive levels, requiring learners to design a solution for a given problem. However, you have to aim for assessments that are balanced on the various cognitive levels. With Solution Development, aim for lower cognitive levels as well. With content that have a more theoretical focus, you need to incorporate higher cognitive levels.

Table 4.1 shows an example of the way in which a test or question paper can be analysed. The table can be compiled with Excel, as you need to do some calculations. To complete the table, list each question number in the first column. Enter the number of marks for each question under the relevant cognitive level (examples are already entered in the first two lines of the table; delete these when doing your own analysis). Calculate the total marks per cognitive level in the second last row. Work out the percentage of marks for each level in the final row (Total for cognitive level/total marks of the assessment x 100). You can then interpret the results to determine whether the assessment is balanced by looking at the percentages of the various cognitive levels.

*Table 4.1    Example: The way in which an assessment can be analysed*

| Description of assessment: | | | | | | |
|---|---|---|---|---|---|---|
| Total marks of the assessment: | | | | | | |
| Question No | Level 1 | Level 2 | Level 3 | Level 4 | Level 5 | Level 6 |
| 1.1.1 (example) | | | 5 | | | |
| 1.1.2 (example) | | 3 | | | | |
| etc. | | | | | | |
| | | | | | | |
| | | | | | | |
| | | | | | | |
| | | | | | | |
| | | | | | | |
| | | | | | | |
| | | | | | | |
| | | | | | | |
| | | | | | | |
| **TOTAL** | | | | | | |
| **Percentage** | | | | | | |

| Question from IT/CAT test | Bloom's taxonomy level |
|---|---|
| Define multi-processing. | This refers to the recall of knowledge without necessarily understanding it. This refers to level 1. |
| Give a simple, practical example of where a user will see multi-processing in action. | This calls for an interpretation and description of knowledge; it can be considered to be on level 2. |
| Add a formula in column E to calculate the profit made on each item the company sells. | The rules and methods to create an Excel formula have to be applied in a new situation (a spreadsheet the learner has not seen before). This is a skill on level 3. |
| Arrange the following storage capacities from the smallest to the largest: 1.2 megabyte; 1.6 terabyte; 1 byte; 2048 gigabytes; 7 bits; 1 kilobyte; 2048 kilobytes; 0.5 exabyte | In this question, the relationship between elements must be recognised; this refers to cognitive level 4. |
| The trend worldwide is to save on natural resources. Educational institutions also have a duty to promote the conservation of resources. Write a proposal to the school to suggest how they can contribute to "green computing". | Elements of knowledge regarding various aspects (hardware as well as software) are combined to create a new product. This is a characteristic of level 5. |

| Question from IT/CAT test | Bloom's taxonomy level |
| --- | --- |
| Someone makes a remark that the USA has recently passed a law that allows officials to confiscate and examine any electronic device at the border when people enter the USA. He thinks that we should implement a similar policy in South Africa. Ethically speaking, discuss what is WRONG with this policy. You MUST give FOUR clear bullet points to support your answer. | An evaluation or recommendation is made and a statement is criticised, therefore it is on level 6. |

# ACTIVITY 4.5

**Visit the Department of Basic Education's website and download one practical and one theoretical paper for your subject (IT/CAT). Analyse both papers according to Bloom's taxonomy. Do you consider the papers to be balanced? Write a short report to express your opinion.**

## 4.6 PLANNING A TEST OR EXAMINATION PAPER

In setting a test or examination, you need to pay attention to the following aspects:

**A) Skills, knowledge, attitudes and values to be assessed**

- Always keep the purpose of the paper in mind, which is to determine whether or not the learners have attained the particular learning objectives

- See to it that the test covers the work that it is supposed to cover. Refer to your work schedule where it is indicated what topics have been covered in the time preceding the test or examination.

- Disseminate questions proportionally according to the amount of time which was allocated to the particular topic in class. For a Grade 12 paper, refer to the layout of the paper provided in documents from the Department of Basic Education, the examination guidelines, as well as the exemplar papers for an indication of the number of marks to be allocated to different topics. Papers for Grades 10 and 11 can be modelled on the Grade 12 papers.

- See to it that no question deals with work which the learners were not supposed to study.

**B) Type of questions to be used**

- Vary the types of questions; all questions should not be multiple choice or fill-in questions. Aim for a test that is balanced with regards to cognitive levels.

- Do not try to pose trick questions. Set questions in such a way as to allow the average learner to obtain at least 50% for the paper. Out of the total number of marks, 10% should be directed at Bloom levels 1 and 2 and 10% at Bloom levels 4, 5 and 6.
- See to it that all questions are formulated clearly in order for learners to know precisely what is expected of them.

**C) Duration of the paper**

- Be fair in the allocation of marks per minute. A general guideline would be to allow approximately one minute per mark for a theory paper, and 1.5 minutes per mark for a practical paper. Take into account the length of a class period as well as the time it takes learners to get to class, to sit, to hand out and to take in the test.

**D) Preparation before the paper is written**

- Compile the memorandum after the paper has been set, but prior to copying the final paper and the writing of the paper. In this way, errors in terms of questions which do not work out may be omitted.
- As far as practical assessments and the marking of projects are concerned, it is important to employ a marking scheme or a marking rubric. This will result in the uniform allocation of marks. You also need to indicate clearly what you allocated marks for when giving feedback to the learner.

## 4.7    ASSESSMENTS AND MARKING INSTRUMENTS

The following should take place before you give an assessment task to a learner. It is also important that you share the information with the learners:

- clarify what learning objectives and content you are going to assess; and
- develop a marking guide to indicate what is expected of the learner.

When the learners are writing a test, you will, of course, not always share the marking guide with them before the test.

Examples of marking guides include checklists, memorandums, rubrics, as well as assessment grids using rating scales and observation sheets. In this section, we are going to provide some general guidelines that you can apply when you set assessment tasks, and also discuss different types of marking guides that are suitable in assessing IT/CAT tasks.

## 4.7.1    Assessments applicable to IT and CAT

A number of different assessment tasks can be used in IT and CAT. (Note that 'assessment' refers to formative as well as summative assessment.) Some of these include written tasks, practical tasks, examinations, tests, presentations, debates, interviews, demonstrations, role-play projects, research tasks and case studies.

# ACTIVITY 4.6

**Describe a suitable IT/CAT assessment task for each of the different types of assessment by completing the following table. (Briefly describe the main content to be addressed and indicate page numbers in the CAPS document that refer to the content.)**

| Subject: (IT or CAT?) | | |
|---|---|---|
| Assessment form | Brief description of the task | Main content to be addressed |
| Written task | | |
| Practical task | | |
| Examination | | |
| Test | | |
| Presentation | | |
| Debate | | |
| Interview | | |
| Demonstration | | |
| Role-play project | | |
| Research task | | |
| Case study | | |

All assessment tasks should be marked or graded, whether by the learners themselves, by a peer and/or by the teacher. To mark or grade the task, you have to develop a marking guide or assessment instrument that can be used to assess the learners' work.

## 4.7.2 Types of marking guides or assessment instruments

Marking guides fall into three broad categories: checklists, rating scales and rubrics (Killen 2007). Whatever guide you use, learners must have access to these before they attempt the task so that they can determine what aspects they will be assessed on, and what the level of difficulty or quality of work will be. This is not always applicable to tests or examination papers, but even for an examination paper, learners need to know what type of questions they will be asked and what content they need to study.

## Checklist

"Checklists contain lists of behaviours, traits, or characteristics that can be scored as either present or absent. They are best suited for complex behaviours or performances that can be divided into a series of clearly defined, specific actions" (Kubiszyn and Borich 2000:196).

Table 4.2 shows a checklist which can be used to assess a practical task such as creating a database. Since certain tasks take longer than others to complete, involve more actions or can be considered to be more difficult, a weight can be assigned to a criterion so that it makes a larger contribution to the final mark. Add a formula in MS Word to calculate the total weight (to check if the total is correct) and to calculate the total mark in order to reduce marking errors. In the feedback column, you can type remarks to indicate why you have assigned a certain mark (do not forget to also include positive, encouraging remarks and to praise good work).

*Table 4.2    Example of a checklist*

| Criteria | ☒☑ | Weight | Mark | Feedback |
|---|---|---|---|---|
| Gave database suitable name | | 1 | | |
| Imported five records | | 3 | | |
| Selected suitable field names | | 2 | | |
| Selected correct field types | | 2 | | |
| Selected appropriate field sizes | | 2 | | |
| Chosen unique field as primary key | | 1 | | |
| TOTAL | | | | |

## Rating scale

"Rating scales are typically used for those aspects of complex performance that do not lend themselves to yes/no or present/absent type judgements. The most common form of a rating scale is one that assigns numbers to categories of performance" (Kubiszyn and Borich 2000).

The rating scale in Table 4.3 (page 84) can form part of the marking guide for a research project.

*Table 4.3    Example of a rating scale*

| Rating Code | 6 | 5 | 4 | 3 | 2 | 1 | |
|---|---|---|---|---|---|---|---|
| Description of competence | Outstanding | Meritorious | Satisfactory | Adequate | Partial | Inadequate | Learner's mark |
| Introduction: Description of the topic | | | | | | | |
| Definition of key concepts pertaining to the topic | | | | | | | |
| Discussion of the topic | | | | | | | |
| Formulation of the conclusion | | | | | | | |
| Layout of document | | | | | | | |
| TOTAL | | | | | | | |
| Feedback/Comments: | | | | | | | |

## Rubric

"A rubric is a special form of rating scale that allows the marker to provide descriptive feedback about the quality of a learner's work, with reference to several specific criteria" (Killen 2007:353). The rubric in Table 4.4 forms an example of a the marking guide for a PowerPoint presentation. In the bottom row, you can provide more detailed feedback to the learner or make comments such as praising good work.

*Table 4.4     Example of a rubric*

| | Level 1 | Level 2 | Level 3 | Level 4 | |
|---|---|---|---|---|---|
| | 0 | 1 | 2 | 3 | Learner's mark |
| Introduction slide (should contain purpose, name of presenter, photo of presenter) | No introduction | Introduction contains only one of the three requirements | Introduction contains only two of the three requirements | Introduction contains purpose of presentation, name of presenter, and photo of presenter | |
| Number of slides included (introduction slide, at least three slides for explanation and a summary slide) | One or two slides | Only three slides included | Only four slides included | Introduction, three or more slides as part of the explanation and a summary slide included | |
| Legibility (font size adequate, font type legible, background letter colour combination) | None of the principles applied | Only one principle applied | Only two principles applied | All three principles applied | |
| PowerPoint skills | No additional effort | Custom animation OR slide transition used | Custom animation and slide transition used but not always in an appropriate manner | Custom animation and slide transition used in a skilful and appropriate manner | |
| Use of pictures | No pictures used | Pictures are not relevant to the explanation | Pictures contribute to the explanation but are of poor quality | Pictures contribute to the explanation and they are clear and well sized | |
| TOTAL | | | | | /15 |
| Feedback/Comments: | | | | | |

A summary of the three categories of marking guides follow in Table 4.5 (adapted from Killen 2007).

*Table 4.5    Summary of the three categories of marking guides or assessment instruments*

| Name | Description | Useful for | Weak points |
|---|---|---|---|
| Checklist | A list of all the evidence/ proof of achieving the learning objectives that you want to see in a learner's performance | Provide basic formative feedback to draw attention to aspects learners may have forgotten or not yet mastered; summative assessment to check if a learner has obtained knowledge or mastered certain skills | Judging the quality of performance such as marking an essay because it cannot measure how well learners expressed ideas or developed arguments |
| Rating scale | A list of criteria learners have to meet, including a rating scale that indicates the level of performance on each criterion | Assessment where the different aspects can be completed at different levels of performance | It does not indicate how the marker will decide which rating scale is appropriate |
| Analytic rubric | A marking guide that includes descriptions that indicate how the marker will judge the quality of each criterion | Assessment where the different aspects can be completed at different levels of performance and where you want to minimise the possibility of biased marking | If the difference between two levels is always one mark, it may not give a true representation of the learners' skills. It may be that the difference between a level 1 and a level 2 performance is not as significant as between a level 3 and a level 4 difference. Another problem may be that the various criteria may not be equally important |

### 4.7.3  Marking guidelines

The following steps should be followed once the tasks have been completed:

1.  Mark a random sample of the assessment to ensure that the marking guide covers all aspects of the learners' work. If more than one person will be involved in marking, each should mark the same random sample and then the markers should have a discussion on how they allocated marks to ensure that they will interpret the marking guidelines in the same way.

2.  Provide feedback to the learners. Ensure that comments are clear and sufficiently detailed to promote learner reflection and enhance learning.

### 4.7.4  Useful tips for marking memoranda

Since both IT and CAT contain 50% practical components, the use of marking memoranda displaying the final layout of documents or programming code is very useful. The following are examples of such marking memoranda.

*Example 4.1   Marking memorandum for an Excel assignment*

*This memorandum can be used as a marking guide. If the assignment is printed out, simply circle the marks for each aspect of the assessment the learner included in his/her task, then add up all the circled marks.*

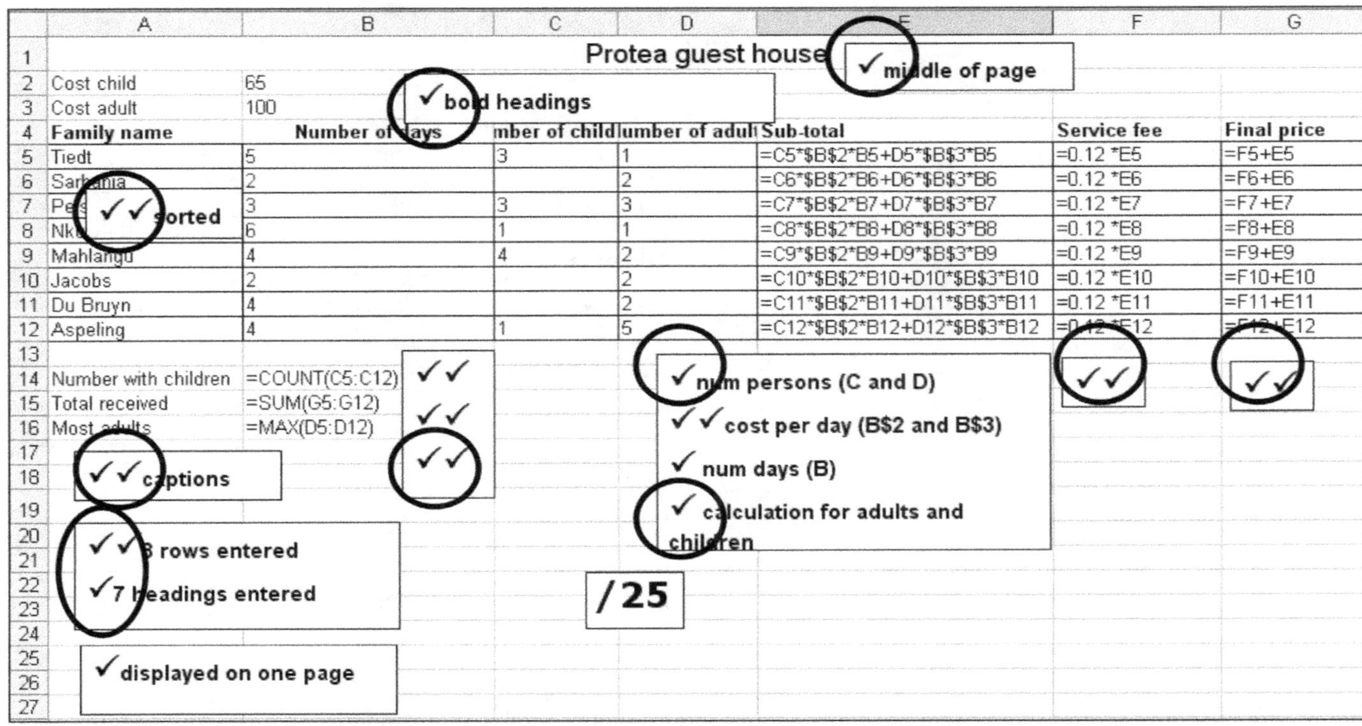



|  | A | B | C | D | E | F | G |
|---|---|---|---|---|---|---|---|
| 1 | | | | | Protea guest house | | |
| 2 | Cost child | 65 | | | | | |
| 3 | Cost adult | 100 | | | | | |
| 4 | Family name | Number of days | mber of child | umber of adul | Sub-total | Service fee | Final price |
| 5 | Tiedt | 5 | 3 | 1 | =C5*$B$2*B5+D5*$B$3*B5 | =0.12 *E5 | =F5+E5 |
| 6 | Sarhania | 2 | | 2 | =C6*$B$2*B6+D6*$B$3*B6 | =0.12 *E6 | =F6+E6 |
| 7 | Pe... | 3 | 3 | 3 | =C7*$B$2*B7+D7*$B$3*B7 | =0.12 *E7 | =F7+E7 |
| 8 | Nk... | 6 | 1 | 1 | =C8*$B$2*B8+D8*$B$3*B8 | =0.12 *E8 | =F8+E8 |
| 9 | Mahlangu | 4 | 4 | 2 | =C9*$B$2*B9+D9*$B$3*B9 | =0.12 *E9 | =F9+E9 |
| 10 | Jacobs | 2 | | 2 | =C10*$B$2*B10+D10*$B$3*B10 | =0.12 *E10 | =F10+E10 |
| 11 | Du Bruyn | 4 | | 2 | =C11*$B$2*B11+D11*$B$3*B11 | =0.12 *E11 | =F11+E11 |
| 12 | Aspeling | 4 | 1 | 5 | =C12*$B$2*B12+D12*$B$3*B12 | =0.12*E12 | =F12+E12 |
| 13 | | | | | | | |
| 14 | Number with children | =COUNT(C5:C12) | | | | | |
| 15 | Total received | =SUM(G5:G12) | | | | | |
| 16 | Most adults | =MAX(D5:D12) | | | | | |

**TOTAL 17/25**

When the assignment has to be marked electronically, the marker still needs to indicate how marks have been allocated. Electronic assignments can, for example, be marked as follows:

1. The Excel sheet can be printed to a PDF file and the teacher can use the marking add-on PDF tool to indicate ticks on the PDF file and to calculate totals. Comments or feedback can be added using the PDF commenting tool.

2. Compile a mark sheet where the question numbers, and correct answers are indicated. The advantage of this mark sheet is that the memorandum is then also available as feedback to the learners. Table 4.6 below is an example of a mark sheet for the Excel assignment indicated in Example 4.1.

*Table 4.6    Example of a marking sheet for an Excel assignment*

| Question No | Question/ Task | Mark | Mark allocated | Feedback/Comment |
|---|---|---|---|---|
| 1 | Bold headings | 1 | | |
| 2 | Centre main heading | 1 | | |
| 3 | Sort according to family name | 2 | | |
| 4 | Calculate service fee (-0.12*E6) | 2 | | |
| Etc. | Etc. | Etc. | | |
| | TOTAL | 25 | | |

A mark sheet as indicated in Table 4.6 is especially handy when marking Access and programming assignments to ensure consistency of marking and to clearly indicate how marks were allocated.

*Example 4.2    Marking memorandum for a Delphi program*

*The following marking memorandum can be used for a programming task where learners had to read an ID number, and change all the letters "I" in the number to the digit 1, and all the letters "O" to the digit 0. They also had to report on the number of changes made for each invalid letter.*

```
procedureTfrmChange.btnChangeID(Sender: TObject);
var
sID : string ;
i, iCountI, iCountO : integer ;
begin
iCountI := 0 ; iCountO := 0 ;
sID := edtID.Text ;
fori := 1 to length(sID) do
begin
ifsID[i] = 'I' then
begin
inc(iCountI);
sID[i] := '1' ;
end ;
ifsID[i] = 'O' then
begin
inc(iCountO) ;
sID[i] := '0';
end ;
end ;

redOut.Lines.Add('The letter I occurred ' + IntToStr(iCountI) +
' times') ;
redOut.Lines.Add('The letter O occurred ' + IntToStr(iCountO) +
' times') ;
end;
```

Variables declared correctly ✓

Set Counters to 0 ✓

Read ID from EditBox✓

Inspect all characters in the string✓

Count I✓

Count O✓

Replace I✓

To provide more detailed feedback and for more complex programming assignments, a mark sheet can similarly be compiled for programming assignments as indicated in Table 4.6.

# ACTIVITY 4.7

(a) The mark sheets for the Grade 12 PAT are a combination of various marking guides. Write a short report on the mark sheets for the PAT of this year. Include the following headings in your report:

- What types of marking guides have been included?
- What is your opinion on the relevancy of the marking guide for each specific type?
- What other types could have been included?
- Can some of the checklists be converted to rating scales?
- Can some of the rating scales be converted to an analytic rubric?

(b) Compile a 30 mark Microsoft Access test (or another relevant solution development topic).

- List the learning objectives that you want to assess.
- Indicate the page number in the policy document that refers to the content and skills being assessed.
- The following should be indicated on the test: Teacher's name, subject, grade, time, number of marks.
- Apply good formatting techniques (tabs, indentation, etc.) and activate the spelling checker to eliminate spelling mistakes.
- Compile a table to determine the distribution of cognitive levels.
- Compile a marking guide as indicated in Table 4.6.

(c) Do some research on online applications, such as Kahoot and Plickers that can be used to do formative assessment in a fun way. Compile an informal assessment on a topic in IT/CAT.

## 4.8    CONCLUSION

In this chapter we showed you how assessment forms part of learning, and that it should not be seen as a once-off procedure that takes place after teaching. We guided you to ensure that you are familiar with the recording and reporting structures that are required by the Department of Basoc Education. We also provided assessment principles, and useful tips on planning and structuring written papers. You are further encouraged to study all official departmental documents regarding assessment, and make sure you know what the implications of all the policies and guidelines are for teaching and assessing IT/CAT. A number of assessment forms and marking guides have been discussed and examples provided. Please note that these are not the only forms and marking guides you should use – they are merely examples you can use to get you started.

# ASSIGNMENT 4

Collect an IT/CAT assessment task and marking guide for each type discussed in this chapter from any source, for example, a teacher you know at a school, a textbook, or from your own portfolio of a previous year of study.

**4.1**    Indicate the learning objectives addressed by each assessment task.

**4.2**    Write a short report on each of the marking guides. Include the following:

   a)   What type or types of marking guide have been used?

   b)   What are the strong points of each marking guide?

   c)   What are the weak points of each marking guide?

   d)   Would you have used a different marking guide or is the current one the best for the particular assessment task?

## REFERENCES

Airasian, P.W. 2005. *Classroom assessment. Concepts and applications*, 5th ed. New York: McGraw Hill.

Black, P. and William, D. 1998. Inside the Black box: Raising standards through classroom assessment. *Phi Delta Kappan*, 80:139-148.

Boud, D. and Molloy, E. 2013. What is the problem with feedback? (In D. Boud and E. Molloy. *Enhancing learning through self-assessment*. London: Kogan Page, pp. 48-63.) https://doi.org/10.4324/9781315041520

Gagné's Nine Events of Instruction. (n.d.). The Chang School Ryerson University: http://de.ryerson.ca/portals/de/assets/resources/Gagne%27s_Nine_Events.pdf (Accessed: 24 April 2012).

International Board of Standards for Training, Performance and Instruction. 2010. Legacy of Robert M. Gagné. R.C. Richey, ed. International Board of Standards for Training, Performance and Instruction: http://www.ibstpi.org/Products/pdf/chapter_4.pdf (Accessed: 27 July 2012).

Killen, R. 2007. *Teaching strategies for outcomes-based education*, 2nd ed. Cape Town: Juta.

Kubiszyn, T. and Borich, G. 2000. *Educational Testing and Measurement*, 9th ed. United States of America: John Wiley & Sons.

Lubbe, A. and Mentz, E. 2021. Self-directed learning-oriented assessment and assessment literacy: Essential for 21st century learning. (In E. Mentz and A. Lubbe. *Learning through assessment: An approach towards self-directed learning*. Cape Town: Aosis, pp. 1-26.) https://doi.org/10.4102/aosis.2021.BK280.01

Manitoba Education. 2006. *Rethinking classroom assessment with purpose in mind: Assessment for learning, assessment as learning, assessment of learning*. Winnipeg, MA: Minister of Education, Citizenship and Youth.

Maree, J.G. and Fraser, W.J. 2004. *Outcomes-based assessment*. Sandown: Heinemann.

Mentz, E. and Lubbe, A. 2021. Value of feedback during the group-individual-group cooperative learning method of assessment. (In E. Mentz and A. Lubbe. *Learning through assessment: An approach towards self-directed learning*. Cape Town: Aosis, pp. 143-164.) https://doi.org/10.4102/aosis.2021.BK280.07

Siebörger, R. and Macintosh, H. 2004. *Transforming assessment: A guide for South African teachers*, 4th ed. Cape Town: Juta.

William, D. 2011. *Embedded formative assessment*. Bloomington, IN: Solution Tree Press.

# CHAPTER 5

# Facilitating problem-solving

**Elsa Mentz, Betty Breed & Marietjie Havenga**

## OBJECTIVES

**After completing this chapter you will be able to:**

- *distinguish between different types of problems and different reasoning techniques;*

- *discuss the kinds of knowledge necessary to solve a problem;*

- *discuss and apply various ways to support learners in solving problems; and*

- *guide learners to implement problem-solving strategies successfully when solving problems.*

## 5.1 INTRODUCTION

Problem-solving may be defined as an active process in which a person attempts to effectuate a change from an initial state to a new, desired state. It is the way in which an individual employs prior knowledge, skills and understanding in order to face the challenges of an unfamiliar situation. The ability to solve problems requires learners to engage in higher-order thinking skills. Although the ability to solve problems depends on the type and nature of problem, the previous experiences of the person solving a problem and various other factors, it is commonly accepted that problem-solving skills can be taught. In this chapter we are going to discuss various ways in which the teacher can facilitate problem-solving in order to improve the learner's problem-solving skills.

Problem-solving is a generic life skill which is required from each learner in any subject. Therefore, it will be of value for the Information Technology (IT) and Computer Applications Technology (CAT) teacher to be aware of ways in which the development of problem-solving skills can be supported in learners.

The main aim of the school subject IT is to enable learners to write correct and high-quality computer programs to solve real-world problems effectively and efficiently. It focuses on activities that deal with creative and logical thinking, the solution of problems and the development of applications by using programming languages. However, programming is a complex and difficult intellectual activity that requires a great number of problem-solving and supportive skills. Computer programming requires the use of specific knowledge, skills and supportive strategies to facilitate the learning process and solve programming problems.

The main aim of the subject CAT also focuses on practical techniques for the efficient use and application of integrated components of a computer system to solve everyday problems.

The use of cognitive and metacognitive activities can direct the thinking processes and can enhance <u>effective</u> solution of problems. The ability to use cognitive activities such as attention, comprehension, reasoning, decision-making, creative thinking and critical thinking will contribute to effective problem-solving. It is therefore essential that teachers should be skilful in supporting learners to use cognitive and metacognitive activities in order to solve problems effectively.

## 5.2 TYPES OF PROBLEMS

Different types of problems exist and they require various approaches to be solved. Learners should understand how problems vary according to so-called well-structured and ill-structured problems. According to Mendonca *et al.* (2009), ill-structured (sometimes referred to as ill-defined) problems are so-called "real world" problems that require additional skills beyond codification. Well-structured problems usually are easy to solve, where all the elements of the problem are present and a possible solution can be found with the application of a limited number of rules or principles. Ill-structured problems are more complex, ambiguous and there are probably more than one answer to such a problem. The teacher needs to discuss and assess both well-structured and ill-structured problems in the class. The teacher should, however, start with well-structured problems and then gradually proceed towards ill-structured problems that are more difficult to solve. One example of a well-structured problem for Grade 10 IT or CAT learners is to determine the average mark of seven subjects. An example of an ill-structured problem for Grade 11 CAT learners is to develop a database for a cellphone company where learners, on their own or in groups, make use of database objects such as tables, forms, queries and reports.

Successful problem-solving depends on domain-specific knowledge that is relevant to the problem-solving task, strategies on how to use the relevant knowledge in problem-solving, and feelings and beliefs regarding one's own interests and abilities to solve the problem (Mayer 1998). Problem-solving therefore depends on cognitive, metacognitive and affective skills that will be discussed subsequently.

## 5.3    KNOWLEDGE FOR PROBLEM-SOLVING

There are four kinds of knowledge that are necessary to solve problems (Pickard 2007), namely factual, conceptual, procedural and metacognitive knowledge.

### 5.3.1    Factual knowledge

Factual knowledge is basic information that learners must have regarding a subject to solve a problem (Pickard 2007). This includes terminology related to the subject, discrete facts, and basic elements. Teachers must decide what information is critical to be remembered and what can be acquired when needed, for example, by using the internet. Factual knowledge plays an important role in learners' understanding of a problem and consequently also in the creation of the solution.

### 5.3.2    Conceptual knowledge

Conceptual knowledge refers to knowledge regarding the interrelationships amongst the basic elements and includes knowledge of classifications and categories, knowledge of principles and generalisations, and knowledge of theories, models and structures (Anderson and Krathwohl 2001). To be able to solve a problem, learners must have acquired the ability to recognise relationships between the basic elements involved, explain the kind of relationship and its relevance with regard to the problem to be solved, and apply the relationship in the problem-solving process (Pickard 2007).

### 5.3.3    Procedural knowledge

Procedural knowledge refers to knowledge of what sequence of steps to follow in solving a problem, including criteria of when to use a specific skill, technique, method or algorithm (Pickard 2007). Procedural knowledge also concerns knowledge of different procedures and alternatives to solve a problem.

## 5.3.4 Metacognitive knowledge

Metacognitive knowledge refers to knowledge of three general factors: knowledge of yourself and your nature as cognitive processor; knowledge of different learning tasks and what they require; and knowledge of appropriate strategies to successfully execute a learning task (Flavell 1979; Schraw 2001). The learning task under consideration in this chapter is the solving of a problem. Learners' ability to think about how, when and why they learn or solve problems in particular ways and what they can do to change ineffective habits can be promoted if the teacher

▸ explicitly promotes the learners' knowledge regarding thinking processes, types of problems and strategies for solving problems; and

▸ consciously creates opportunities in class for the learners to contemplate what they know about themselves as learners, what they know about different types of problems and their requirements, and what they know about appropriate strategies to successfully solve a problem.

### 5.3.4.1 Knowledge of yourself and the way you do cognitive processing

Knowledge of yourself firstly refers to *what* you know about your own learning and thinking processes, factors that influence your performance, and what your own strengths and weaknesses are, e.g. "I can remember information well; I cannot learn if my work is not ordered; I am good at organising new information". Knowledge of yourself also concerns knowledge of *how* you learn and think, *when* and *why* your performance is influenced, and *when* and *why* your strengths/weaknesses play a role, e.g. "I know when and why my performance is influenced; I know when and why information should be chunked and categorised".

### 5.3.4.2 Knowledge of different types of problems and their requirements

Knowledge of the requirements of different problem-solving tasks firstly refers to learners' knowledge of the fact that different problem-solving tasks require different strategies, e.g. "This type of task requires that I should first do an information search; this type of problem requires a sorting algorithm (in IT) or the creation of a template (in CAT)". Knowledge of different problem-solving tasks also refers to knowledge of *how* to perform the task, e.g. "I know how to do different information searches; I know different algorithms (in IT) or how to create a template (in CAT)". Further it is important to know *when* and *why* the task must be performed, e.g. "I will do an information search before I start writing the report so that I have all the information available to complete the report".

### 5.3.4.3 Knowledge of appropriate problem-solving strategies

Knowledge of appropriate problem-solving strategies refers to knowledge of specific strategies that can be implemented to successfully perform a problem-solving task, e.g. "I know the following methods to do information searches; I know the following algorithms (in IT) or I can create a template (in CAT)". It further concerns knowing how to use the strategy, e.g. "I know how to do an information search on this topic; I know how to use a specific algorithm (in IT) or how to create a specific template (in CAT)". Lastly, knowledge of appropriate strategies concerns knowledge of the circumstances under which specific strategies can be successfully implemented, in other words *when* and *why* implementation of a specific strategy could be successful, e.g. "I know that an internet search is the best method to get the latest information on this topic; I know that in these circumstances this sort of algorithm will yield results the fastest (in IT) or that a template will ensure uniformity of the required documents (in CAT)".

## ACTIVITY 5.1

**Write a report in which you make recommendations on activities that a teacher can use in class to promote learners':**

**(a) knowledge of themselves and the way they learn or complete problem-solving tasks;**

**(b) knowledge of different problem-solving tasks and their requirements; and**

**(c) knowledge of appropriate problem-solving strategies.**

## 5.4   COGNITIVE STRATEGIES AND TECHNIQUES FOR PROBLEM-SOLVING

Although various techniques and strategies can be used for solving problems, it should be remembered that learners will not necessarily use the same strategies and the teacher therefore needs to provide and discuss a variety thereof to enhance the thinking process. Some reasoning techniques for problem-solving will be briefly discussed, followed by a discussion on different inference techniques.

### 5.4.1   Reasoning techniques for problem-solving

To solve a problem, you need to combine and integrate given facts with your knowledge base. The way in which a person is able to combine facts of a specific problem with their existing knowledge and reach a logical conclusion, relates to the person's reasoning skills. Logical reasoning can be described as the science of reasoning which tries to discover conditions by which conclusions are justified and indicated as correct (Eysink, Dijkstra and Kuper 2002). It is concerned with distinguishing correct from incorrect reasoning. Different reasoning techniques can be used to assist in solving problems.

### 5.4.1.1 Deductive reasoning

With deductive reasoning, facts, rules and related knowledge are used to arrive at new knowledge. Deductive reasoning is useful because it helps learners to connect various propositions and draw conclusions from it. One example of deductive reasoning is conditional reasoning: *if … then*. A simple example of this kind of reasoning is when two facts are given:

**Fact A:** If it rains, the grass is wet.

**Fact B:** It is raining.

**Conclusion:** If Fact B is true (it is raining), then the grass is wet. However, if the grass is wet, it is not necessarily raining. There may be other reasons for the grass to be wet.

In this way, new information can be derived from the given data. In problem-solving, it is important to get as much information as possible from the given data. Learners should be aware of this fact when solving problems.

### 5.4.1.2 Inductive reasoning

Inductive reasoning can be used to reach a solution with limited facts through generalisation. It implies that if X is true for A and X is true for B and X is true for C, then X is true for all values. Learners need to be very careful with this kind of reasoning as the chances of conclusions being false are significantly higher. For example: If all the monkeys in the Pretoria Zoo like peanuts and all the monkeys in the Durban Zoo like peanuts, it is not necessarily true that all the monkeys in the world like peanuts. If I always go on holiday every year and all our employees always go on holiday every year, it is not necessarily true that all employees go on holiday every year. An example of how inductive reasoning can well be used is:

**Fact A:** 60% of people in Africa are overweight.

**Fact B:** South Africans live in Africa.

**Conclusion:** Therefore, the probability that people in South Africa are overweight is 60%.

### 5.4.1.3  Backward chain as reasoning technique in problem-solving

With this technique, the learners need to consider what would be a reasonable step or argument just prior to reaching the goal. Thereafter they need to consider what would be the step prior to that and carry on until they research the initial state. Backward chain can be explained by beginning with the end, working backwards and eventually reaching the initial condition of the problem (Martinez 1998).

**For example:** If the following rules are true and only A and B are given in the problem statement as true, backwards chain can be used to prove that F is true.

> **Rule 1:** If A and B then E.
>
> **Rule 2:** If B then C.
>
> **Rule 3:** If C and E then F.

**Conclusion:** If F needs to be true, C and E need to be true. For C to be true, B needs to be true, which is given. Thus, C is true. For E to be true, A and B need to be true, which is also given. Thus, E is true. This implies that F is true.

### 5.4.1.4  Forward chain as reasoning technique in problem-solving

With forward chain, new facts are derived from the given information through the application of known rules and conditions that fit the information at hand.

**For example:** If the following rules are true and only A and B are given in the problem statement as true, forward-chaining can be used to prove that F is true.

> **Rule 1:** If A and B then E.
>
> **Rule 2:** If B then C.
>
> **Rule 3:** If C and E then F.

**Conclusion:** A and B imply E is true, B implies C is true. E and C imply that F is true.

### 5.4.1.5  Logic

Logic can be described as the study of the principles of correct reasoning. Within computer science, all yes-no/true-false decisions can be seen as logic. It is all about the validity of your arguments and conclusions. Conclusions always need to follow from given assumptions. If learners are exposed to the principles of logic, it helps them to identify patterns of good and bad reasoning. Logic goes hand in hand with critical thinking and can be improved by practise and regular exposure to this kind of reasoning.

Examples of logic:

---

**Fact 1:** All human beings can communicate.

**Fact 2:** Einstein is a human being.

**Conclusion:** Einstein could communicate.

---

**Fact 1:** All Fox Terriers are dogs.

**Fact 2:** Vlekkie is a Fox Terrier.

**Conclusion:** Vlekkie is a dog.

---

**Fact 1:** Pete is always absent when it rains.

**Fact 2:** It is raining today.

**Conclusion:** Pete will be absent today.

---

The more teachers can expose their learners to logical reasoning, the better problem-solvers they will be. Therefore, it is good practice to give learners a three-minute assignment in logical reasoning as a warm-up exercise before starting a lesson. It is also a good idea to use cooperative pairs for such an assignment.

## ACTIVITY 5.2

**Develop three examples of logical reasoning which you can apply in your classes to assist learners with problem-solving.**

### 5.4.2 Searching for the solution

The process of finding a solution can be explained as a search through the problem space to find the correct path which leads to the goal (Chi and Glaser 1985). Some search techniques and problem-solving approaches will subsequently be discussed. Search techniques break a problem into parts which help to transform the problem into manageable sub-problems.

#### 5.4.2.1 Depth-first analysis

With depth-first analysis, the learner needs to search a specific path in the problem space all the way to the bottom or until it is proven to be the wrong path, before choosing a new path. When the search in a specific direction does not reach the goal, the learner needs to go back to the previous decision point and work from there with a new possibility to reach the goal. This technique helps the learner to realise that there are many ways to think about solving the problem, but not all the ideas will eventually lead to the goal. A graphical presentation of depth-first can be seen in Figure 5.1. If you, for example, want to determine the name of a large white bird, you will first look at (2) and if (2) specifies a large bird, you will go to (3). If (3) is a black bird, you will return to (4), and if (4) are white birds, you will go to (5) to reach the name of the bird. If the bird you are looking for is not a large bird, you will go directly from (2) to (6), and if (6) does not have specifications of the bird, you will go to (8).

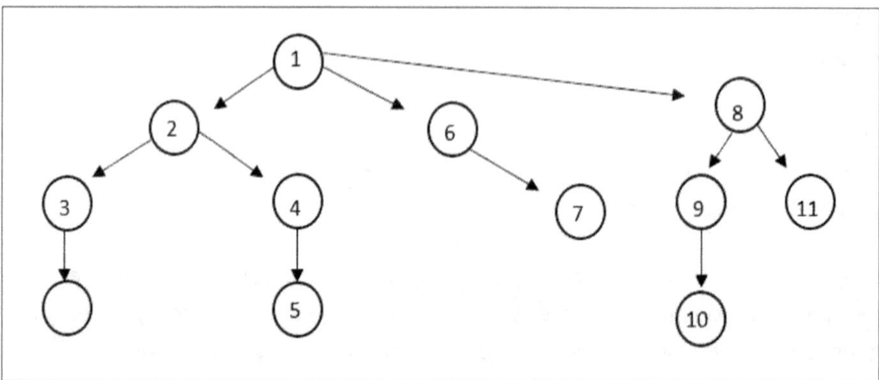

Figure 5.1     Depth-first analysis

### 5.4.2.2  Breadth-first analysis

Breadth-first analysis looks at all possible solutions to reach the goal by discovering them together until one of them prove not to be a successful option. An example where breadth-first can be used in problem-solving is when a doctor needs to diagnose a patient from the given symptoms. The doctor can quickly identify a couple of symptoms associated with that illness (1, 2 and 3 in Figure 5.2), but needs to go further in studying each of the symptoms (4, 5, 6, 7 and 8 in Figure 5.2) and their causes (9, 10 and 11 in Figure 5.2) to determine the most likely illness in order to prescribe the correct medicine. A graphical representation of breadth-first can be seen in Figure 5.2.

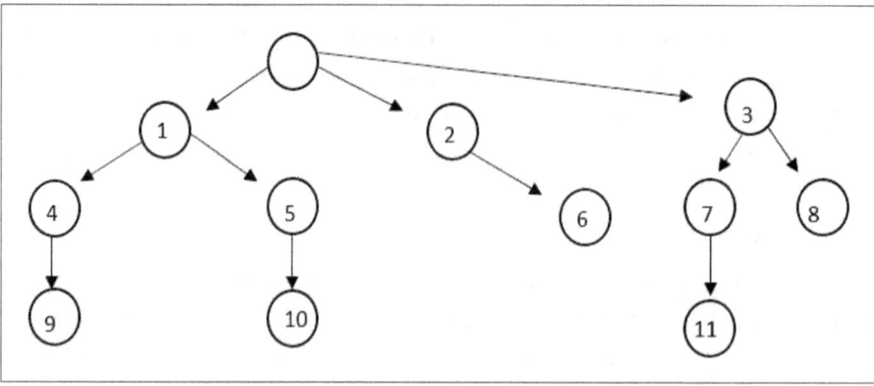

Figure 5.2     Breadth-first analysis

### 5.4.2.3 Means/ends analysis

With means/ends analysis a sub-goal is formed to reduce the discrepancy between the present state and the goal. Steps taken are not blind or random, but based on the best way to achieve the goal. Teachers should ask learners to try and break up problems into manageable sub-problems and then solve different sub-problems in order to solve the initial problem.

### 5.4.2.4 Generate and test

A technique for solving problems which can be used by novice problem-solvers is to generate as many solutions as possible and then test every solution in order to determine the best one.

### 5.4.2.5 Bottom-up strategies

This involves the planning of individual parts of a problem which are combined to form a solution for a problem. By using the bottom-up strategy a learner may for example design four individual web pages and thereafter integrate these within one website.

### 5.4.2.6 Top-down strategies

It focuses on the "big picture" and then breaks it down into smaller sub-problems. In the top-down strategy, high-level planning and understanding of the complete system are addressed upfront, without initially going into low-level details. By using the top-down strategy, a learner may design a complete website before attending to the details of each web page.

### 5.4.2.7 Integrated strategies

This implies using both bottom-up and top-down approaches during problem-solving. The problem-solver may switch between different strategies. When applying the integrated approach, a learner may design a website with individual web pages simultaneously.

### 5.4.2.8 Trial-and-error strategies

It refers to an approach where a learner reaches a solution without any explicit planning. This strategy is used when a part of the solution fails to work, where the problem-solver experiences difficulties, or is confused. Novice problem-solvers tend to rely on trial-and-error strategies. Teachers should not encourage learners to use this strategy as it is not a good way to solve any problem. It could take longer to solve and will not necessarily be a good or the best solution to the problem. This method also demotivates learners when they cannot find a suitable solution to the problem at hand.

## ACTIVITY 5.3

**Choose a specific search technique and explain with an example from your subject how you will incorporate that technique in problem-solving in an IT or CAT lesson.**

### 5.4.3 Represent the problem

Knowledge representation techniques allow us to present specific information regarding a problem visually, using a set of symbols. The representation of problems can display more details and complexity than we can hold in our mind at a given moment in time. Therefore, it helps to see the problem in a new way. Sometimes a graphical or picture representation makes more sense than many words. Different kinds of representations can be used, however, it depends on the type of problem as well as the personality and interest of each individual.

Problems can be represented by using pictures, diagrams, graphs, mind maps, and models – to name but a few.

#### 5.4.3.1 Mind maps

The use of mind maps is a visual way in which a problem can be structured by beginning with a main idea in the centre of the page and elaborating on that idea by branching in different directions. Lines connect the different ideas, concepts or objects with each other. Words, objects and symbols can be used to represent knowledge in this format. It can be used for initial brainstorming before solving the problem. The aim is to indicate connections between portions of information. Always begin in the centre and expand different concepts on different lines. Use different colours to indicate associations in the mind map and connect the branches in a logical order. Each person should develop their own personal style when creating a mind map. An example of a mind map is given in Figure 5.3.

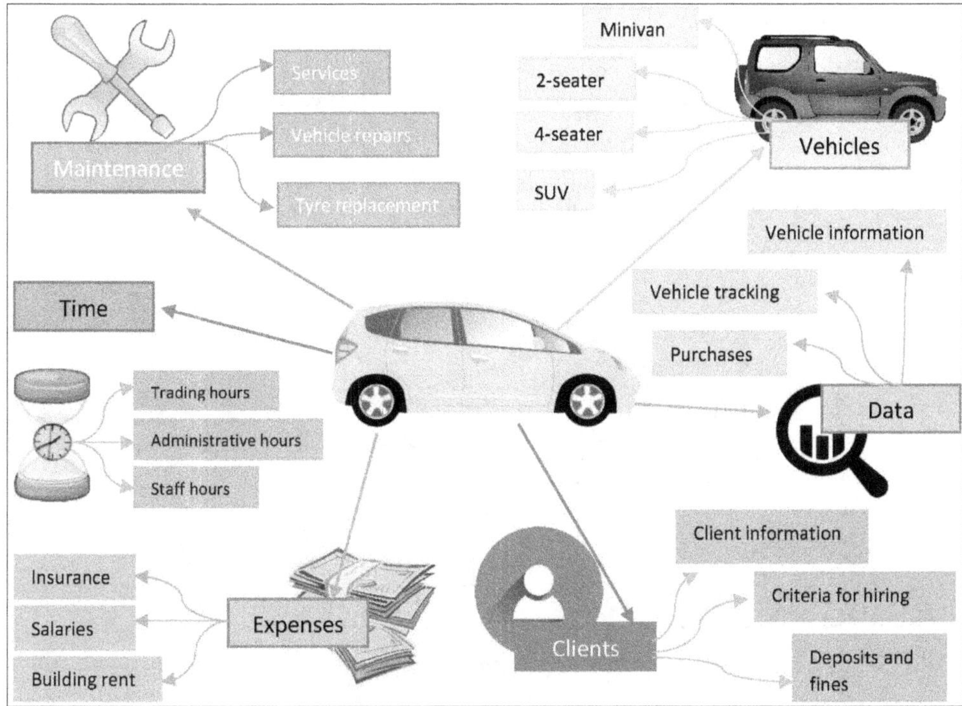


Figure 5.3    An example of a mind map to create a database for a car rental company

## 5.4.3.2  Models

Models can be used to communicate ideas to others while doing problem-solving and to stimulate new ideas to solve problems. It is a valuable method to organise and structure information and show missing links. An example of a model can be seen in Figure 5.4.

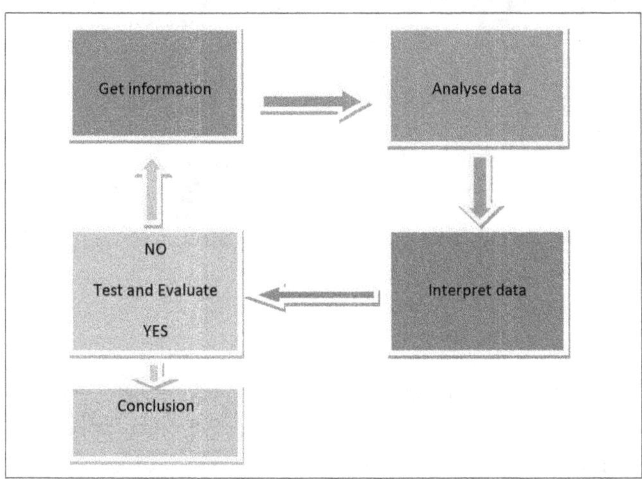


Figure 5.4    An example of a model

### 5.4.3.3  Tree diagrams

A tree diagram consists of different nodes linked together from a parent node at the top, down to child nodes in a tree-like shape. Tree diagrams are commonly used for decision-making or to display an algorithm visually (see Figure 5.5). When used for decision-making, the nodes can also be shaped differently (decision trees) using flowchart symbols, e.g. start and end nodes as circles or rectangles and decisions as diamonds (see Figure 5.6).

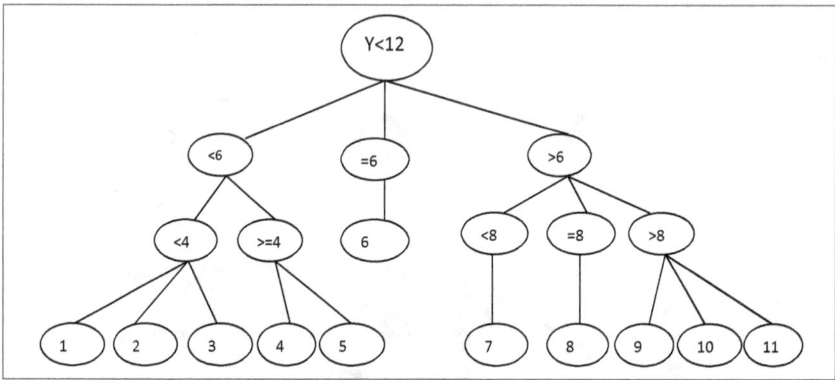

Figure 5.5      An example of a general tree diagram

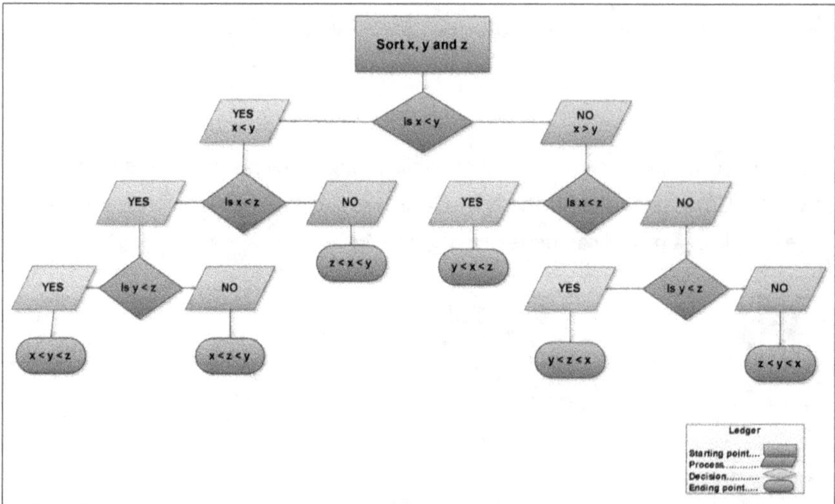

Figure 5.6      An example of a decision tree

### 5.4.3.4  Venn diagrams

With a Venn diagram, possible relationships between objects can be presented visually. It is a very useful tool when explaining the AND, OR, and NOT concepts to learners. Then they can classify various objects into different categories and indicate the overlapping properties. Learners can also use different colour pens to indicate the different sets to which the objects belong, for example, one can look at the situation when learners have to search the internet regarding a topic. They are required to decide on the use of AND/OR/NOT and the implication thereof on the search results, e.g. "HIV Aids AND Tuberculosis" vs. "HIV Aids OR Tuberculosis", which will render different search results.

In Figure 5.7, the relationships between a dog, a bird and a fish are visually displayed. They all have tails and eyes. However, there are also unique properties to each of them and properties which two of them share. Dogs and birds, for example, have legs.

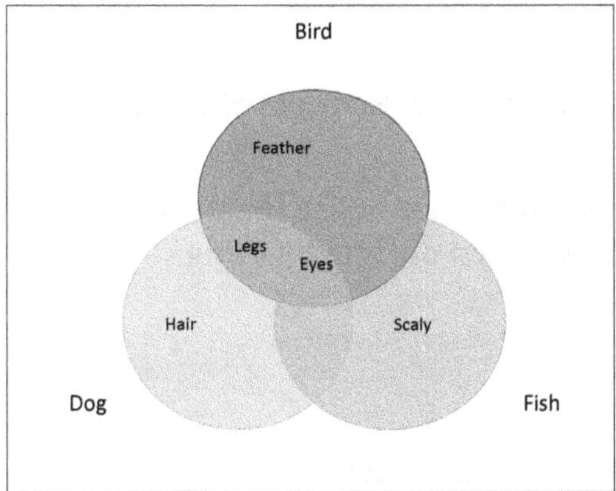


Figure 5.7     An example of a Venn diagram

### 5.4.3.5  Semantic nets

Another way to present knowledge when the objects given are related to each other is to draw a semantic net. A semantic net consists of nodes and links, where the nodes represent the objects, facts or concepts and the links the relationships or association between concepts or objects. An example of a semantic net can be seen in Figure 5.8.

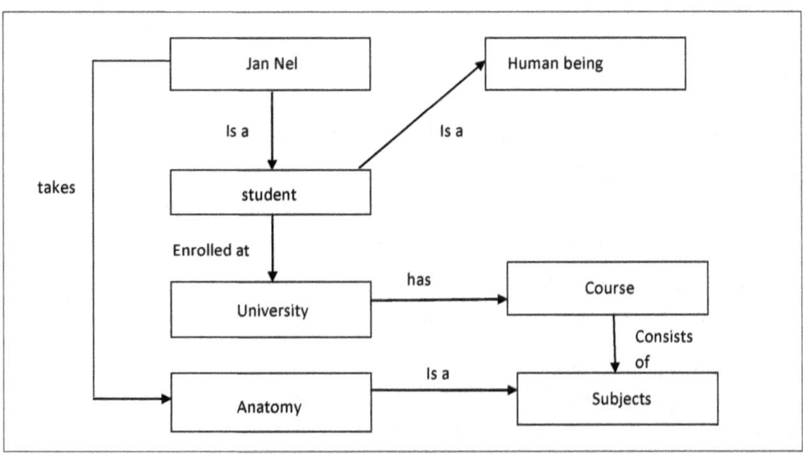


Figure 5.8     An example of a semantic net

A conclusion from Figure 5.8 is: Because Jan Nel is a student, and students are human beings, Jan Nel is a human being.

## ACTIVITY 5.4

(a) Formulate an assignment for your IT or CAT class in which learners need to represent the problem at hand in the form of a mind map, model or semantic net. Create your own mind map, model or semantic net as an example of what you expect from the learners.

(b) Develop an assignment for learners to practise their understanding of the relationship between objects by using a Venn diagram.

## 5.5 METACOGNITIVE STRATEGIES FOR PROBLEM-SOLVING

Metacognitive strategies are meant to help learners to manage their own learning. These strategies relate to planning before beginning a problem-solving task, monitoring while working on the task, and evaluation after completing the task, as well as active reflection on what occurs throughout the execution of the task (Schunk 2000). Because metacognitive strategies seem obvious, teachers might believe that the learners know all about them and are experienced in using them. However, most learners are unaware of metacognition and therefore it needs to be developed. Initially, the teaching and practice of metacognitive strategies may be quite time-consuming, but the outcome thereof will prove worthwhile.

### 5.5.1 Planning

Planning of a problem-solving task includes metacognitive strategies regarding goal-setting, selecting cognitive strategies/procedures to reach the goal and identifying possible obstacles. The teacher should encourage learners to first read through the problem to get an overall view and to ensure that all terminology is known, to analyse the problem in order to identify the most important information given, and to determine the specific expected outcome. Then, through modelling and practice, the teacher should support the learners to practise the following metacognitive strategies:

- Reflection on previous knowledge – determining the relation to own experiences; making connections with aspects of the problem that are already known; thinking about how knowledge of similar problems that were solved previously can help to solve the current problem;

- Setting the goals to be reached with the solution of the problem – predicting outcomes helps learners to understand what information they need to solve the problem (Darling-Hammond *et al.* 2008);

- Planning the time to be spent;
- Assigning the appropriate resources;
- Choosing the cognitive strategies/procedures that are appropriate to solve the problem;
- Deciding on a solution to solve the problem and on the sequence in which the strategies/procedures will be applied.

To practise these activities, learners can write their planning details in a journal, making short notes on their intentions, including problems anticipated with specific aspects of the problem-solving process. Alternatively they can be provided with a list of questions that they can use for self-questioning to ensure that they have attended to the necessary metacognitive activities. Questions that learners can ask themselves while they are busy with the planning of a problem-solving task include: "What are the outcomes I have to reach with the solution of this problem?", "What aspects of the problem are already known to me?", "What resources can help me with the solution of the problem?", "What strategies/procedures do I know that are appropriate to solve the problem?", and "In which sequence must the strategies/procedures be applied?"

## 5.5.2  Monitoring

Monitoring of a problem-solving task comprises an awareness of what you are busy doing, where the current action fits into the sequence of steps, and an anticipation of what has to be done next. Again the teacher should initially support the learners to practise the following metacognitive strategies:

- Regular re-consideration of whether what is being done is still understood;
- Regular re-consideration of whether the process is still in accordance with the planning;
- Thinking about how each step fits into the problem-solving process;
- Anticipation of what has to be done next;
- Monitoring the progress that is made;
- Identification and correction of errors as the task progresses;
- Changing the planning, if necessary, and investigating alternatives;
- Asking for help or consulting resources, if necessary – discussion of ideas with other students or the teacher can help to clear uncertainties;
- Checking the time spent.

To initially practise these activities, learners again can be provided with a list of questions for self-questioning, checking that they have attended to the necessary metacognitive activities, until they have come into the habit of doing it. Self-questions that learners can use during their execution of the problem-solving task include: "Do I still understand what I am doing?", "Am I still on the right track?", "How does this step fit into what has already been done and what needs to be done next?", "Am I identifying and rectifying errors as the task progresses?", "Is it necessary to change the planning?", "Am I making progress with the task?", and "What resources are available if I need help?".

The teacher can contribute by asking students questions as they work, such as: "What are you working on now?", "Why are you using that specific strategy?", and "How does it help you?" (Darling-Hammond *et al.* 2008).

## 5.5.3 Evaluation

Evaluation of a problem-solving task includes determining the success and effectiveness of the product and the process of solving the problem so that it can be changed or adapted, if necessary, when used in a similar task in future. At first, the teacher would have to support the learners to practise the following metacognitive strategies, and finally expect from them to do it on completion of each of their problem-solving tasks:

- Evaluation of the product to determine if the expected outcome was attained;
- Evaluation of the extent to which the set goals were reached;
- Evaluating the effectiveness of the strategies/procedures that were used;
- Reflecting on what could have been done differently;
- Identifying changes that will be made the next time a similar problem has to be solved;
- Reflecting on what was learned from solving the specific problem.

To practise these activities, learners can again write their evaluation details in their journals, making short notes on how they evaluate the product of the task and the extent to which they have reached their goals. Learners should also formulate their own opinion on the effectiveness of the strategies they have used and what they would do different next time they have to solve a similar problem. Questions that learners can ask themselves while evaluating their execution of the problem-solving task include: "Have I reached the expected outcomes?", "Have I used the best possible strategies/ procedures to solve the problem?", "What could possibly have been done in a different way?", "Will I apply the same strategies for similar problems in future?", and "What have I learned from solving this specific problem?".

Evaluating and reviewing their work helps learners to determine where their strengths and weaknesses lie within their work (Darling-Hammond *et al.* 2008). The teacher contributes by providing feedback to the students on their work.

## 5.5.4 Reflection

Reflection is a critical element of effective problem-solving and should take place through every step and phase of the problem-solving process. Continuous reflection during all the steps and phases of problem-solving is a dynamic process of receiving feedback on every action, eventually leading to successful completion of the task. Reflection makes it possible for learners to apply the metacognitive knowledge, skills and strategies gained from previous experiences and transfer them successfully into new problem-solving situations. Reflection strategies include:

- Continuous self-questioning (as previously discussed).

- Using a reflective journal that gives learners the opportunity to make brief notes about their feelings, frustrations, expectations, goals and problems in specific aspects of problem-solving. This is an effective way to reflect on their problem-solving tasks. Learners may use a weekly diary to reflect upon their activities during the week. The teacher should do spot-checks from time to time by reading from learners' journals and offering informative feedback where problems have occurred.

## ACTIVITY 5.5

**Write a report in which you make recommendations on how a teacher can create a socially supporting environment in which learners can practise and evaluate their use of metacognitive skills. Motivate your recommendations with specific examples of activities that will promote a metacognitive learning environment.**

## 5.6  COMPUTATIONAL THINKING

Computational thinking (CT) has been associated with the development of essential knowledge and skills for the Fourth Industrial Revolution (4IR). Papert (1980:4), one of the pioneers, mentions that "the computer presence could contribute to mental processes not only instrumentally but in more essential, conceptual ways, influencing how people think even when they are far removed from physical contact with a computer". Therefore, CT allows people to understand a complex problem by using a particular way of thinking that does not necessarily include the use of a computer. CT was populated by Wing (2006) as an essential competency to solve challenging problems. Fundamental to CT are the following main principles namely, abstraction, problem decomposition, algorithmic thinking, and pattern recognition (some scholars add additional principles to be part of CT).

### 5.6.1  Abstraction

This involves focusing on essential information only and ignoring aspects that are not necessarily relevant to the problem. For example, using a formula in Excel to solve a problem implies locating only the relevant data. Note in the following examples the focus is on "computational thinking" rather than using a computer. One example is to calculate the number of "working days" (ignoring Saturdays and Sundays) between two dates using the NETWORKDAYS ( ) function in Excel:

```
=NETWORKDAYS(F1,F2)
where F1 = the startDate and F2 = the endDate
```

## 5.6.2  Problem decomposition

Refers to the activity by breaking down a challenging problem into sections that can be solved more easily (see section 5.4.2). Each of the smaller sections can be addressed individually. For example, the VLOOKUP( ) function in Excel can be used to look up data in an organised table.

**=VLOOKUP (lookupValue, tableArray, columnIndexNum, [rangeLookup])**

Where the:

-**lookupValue** refers to the value looking for in the first column of the table
-**tableArray** refers to the table that is involved to retrieve a particular value
-**columnIndexNum** refers to a particular column in the table from which the value is retrieved
-**[rangeLookup]** returns TRUE (if the value matches) or FALSE

## 5.6.3  Algorithmic thinking

This relates to developing a solution by using particular steps. This can be done in Excel when compiling a formula to determine a particular symbol that a learner obtains for the exam. For example:

Algorithm:

**If mark >= 75 then write "Distinction"**
**If mark >= 60 then write "Average"**
**If mark >= 50 then write "Pass"**
**else write "Fail"**

Corresponding formula in Excel:

**=IF(B2>=75, "Distinction", IF(B2>=60, "Average", IF(B2>=50, "Pass", "Fail")))**

## 5.6.4  Pattern recognition

This way of thinking is related to similarities amongst various problems. The function COUNT() counts how many cells in a particular range contain numbers. SUM() is used to add values and calculate the sum thereof, whereas the COUNTIF() function counts the number of cells that meet a particular criterion. In the example below, a student has to obtain at least 70% (criterion) for each class test. Only one student met this criterion,

**=COUNTIF(F3:F5,">=21")**

| F7 | | | | $fx$ | =COUNTIF(F3:F5,">=21") |
| --- | --- | --- | --- | --- | --- |
| | A | B | C | D | E | F |
| 1 | Name | | Mark#1 | Mark#2 | Mark#3 | Sum |
| 2 | | | 10 | 10 | 10 | |
| 3 | Cronje | John | 7 | 8 | 9 | 24 |
| 4 | De Waal | Ann | 5 | 6 | 7 | 18 |
| 5 | Mosiane | Patience | 7 | 6 | 4 | 17 |
| 6 | | | | | | |
| 7 | | | | | | 1 |

*Figure 5.9    Excel example of pattern recognition*

## 5.7    CLASSROOM PRACTICES

### 5.7.1  Facilitating the steps in problem-solving

Although you now have knowledge regarding problems and ways in which to assist learners in solving them, it is required to direct the problem-solving process by using five steps to support the learners. These five steps must not be seen as sequential, but rather as a cyclic process as shown in Figure 5.10:

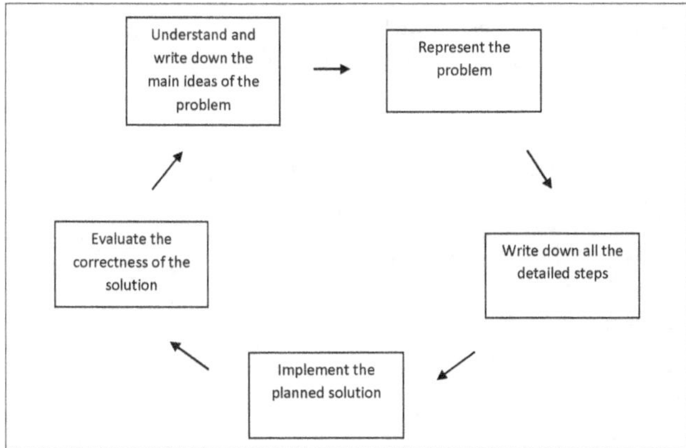


*Figure 5.10    A cyclic representation of the problem-solving steps*

1. **Understand and write down the main ideas as outlined in the problem.**
   - The first step in problem-solving is to understand the problem at hand. The three basic steps to assist learners to understand the problem are:
     - Read the problem and **underline** all the important concepts. Read the problem again to **clearly understand** and interpret the question.
     - Write down the problem in your own words.
     - What is difficult and what do you not understand?

2. **Represent the problem.**

   ▶ When the problem-solver understands the problem, he/she should be able to make a representation of the problem. A detailed, correct representation can support the solution process. Remember that the same problem can be represented in different ways.

   ▶ The problem can be represented by using a diagram, picture, mind map, flow chart, table, figure, concept map, or any other method to indicate your representation of the problem. All these representations can be drawn, based on an individual's own preferences (see section 5.4.3).

3. **Write down all the detailed steps to solve the problem.**

   ▶ The problem-solver should write out the planned solution in a step-by-step manner.

   ▶ IT learners should write an algorithm to solve the programming problem (see Chapter 7). The IT learner needs to think about the following questions to direct the process:

     – Which constructs will you use to input the data? (when applicable)

     – Which variables need to be declared and what are their scope?

     – Which statements will you use to process or calculate the data?

     – Which constructs will you use to display the program output?

     – How can I determine the correctness of my program?

4. **Implement the planned solution.**

   ▶ The implementation of the solution will now depend on the specific subject or field of study.

   ▶ In the IT class it will be the stage when the learners type the code into the computer, compile the program and correct the programming and syntax errors, while in the CAT class it could, for example, be that the actual website is created according to the planning that was done.

5. **Evaluate the correctness of the solution.**

   ▶ During this step, learners need to go back to the problem and evaluate the correctness of their answer.

   ▶ In the IT class the learner should ask and answer the following questions:

     – Which **test data** can I use and how can I ensure that the extreme cases of the test data are included?

     – How should I **correct** the programming **errors**?

     – Did I use the necessary **resources** to support my programming process? (Books, group members, the teacher).

     – Am I satisfied with my solution? Explain why.

     – Did I solve the problem?

## 5.7.2 Facilitating learners' critical thinking skills

Critical thinking is a basic life skill. However, learners do not automatically learn to think critically and therefore teachers need to support learners to think critically. It can be done by asking questions that require critical thinking or by encouraging learners to ask critical thinking questions and to reflect on other learners' explanations and answers in a critical manner. Take, for example, the following scenario:

---

**We need to transfer an elephant from one place to another. There are three containers: a large cubic container, a four-ton truck, and a freezer. Which one will you use to transfer the elephant?**

---

In this scenario, there will be learners who will select the truck, without questioning whether a four-ton truck will have enough space to move the elephant. Others will select the cubic container because the elephant fits into the cage. When the teacher does not focus only on the correct answer, and requires a discussion, learners will engage in critical thinking as one question leads to another. Possible questions that can be asked include: "How will the cubic container be moved?", "Will the elephant fit onto a four ton truck?", "Is the elephant dead or alive?".

Learners are required to not take everything for granted, but to think about alternatives. They should also distinguish between possible and impossible, wrong and right, suitable and not suitable, realistic and unrealistic, fair and unfair, good and bad, etc.

### 5.7.3  Pair problem-solving

As early as 1982, Whimbey and Lockhead defined pair problem-solving as a form of active learning which aims to improve learners' problem-solving ability. It consists of two participants, a problem-solver and a listener, working through a problem together. The problem-solver solves the problem step-by-step, while explaining each step in detail. The verbal explanation of each step is crucial to the understanding of the process, for both the problem-solver and the listener. The listener follows the problem-solver's steps carefully, verifies each step, and asks for clarification when necessary. The listener also points out errors and learns problem-solving by seeing the process in action. The problem-solver benefits from pair problem-solving because he/she needs to slow down and give reasons for each step, investigating more deeply the reasons for taking a specific step, and this results in better understanding of the problem-solving process. It can be used when a step-by-step solution to a problem is required and works well in IT with the principles of pair programming (see Chapter 6).

### 5.7.4  Guidelines to the teacher

There are a number of handy practical hints when you want to improve your learners' problem-solving skills:

- Set up a class discussion; let learners explain how they will solve a problem and why they have selected a specific approach. Allow learners to communicate with each other about the problem-solving process.

- Always try to guide learners to realise that there is not necessarily only one method to solve a problem, however, there may be a best way to solve it.

- Encourage learners to think about different ways to solve the same problem. Then, allow them to prioritise the solutions and select the best approach. It fosters critical thinking and can result in an important class discussion. This will be a valuable experience to learners which they can use in solving future problems.

- Always give time for reflection after a problem is solved.

- Select problems that are interesting to the learners. Then they will work harder and be more motivated.

- Encourage students not to be demotivated by failure. They need to understand that failure could be linked to a lack of effort, rather than a lack of ability.

# ACTIVITY 5.6

**Write a three-page essay on the value of teaching critical thinking skills to IT or CAT learners. The following criteria will be used when assessing the essay:**

**(a) An introductory statement of the issue focused on and clear definitions of the concepts used.**

**(b) A summary of the theory or conceptual framework used to understand the issue.**

**(c) A summary of major research on this topic.**

**(d) A brief description of one relevant study that should be conducted on this topic.**

**(e) Your own conclusion from this research.**

## 5.8    CONCLUSION

In this chapter, the importance of teaching problem-solving to learners was emphasised. Teachers need to know how to assist learners in the acquisition of the necessary skills to solve problems effectively. It is important to keep in mind that acquiring the skills necessary for effective problem-solving is not a once-off process, but that the entire process of problem-solving and the associated knowledge and strategies need to be practised on a continuous basis.

# REFERENCES

Anderson, L. and Krathwohl, D.E. 2001. *A taxonomy for learning and teaching: A revision of Bloom's taxonomy of educational objectives*. New York: Addison Wesley Longman, Inc.

Chi, T.H. and Glaser, R. 1985. Problem-solving ability. (In R. Sternberg, ed. *Human abilities: An information-processing approach*. San Francisco, CA: W.H. Freeman & Co, pp. 227-257.)

Darling-Hammond, L., Austin, K., Cheung, M. and Martin, D. 2008. Thinking about thinking: metacognition. https://bit.ly/3k8W8wd

Eysink, T.H.S., Dijkstra, S. and Kuper, J. 2002. The role of guidance in computer-based problem solving for the development of concepts of logic. *Instructional Science*, 30(4):307-333. https://doi.org/10.1023/A:1016018210897

Flavell, J.H. 1979. Metacognition and cognitive monitoring: A new area of cognitive-developmental inquiry. *American psychologist*, 34(10):906-911. https://doi.org/10.1037/0003-066X.34.10.906

Lockhead, J. 1985. Teaching analytic reasoning skills through pair problem solving. (In J. Segal, S. Chipman and R. Glaser, eds. *Thinking and learning skills. Volume 1: Relating instruction to research*. Hillsdail, NJ: Erlbaum, pp. 109-131.)

Martinez, M.E. 1998. What is problem solving? *Phi Delta Kappa*, 89(8):605-609.

Mayer, R.E. 1998. Cognitive, metacognitive, and motivational aspects of problem solving. *Instructional Science*, 26:49-63. https://doi.org/10.1023/A:1003088013286

Mendonca, A., De Oliveira, C., Guerrero, D. and Costa, E. 2009. Difficulties in solving ill-defined problems: A case study with introductory computer programming students. (In *Proceedings of the 39th IEEE Frontiers in Education Conference*, 18-21 October, San Antonio, Texas. Piscataway, NJ: IEEE Press, pp. 1171-1176.) https://doi.org/10.1109/FIE.2009.5350628

Pickard, M.J. 2007. The new Bloom's taxonomy: An overview for family and consumer sciences. *Journal of family and consumer sciences education*, 25(1):45-55.

Schraw, G. 2001. Promoting general metacognitive awareness. (In H.J. Hartman, ed. *Metacognition in learning and instruction: theory, research and practice*. Dordrecht: Kluwer, pp. 3-16.) https://doi.org/10.1007/978-94-017-2243-8_1

Schunk, D. 2000. *Learning theories: An educational perspective*, 3rd ed. Upper Saddle River, NJ: Prentice Hall.

# CHAPTER 6

# Cooperative learning in IT and CAT classes

**Elsa Mentz & Leila Goosen**

# OBJECTIVES

**After completing this chapter, you should be able to:**

- *define and discuss the term cooperative learning;*

- *discuss the key elements of cooperative learning;*

- *discuss the advantages for IT/CAT teachers when using cooperative learning;*

- *explain why it is helpful to use cooperative learning in the classroom;*

- *name ways in which cooperative learning can be implemented; and*

- *discuss the benefits and limitations of pair programming.*

## 6.1 INTRODUCTION

This chapter will offer an overview of the principles of cooperative learning for implementation in IT and CAT classes during practical as well as theoretical work. Special reference will be made to pair programming as a specific cooperative learning strategy for teaching and learning of programming skills in the IT class. The aim is to explain how to use cooperative learning strategies in IT and CAT classrooms in South Africa.

According to Geldenhuys (2012), it is of the highest importance that people have the skills needed to communicate, which are specifically used when taking part in social interactions. Due to the impact that unified communication and collaboration technologies are having on productivity and innovation and the need for promotion towards the fourth industrial revolution (Bolton, Goosen and Kritzinger 2021), Agrawal, Joshi and Purohit (2020) pointed to the similarly growing need for a cooperative communications framework that can be applied across different industrial applications. Learners therefore need to be empowered with the knowledge and skills they need in such contexts (Du Toit 2019).

## 6.2 WHAT IS COOPERATIVE LEARNING?

Researchers often use the terms "cooperative learning", "collaborative learning" and group work interchangeably when referring to learners working together on a task. Both the cooperative and collaborative approaches are examples of social learning where groups of learners communicate with each other under conditions where they work together to complete specific, commonly assigned tasks or projects. Johnson and Johnson (2009a), Tran (2013), as well as Johnson and Johnson (2018), state that cooperative learning has its roots in the social interdependence theory, the cognitive development theory, and the behavioural-social theory; whereas Barkley, Cross and Major (2014) state that collaborative learning has its home in the social constructivist theory. With both cooperative and collaborative learning, students work in a group and engage actively towards a stated objective while working together.

Barkley, Cross and Major (2014:4) define collaborative learning as two or more students working together and sharing the workload equitably as they progress towards intended learning outcomes. Meaningful learning should take place whereby all students should increase their knowledge or deepen their understanding of the course curriculum. The responsibility for learning is shifting from the teacher to the students (Barkley, Cross and Major 2014:4).

Cooperative learning is defined by Johnson and Johnson (2018) as "the instructional use of small groups so that students work together to maximize their own and each other's learning". Students in a cooperative group should have a common goal to achieve, which creates a high commitment from every member of the group. They should communicate effectively and accept individual and group responsibility for the completion of the task. Cooperative learning is directed at the effectiveness with which the different resources in the group can be shared and used in the best possible way to the benefit of all the members of the group. Five basic elements need to be present for any group to be a cooperative learning group, namely positive interdependence, individual accountability, promotive face to face interaction, interpersonal and small-group skills, and group processing (Johnson, Johnson and Holubec 2007; Johnson and Johnson 2019). Whereas researchers agree that cooperative learning can be identified through the presence of the five basic elements, researchers are not in agreement on the distinct elements of a collaborative learning environment, except for the fact that individuals do not work alone. It could be stated that all cooperative learning is also collaborative, but all collaborative learning is not necessarily cooperative. Millis and Cottell (1998) view cooperative learning as a more structured strategy than collaborative learning.

Thus, group work can be cooperative or collaborative. Cooperative learning groups is only one of the many types of groups that can be used in the classroom. Johnson, Johnson and Holubec (2007) distinguish between pseudo-learning groups, traditional classroom learning groups, cooperative learning groups, and high-performance cooperative learning groups. Not all types of groups facilitate learning and increase the quality of learning in the classroom equally. According to Johnson, Johnson and Holubec (2007), only in cooperative learning groups the academic achievement of the individual members of the group are higher than if they would have worked alone. The difference lies in the application of the five elements of cooperative learning.

## 6.3    KEY ELEMENTS OF COOPERATIVE LEARNING

Those with experience in using groups appreciate that successful group work "does not just happen" (Sudweeks 2003:1440) when learners are simply assigned to groups and told to work together. This does not automatically mean that learners will "naturally" work well together (Gillies 2016:51). Most literature cites work by Johnson and Johnson (e.g. 2005, 2009a) that highlights the significance of organising small groups for success by making sure that the following five elements are present:

a.  **Positive interdependence:** According to Johnson *et al.* (2014), explicitly structuring positive interdependence in groups is vital for cooperative learning to thrive. The interdependence of group members must be dealt with in such a way that they realise that they will not achieve success unless all the members of the group achieve success. Mutuality needs to be established in terms of common goals and "benefits from achieving goals" (Johnson and Johnson 2005:285). Having the completion of the project as a common goal should serve as one of the main factors in uniting group members in a joint effort. This mutual goal should be relevant and convincing enough to overcome learners' possible competing agendas and any conflict that might arise within the group.

    The relationship between group members should bring about the understanding that they cannot succeed as individuals if everyone in the group does not succeed, and vice versa. It is all about the understanding that they need to coordinate their efforts to achieve the goal. It is the so-called 'all for one and one for all' mentality where the individual realises that he/she cannot achieve the goal without the group (Mentz 2011). Members of a cooperative group have two main responsibilities: to reach the goal individually and to ensure that all members of the group reach the goal (Kishore 2012). Every member has a contribution to make to the joint effort of the group which implies that there can be no social loafing. If positive interdependence in a group is high, it has an effect on individual group members' motivation and productivity (Johnson and Johnson 2009b).

**b.** **Individual and group accountability:** Each group member needs to be involved in providing his/her individual input towards the group's work and learning and understands his/her responsibility to the success of the group. The slogan 'individuals work together, but perform alone' is applicable. The performance of each individual member needs to be assessed and given back to the individual and the group. The group needs to hold the individual accountable for his/her contribution to the group's success. Group accountability can be fostered by assessing the performance of the group and when given back to the group, the group needs to compare the results against a certain standard of performance decided upon by the group. Each member needs to feel a personal responsibility for the success of the group (Johnson and Johnson 2009a). Laal, Geranpaye and Daemi (2013) and Meijer *et al.* (2020) stress the importance of assessing for individual accountability to ensure that all group members participate. Individual accountability is important for group success, since some members tend to dominate and some to withdraw, unless mechanisms are in place forcing everyone to participate.

**c.** **Promotive interaction** is demonstrated when group members support and encourage each other's efforts to achieve the goal. It results in a caring and committed relationship where individuals assist each other, share each other's resources, challenge each other's conclusions and reasoning, and motivate each other in their efforts to achieve the goal. They will need to provide explanations and elaboration to help other group members understand key principles and concepts. Promotive interaction provides a safe environment where members are encouraged to ask questions and give their own opinions. It motivates group members to achieve the mutual goals and reduces their stress and anxiety (Johnson and Johnson 2009b; Kishore 2012).

**d.** **Interpersonal and small-group skills:** It is necessary to ensure that learners are trained in the interpersonal and small-group skills that facilitate learning in cooperative groups. Group members must be taught to use appropriate social skills which include good communication and listening skills, conflict resolution skills, effective leadership skills, and decision-making skills. Learners need to know how to communicate with each other and incorporate the concepts of compromise, participation, interaction and cooperation. It is also important to teach group members how to avoid negative comments, and to present their criticism in a positive way (Pollock and Jochen 2001). According to Johnson and Johnson (2009b, 2019a), good social skills promote higher achievement and positive relationships amongst group members. Buchs and Butera (2015:2) argue that social skills development is important to "enhances the efficacy of group work in terms of cognitive/academic outcomes".

**e.** **Group processing:** The group is expected to reflect upon their performance as a group and to plan how to improve it. It includes reflection on the input and assistance of each member of the group in order to determine which actions contribute to the achievement of the goal and which actions should be avoided in future. Group processing provides a structure to members of a group to hold each other accountable for their actions. An important part of group processing is the celebration of group successes which enhance the quality of the group cooperation as it acts as an intrinsic motivation amongst group members (Johnson and Johnson 2019a).

## 6.4 ADVANTAGES OF COOPERATIVE LEARNING

According to Gillies (2019), interest in the key role that is taking place in constructing knowledge, understanding and learning has gained momentum in the past few years as research had demonstrated how learners learn from each other and how teachers, in turn, can use this information to structure their classroom experiences in order to promote students' participation and productive dialogue. A number of advantages of cooperative learning have been identified by researchers over many years (Terwel 2003; Johnson, Johnson and Stanne 2000; Johnson and Johnson 2019). The biggest contribution lies in higher achievement and improved interpersonal and social skills. We will only name and summarise a few:

- ▶ Learners are exposed to different opinions, perspectives, viewpoints and ways in which to solve problems. It creates the willingness to adjust a learner's individual solution, which results in higher order critical thinking and reasoning;
- ▶ Learners benefit from the knowledge, skills, resources and experiences of the other members of the group;
- ▶ The fact that learners need to communicate and explain their thoughts and thought processes with others results in a clearer understanding of concepts;
- ▶ Cooperative learning results in higher academic achievement in higher-level learning tasks than in competitive or individualistic learning, and in improved social and interpersonal skills.
- ▶ It enhances learning skills, improves learner motivation, and produces significant positive gains in learners' attitudes towards the specific subject matter.

Working together in groups can provide learners with important learning experiences to help them realise the contribution that working in a group can make as a tool for achieving success. Although the same learning content is covered as with conventional methods, positive interpersonal relationships and skills are developed at the same time. With cooperative learning, learners experience the social growth and develop the skills needed to work effectively with others (Chiriac 2014). The mutual support that learners receive when they help and are helped by their peers when they work together in groups enables them to experience the satisfaction of both encouraging and challenging each other. Dialogue and communication are important activities in the process of creating an environment where the learner can be actively involved in exploratory learning. Increased learner interaction and dialogue (Whatley *et al.* 2005) also promotes deep learning and self-directed learning (Mentz and Van Zyl 2016). Cooperative learning significantly fosters the development of a wider breadth of knowledge by helping the members of the group to clarify their ideas through discussion and debate and by evaluating each other's ideas. Academically stronger learners, in particular, report a deeper understanding of new concepts and ideas after having had opportunities to talk about and explain these to other group members (Alfares 2017).

Advantages mentioned by Nuutila, Törmä and Malmi (2005) include the fact that when group members analyse problems together from different perspectives, it not only helps them to understand difficult issues, but they also get support from their peers that helps in relieving some of the anxiety caused by these topics. The application of cooperative activities to reinforce learning, therefore has obvious advantages over individual systems, due to shared information (Raveh and Meir 2020).

Although evidence from research demonstrates the advantages of learners working together in groups, Mentz and Goosen (2007) found that group work is not commonly used in South African IT classrooms. Teachers still show a strong tendency to depend on teaching strategies aimed at individual learners for teaching programming skills, requiring their learners to solve problems and practise their programming skills individually. Ignorance of the possible advantages of cooperative learning strategies could be one of the important reasons why cooperative learning is generally not used for teaching computer skills. Therefore, in the remainder of this chapter we will focus on the role that cooperative learning can play by assisting teachers to apply it effectively in South African IT and CAT classrooms.

# ACTIVITY 6.1

**The effectiveness of cooperative learning has been confirmed by research over a number of years.  Find any article which supports the use of cooperative over competitive or individualistic learning. Also find an article that indicates the importance of the incorporation of any of the five basic elements of cooperative learning. Write a short summary of the main findings of both articles to present to the class. Also include your own view on the scientific value of each article.**

## 6.5 USING COOPERATIVE LEARNING IN IT AND CAT CLASSES

### 6.5.1 Why use cooperative learning?

Groups are increasingly being used as strategic work units in most IT companies because of the increase in popularity of agile software development and other collaborative practices (Smite *et al.* 2021). The software industry consequently needs graduates who have had significant and meaningful experiences with teamwork (Samary and Ochoa 2014), which will enable them to exhibit these skills as part of their professional repertoire (McKinney and Denton 2005).

One of the new methodologies of modern software development is Extreme Programming. One of the 12 primary principles typical of the practice of Extreme Programming is pair programming (Venkatesan and Sankar 2010). Smite *et al.* (2021) indicated in their research that pair programming in the industry outperforms individual programming. A pair produces code of a higher standard, is more productive, and works faster on an assignment than an individual. One problem with implementing pair programming in the industry is that most programmers still prefer to work individually. They are not used to working in pairs. The new requirements of the industry forces higher education institutions to train programmers with the necessary social and interpersonal skills in order for them to apply pair programming in the workplace. This requirement obviously also applies to other work environments.

It is advisable that teachers incorporate cooperative learning strategies such as pair programming and pair problem-solving in their classes in order to equip learners with the necessary skills. While direct instruction usually involves individualistic, competitive approaches (Mentz 2011), it is often removed from the environment our learners will most likely encounter when they join private industry after graduation.

In the context of teaching and learning IT or CAT, studies into many possibilities for implementation have shown cooperative learning to be an effective pedagogy (Mentz, Van der Walt and Goosen 2008; Mentz 2011, 2016). Learners also contribute to their own and each other's conceptual learning and the process of constructing new knowledge when they argue and negotiate about different points of view on problem solution. This makes it possible for learners to discover external knowledge and internalise it by transforming it into concepts they can relate to (Panitz 2001; Whatley *et al.* 2005). Possibilities are then created for reconstructing and expanding their own perceptions and answers through new learning experiences (Nuutila, Törmä and Malmi 2005). The pedagogical advantages of cooperative learning, including stimulating the development of communication and problem-solving skills, high-level and critical thinking skills, reflection and the ability to explain are thus converted into tools for intellectual functioning in the IT and CAT classes.

## 6.5.2 How to implement cooperative learning

The implementation of the cooperative learning activities in this chapter will be modelled by taking into account the basic elements of cooperative learning, as defined by Johnson and Johnson (2009a, 2019). Johnson, Johnson and Holubec (2008:1:11) define the elements as "discipline that you have to rigorously apply to produce the conditions for effective cooperative action".

Although most of the specific examples mentioned in this chapter relate to using group work when programming or when working on projects, they can also be useful for teaching and learning other aspects of the IT and CAT curriculum.

### 6.5.2.1 *Positive interdependence*

The teacher can foster positive interdependence amongst group members by establishing at least two of the following:

▶ assigning clear group goals in such a way that everyone in the group realises that they can only achieve the goal if everyone in the group achieves the goal (positive goal interdependence);

▶ giving a joint reward for successful group work (positive reward interdependence);

▶ giving different resources to different members of the group (positive resource interdependence), which the group needs to combine to achieve the goal;

▶ assigning different roles to different members of the group (positive role interdependence); and

▶ assigning different tasks to different members (positive task interdependence) where the members of the group realise that they need each other in order to achieve the goal or complete the given task.

### 6.5.2.2 *Individual accountability*

All group members need to be individually responsible for demonstrating their own knowledge and skills obtained in the group through an individual test or presentation in front of the class. The results of the individual tests should also be communicated to the rest of the group.

### 6.5.2.3   Interpersonal and small-group skills

During the first period allocated to the project, learners should receive training in small group skills by participating in various activities and games. These should illustrate the elements of good group organisation, including having a clear purpose, how to define group goals, and planning the project well (Nipp and Palenque 2017). Innovative teachers should be able to source any number of such activities and games in literature on cooperative work.

The actual 'planning meeting' will take place in the second period allocated to the project. Teachers need to ensure that the time allocated for planning the cooperative group work (at least one period) is spent on appropriate discussion and thorough planning, as this planning is important in order for everyone to know exactly what they will be doing (Goosen and Mentz 2007). Each group should provide an account of how they have planned their work, with details written down, such as the division of tasks between various members. If careful planning is not put into place, a group might take very long to really get started, and spend too long changing their minds about what to do. As a result, they might not have enough time to complete their projects to the extent that they would have preferred.

During the planning meeting, these learners will also be responsible for ensuring that appropriate ground rules for behaviour in the group are developed through discussion within the group (Gillies 2003). These guidelines will govern behaviour during the meetings, and will be reported on as part of group processing. Learners should be able to handle any conflict that might occur in their groups by both understanding conflict itself and resolution concepts, and willingly and appropriately choosing to use conflict resolution skills to resolve problems when they arise in cooperative learning situations.

### 6.5.2.4   Promotive interaction

Promotive interaction is supposed to take place each time the groups meet. Sitting together in their groups give learners an efficient way of communicating and assisting each other in order to achieve their group goals. A situation needs to be created in which learners realise that effective learning is a shared responsibility. It is important that they learn from each other to share their resources, provide mutual support and encouragement to achieve success (Kristiansen *et al.* 2019).

### 6.5.2.5   Group processing

In order to effectively monitor group processing (McKinney and Denton 2005), learners' mastery and application of cooperative skills will be monitored regularly through teacher observation, as well as by having learners submit detailed self and peer assessment reports, in a rubric format, at the end of each cycle. The assessment instrument consists of items specifying positive contributions from different group members towards the project, possible weak spots identified, and an indication of the contribution level for each group member. Then, these assessments will be used to provide timely and appropriate feedback to learners, reflecting observations from their peers and the teacher, about how they are doing as group members (McKinney and Denton 2005).

Disruptive group members could at times appear to be bored and do not always interact well within their groups. Sometimes their effort and interest are minimal in comparison to other group members. Occasionally it can be difficult to get and then hold their attention. These learners might do well to realise the importance of being willing to listen to others in the group and find out about their ideas, for optimal group functioning. This kind of behaviour illustrates that teachers should not only be trained in how to handle the "trouble-makers" in groups, but also how to teach the learners how to handle uncooperative group members (Goosen and Mentz 2007).

If the results of group processing show that some group members act disrespectfully or uncooperatively, it is important that swift corrective action is taken to correct such situations. Persistently disrespectful or uncooperative learners could eventually be required to work alone, or amongst themselves, "rather than be an undue burden to other learners' group experiences" (McKinney and Denton 2005:468).

If teachers are well trained in ensuring that the elements discussed above are successfully implemented in their learners' groups, many of the problems experienced in IT or CAT classes when implementing cooperative groups could disappear. The presence of the cooperative elements should enable groups to work effectively to submit required group projects according to specifications and initial planning (Goosen and Mentz 2007).

### 6.5.3 The role of the teacher in the planning and execution of teaching and learning activities

For learners to successfully achieve their cooperative learning outcomes, the application of this pedagogy in IT or CAT classrooms demands that the teacher be thoroughly prepared by carefully designing and structuring group activities to accommodate the required learning strategies. In addition, it is important for the successful implementation of cooperative group learning that instruction is adapted to the needs of the group (Mentz 2011) by setting specific outcomes for the group, as well as setting and emphasising individual responsibilities for each group member.

In order to maximise all learners' involvement in the project, it is important to pitch the project just right: while some of the tasks should provide a challenge to learners, other tasks need to require the use of skills that they feel capable of using comfortably.

While the group work activities are taking place, it is necessary that the teacher closely monitor the involvement of various learners in the actual learning activities. The teacher should also be available for consultation to provide learners with guidance for their group processes, and to provide corrections where needed.

It should also be emphasised that learners will only gain from working in group contexts if teachers manage these activities effectively. It is of the utmost importance that teachers are knowledgeable about different aspects of group dynamics to support groups in the promotion of positive inter-dependence and the establishment of effective small group communication networks.

### 6.5.4  Ideal group size

The typical group size of a cooperative group should not be larger than four members, but according to Johnson and Johnson (2019a:42), "the smaller the better". A review of research by Gillies (2016) states that the benefits of cooperative learning are enhanced when group size does not exceed four members, as the possibility of free riding (see section 6.5.6) increases significantly with additional members added to the group. Johnson, Johnson and Holubec (2007) name a few principles to keep in mind when deciding upon the group size:

▸ if you want to increase the interpersonal resources available to the group, increase the group size;

▸ if you want to strengthen positive interdependence or individual accountability, decrease the group size;

▸ if the physical resources are limited, increase the group size;

▸ if your instructional time is very limited, decrease the group size; and

▸ if your learners are not very skilled in working together, decrease the group size.

### 6.5.5  Group formation

Having groups that are diverse in terms of knowledge and experience could contribute towards the richness of the learning process (Nhan and Nhan 2019). However, comments from teachers (Mentz and Goosen 2007) regarding group formation and the research by Nhan and Nhan (2019) specifically indicate that students. especially high school learners, do not want to be divided into groups by the teacher, but instead want to establish group membership themselves. These wishes are centred around the learners' desire for control and responsibility. This kind of group formation tends to not have the best results. According to Johnson, Johnson and Holubec (2007) and Nhan and Nhan (2019), random assignment of learners to groups is the easiest and most effective way. If learners know that group formation will be changed on a regular basis, they realise that they will be working with everybody in the class over time and tend to not demand choosing their own groups.

### 6.5.6  Group member roles

Learners need to experience that they will need to effectively implement several member roles in order to successfully maximise their group's interaction and accomplishments. The main aim of these roles is the assignment of different responsibilities to group members and determining how group members are to act and/or function within the group (Smarkusky *et al.* 2005). In this way, "poor drivers" can be avoided – they usually have domineering personalities, leading to their not knowing how to delegate responsibilities, but instead wanting to do everything themselves. The opposite would be learners who become "free riders", avoiding responsibility and/or making contributions by letting others handle all the work (Nuutila, Törmä and Malmi 2005; Chiriac 2014).

Since the only role that teachers usually assign to group members is that of group leader, learners need to be exposed to some of the common pitfalls that could occur when they are group leaders and how to take responsibility. Since teachers generally do not know of other roles that can be assigned to learners when working in groups (Mentz and Goosen 2007), they do not enforce the use of different roles.

The scribe/recorder/secretary is responsible for documenting the group conversation and providing the group consensus solution for the problem. Other positions in a group are the speaker/presenter, who presents the group's answer to the class, and the facilitator, in charge of encouraging everyone to participate. The role of a planner/timer, to outline where and how the group is proceeding through the assignment, can be added. Learners will be required to rotate between different roles which can be fulfilled within the group (McKinney and Denton 2005). Roles can also be defined according to the nature of the task. Other roles like devil's advocate, motivator, checker for correctness, or innovator might also be applicable for certain tasks.

### 6.5.7  Assessment in group context

Many arguments put forward why teachers do not often use cooperative groups in IT/CAT centre on perceptions that assessment in group context and the administration of group work is difficult (Mentz and Goosen 2007; Veenman *et al.* 2002). Teachers need to use techniques that they can implement to obtain information for the assessment of individual learners in the group project situation.

One of the queries most often encountered with group work is the assessment of individual involvement when the product of group work is a single project (Forsell, Frykedal and Chariac 2021). This aspect is intricately linked to the elements of positive interdependence and individual accountability mentioned in previous sections. Teachers need to keep in mind that the aim of cooperative learning is for learners to *learn together*, but to *achieve alone*. If positive interdependence and individual accountability can be fostered in any other way than to formally assess and score the group performance, it will be advisable. Individual assessment remains the number one assessment in cooperative learning. That is why the individual marks of group members should be given back to the group to reflect upon. Teachers should not use cooperative learning only to reduce the number of assignments that need to be assessed. Keep in mind that a project simply given to learners to complete in groups in their own time, without ensuring that the five elements of cooperative learning are adhered to, is not cooperative learning.

When the teacher needs to assess the groups' work, a final cumulative peer assessment instrument can be used that explicitly asks each learner to rate each group member on group skills such as communication and cooperation (Forsell, Frykedal and Chariac 2021). Pollock and Jochen (2001) suggest that when marking group projects, the teacher needs to start all group members with the same grade, but that grade will be adjusted for each member, in accordance with their individual contribution as reflected in their peer assessment. The fact that most learners hesitate to give a bad rating to their partners shows that this kind of assessment does not always work well. It should also be compared with the individual assessment. If the group has the opportunity to discuss each other's involvement in the group during group processing and are given the opportunity to celebrate their successes, it strengthens the positive interdependence of the group, as well as the individual accountability of each member of the group.

## 6.5.8   Different cooperative learning methods

As mentioned in Chapter 2, cooperative learning is a teaching-learning strategy in which different methods can be used. Examples of these methods include Group Investigation, Jigsaw, Student Teams Achievement Divisions (STAD) and Teams-Games-Tournament (TGT) (Garcia 2021), and are illustrated in Chapter 9 for use with theoretical content. Other cooperative learning methods which Johnson, Johnson and Holubec (2008) refer to include Academic Controversy, Cooperative Note-Taking Pairs, Read and Explain Pairs, and Reading Comprehension Triads. Numerous different cooperative learning methods exist which should be selected keeping in mind the content and objectives of the learning situation.

## ACTIVITY 6.2

**Study any cooperative learning method of your choice (see section 6.5.8) and design your own cooperative learning lesson on any theoretical topic in the IT or CAT curriculum where you incorporate the method into your lesson. You need to indicate how you plan to include the five basic elements into your lesson.**

## 6.6   USING PAIR PROGRAMMING AS COOPERATIVE LEARNING METHOD IN THE IT CLASS

The next section describes the use of pair programming as cooperative learning method in the IT class. Please note that pair problem-solving can use the same principles and can be used in IT and CAT classes.

## 6.6.1   What is pair programming?

As opportunities for computer science education for school learners increase, there is also growing interest in pair programming as cooperative learning method in IT classrooms (Tsan *et al.* 2020). Any experienced IT teacher will agree that the best way to learn programming is through practice. This practice includes getting it wrong the first time and learning from mistakes. There is agreement in academic environments that pair programming is a promising strategy through which to exercise this practice. In pair programming, learners can apply basic syntax and semantics practically to enhance the level of deep learning by cooperating with each other on programming assignments.

Pair programming could be defined as a style of programming in which two programmers work at the same computer, execute the programming task together, and collaborate on the same design, algorithm and code. One programmer is called the 'driver', and the other, the 'navigator'. The driver operates the pen or pencil, keyboard and mouse, writes the algorithm, or designs and types the code. The navigator points out the programming direction, actively examines the work of the driver, reviews the code, and identifies defects and errors in the code. It is the navigator's responsibility to suggest strategies for solving a problem, to think of alternatives, to look up resources and to consider the strategic implications of their work. The navigator is the person in charge of programming language reference materials and acts as a strategic, long-range thinker (Williams and Kessler 2003; Bipp, Lepper and Schmedding 2007; Venkatesan and Annamalali 2010). Table 6.2 shows the roles of the driver and the navigator (Hahn 2008) and Figure 6.1 offers a schematic diagram of the responsibilities of the driver and the navigator within the problem space. Always keep in mind that these roles cannot be performed without interaction between them. Both members of the team should work together at all times. The philosophy of pair programming as a form of cooperative learning is that the individual, although in interaction with another, is still responsible for his/her own learning, but respects the capabilities and contributions of the other (Panitz 1997).

*Table 6.2    Roles of the driver and navigator in pair programming (Hahn 2008)*

| Steps in programming | The role of the driver | The role of the navigator |
|---|---|---|
| Objective of program | Write the objective of the program on a piece of paper. | Communicate with driver to clarify objectives; communicate with teacher/facilitator if necessary. |
| The IPO table | Write the input, processing and output in the particular spaces of the IPO table; modify table as needed. | Verify if data is written in the correct spaces; ensure that the processing that is written will produce the necessary output required; use resources to find alternative methods; propose alternatives. |
| Program design | Write an algorithm on paper. | Evaluate every step written in the algorithm; determine whether it is the most logical route that can be followed. |
| Validation of design | Complete the trace table and compare answers with expected output. | Supply test data and expected output for each set of data; find logical errors and correct the errors. |
| Implementation of design | Control the keyboard and mouse; responsible for the typing of programming code. | Check correctness of code; reflect on code and process; ensure that programming happens according to plan; propose corrections. |
| Test of solution | Implement corrections on programming code and/or algorithm, where needed. | Compare the algorithm with the program; propose alternative ways to correct errors. |
| Document the program | Compile documentation on the functionality of the program. | Ensure that documentation is clear and understandable to the teacher/facilitator and other programmers/pairs. |

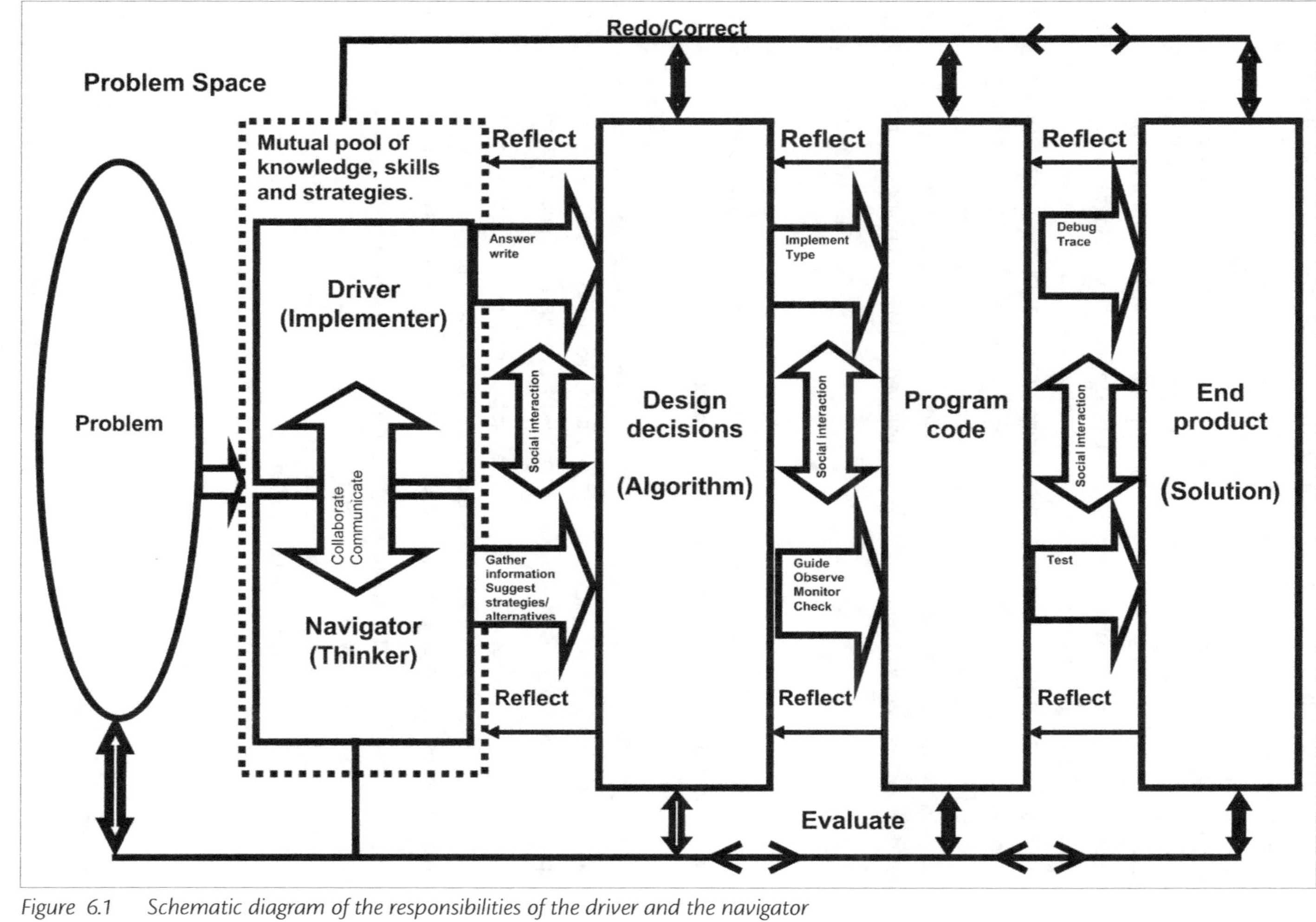



Figure 6.1    *Schematic diagram of the responsibilities of the driver and the navigator*

## 6.6.2   The implementation of pair programming in the IT class

In this section, some guidelines for the implementation of pair programming in the IT class will be provided.

### 6.6.2.1   General principles of pair programming

As with the theory on cooperative learning discussed in this chapter, pair programming demands specific social skills and active communication in order to be able to share one's thinking processes with a partner. The fact that the learners have to communicate what they know and understand to each other, gives them a clear picture of what they do not know, and what they need to ask their partner. Partners serve as resources for each other (Yerion and Rinehart 1995).

A pair that functions well should constantly communicate with each other. They should have the confidence to ask questions and assist each other in understanding and solving the problem. All the social skills applicable for cooperative learning also apply to pair programming.

The role of navigator and driver should be switched regularly in order to give both partners the opportunity to learn the skills of the particular role. The navigator should not use the mouse or keyboard without the permission of the driver and the driver should not use the reference material without the permission of the navigator.

As pair programming can be seen as a cooperative learning strategy, the implementation of pair programming is based on cooperative learning principles, which will be discussed in more detail in the sections that follow.

### 6.6.2.2   Pair formation

Many studies have applied skills level or personality type as criteria for forming pairs. Williams and Kessler (2003), as well as Chapparro *et al.* (2005), found evidence that students produce their best work when they are paired with someone with the same skills level.  Alternatively, Katira *et al.* (2004) found that pair compatibility in beginning courses may increase if pairs are formed by joining students of different personality types. Jensen (2005) confirms that the same experience and capability level is often counter-productive in pair programming. Jensen (2005) found that teams functioned better if one member was slightly more capable than the other. It is true that two high achievers approach the task differently from a high and low achiever or two low achievers, but they gain different positive learning experiences from them all. Within a teaching and learning environment with novice learners where partners were rotated regularly, there was no significant difference between different groupings. As long as the skills level gap is not too big, Chapparro *et al.* (2005) found that students still seem to enjoy and benefit from pairing. According to Williams and Kessler (2003), gender and cultural differences between pairs generally are not problematic, though, in school learners it still may be problematic and teachers need to be aware of possible gender problems, such as boys dominating the learning experience. Sometimes, for different reasons, learners are not compatible with their partners and need to be regrouped to attain optimal learning. Teachers should be sensitive to such cases and identify them early on, and switch pairs to avoid any counter-productivity in the classroom.

Some researchers prefer to allow students to choose their own partners, while others assign partners at random. Researchers disagree on whether self-selected pairs or chosen pairs work best. The main disadvantage of self-selected pairs is that students learn each other's way of working and also learn to cover for each other. At first, they are more confident in asking questions and communicate with each other, but if students get used to working in pairs they learn to question regardless of whom their partner is. If pairs rotate regularly and each member of the class gets the opportunity to work with different personality types and skills levels, learners gain most in terms of social skills and the ability to adjust to different social environments. When students know that they will have an opportunity to pair with everybody in the class, they do not complain or ask to select their own partners. It also creates a good learning environment where they get to know one another, are willing to share their knowledge, and can assist those who struggle to understand the work.

### 6.6.2.3  How to rotate between the roles of navigator and driver

It is important to rotate the roles within the pair on a regular basis to give learners the opportunity to perform in each of the two different roles. Role switching is an informal process and the interval depends mostly on the task at hand and the time available. Some researchers prefer an interval of 20 minutes; others prefer to complete a specific part of the programming assignment before rotating. When rotating, the partners physically get up and change positions. The navigator always sits on the opposite side of the mouse, with the screen turned so that both can see it clearly. For small assignments, it could be best to give two assignments to be completed by one pair, rotating after the completion of the first assignment. The advantage of the second strategy is that the strategic thinking of the navigator is not interrupted.

### 6.6.2.4  Implementing the key elements of cooperative learning in pair programming

➜    *Positive interdependence in pair programming*

To achieve positive interdependence in pair programming, the navigator and the driver need to be linked in such a way that they realise that one cannot succeed unless they both do. They need to coordinate their efforts to complete a task (Johnson and Johnson 2018) and jointly assume ownership for the completion of the task (Werner, Denner and Bean 2004). The key to fostering positive interdependence lies in goal setting, the assessment of the team's work, and control over role performance. Clear goal setting and good assessment methods lead to a situation in which the learners realise that effective learning is a collective responsibility, where resources must be shared and support and encouragement for each other will contribute to their success (Veenman *et al.* 2002). If the pair knows that their work will be assessed and that each of them has a specific role to perform to achieve their goals, it fosters positive interdependence between the pair members.

It is preferable that learners receive a timeframe for completing the assignment. If they know that they have to complete the program before the end of the session or period, it creates a motivation towards task completion, and as a result, learners are actively involved in their own learning for the duration of the session. Positive reward interdependence can be fostered by rewarding bonus points when both members of the pair, for example, achieve above a certain percentage for the individual test. If the pair knows that one of them will be selected to present the solution to the class, and that they will receive marks for the presentation, it creates a positive interdependence between them. Assessment of the end product is necessary, as well as assessing each individual's contribution to the end product. Positive interdependence counteracts competitive behaviour, allowing learners to realise that they depend on each other for their success as individuals and as partners.

### ➡ *Individual accountability in pair programming*

Individual accountability exists when each member of the pair contributes to the success of the pair and shares his/her knowledge and skills (Mentz 2011). To successfully achieve individual and pair accountability, the performance of each individual member of the pair needs to be assessed and the results be given back to both individuals, and the pair, to reflect upon.

Each member of the pair needs to realise that they not only need to achieve the goal set for the pair, by solving the problem and creating a running program, but they also need to assist each other to achieve the outcomes to solve a similar problem individually. Such feelings of responsibility increase a person's motivation to perform well (Johnson and Johnson 2009b). Each member of the pair should realise that they will be held responsible for their work within the pair and each of them must individually achieve the desired outcomes. Assessing students individually by means of a test can determine if each member has achieved the required outcomes. Mechanisms should be put in place which will motivate both members of the pair to be actively involved and to ensure that no one member is going to have an easy ride on the other one's back, or to completely withdraw from or dominate the situation (Tsompanoudi, Satratzemi and Xinogalos 2015). It can be done by giving feedback of individual assessment back to the pair to reflect on what they have achieved. If one of them did not achieve the desired outcome, both fail as they should support and assist each other in order to perform a similar problem by themselves as well.

Learners can also access each other's input and contribution and it can be compared with the individual test of each member. A penalty can be built in if the two marks do not correlate. In this way, partners are forced to assess each other honestly.

### ➡ *Interpersonal and small-group skills in pair programming*

For effective pair programming it is important that each member of the pair is trained in good social skills, which include good communication, listening and interpersonal skills. They need to be motivated to use social skills to get to know and trust each other, communicate ideas accurately and clearly, and to resolve conflict constructively. Members of a pair need to learn to formulate thoughts and ideas about programming clearly and explain it in a logical way to their partners.

They also need to learn to appreciate and accept alternative suggestions by partners. It is important that members of the pair accept the fact that they have to consider different ideas, that their own idea is not necessarily the best idea, and not to be defensive when receiving criticism (Williams and Kessler 2000). Programmers need to ask each other questions, argue with each other about the outcome of a specific action, have confidence in making alternative suggestions to solve a problem, and describe in their own words how they think a problem could be solved. A good pair should be communicating continually during programming, and pay close attention to each other by looking at each other when talking and by listening carefully. Sharing what they know exposes what they do not know and therefore each member of the pair serves as resources for the other member (Yerion and Rinehart 1995). Partners need to make sure that the other member understands what is going on, and should be respectful of the other's opinions. With pair programming, the specific roles of the navigator and driver force students to interact, therefore it is important to facilitate the correct application of roles. As social skills improve, the enjoyment factor increases and students became more motivated about programming. Disagreements do occur but should be resolved respectfully.

### ➜ *Promotive interaction in pair programming*

Promotive interaction in pair programming will result in conducive interaction between members where they provide assistance to each other, gain confidence in asking questions, challenge each other's reasoning, and encourage each other to succeed. Effective promotive interaction results in mutual motivation and the creation of trust in each other's opinions and actions. It develops confidence to venture and communicate and reduces learner stress and anxiety, especially when a novice programmer is paired with an expert. They both have the responsibility to see to it that they both achieve the desired outcomes.

### ➜ *Group processing in pair programming*

After completion of a task, pairs need to reflect on how well they have functioned; on actions that were helpful; on actions that wasted their time; on actions that were unacceptable; and on how they plan to improve their progress. They also need to think about what works well in order to apply that in further programming actions and to change actions that did not work well. Group processing provides feedback to each other regarding their actions and contribution. It also acts as a means of celebrating the successes of the pair.

Feedback from the pair can also indicate to the teacher which aspects were difficult and therefore need extra attention. Self and partner assessment can also be discussed during this reflection.

It is of the utmost importance within a pair-programming environment that partners share ownership of their project (Werner, Denner and Bean 2004; Sedano, Peraire and Ralph 2016). They, therefore, need to encourage each other and praise each other for work well done.

### 6.6.2.5  The role of the teacher in planning and execution of pair programming

Achieving well-functioning pair structures for teaching and learning programming skills require a teacher to be committed to pair programming, and one who is well prepared. This implies a teacher's active involvement in the process. The teacher needs to inform the learners how to work in pairs, plan, guide and monitor the learning activity carefully, and perform assessment of work done in a reliable way. Each of these steps will be discussed in more detail now.

➜　　*Explain pair programming*

Often learners are reluctant to work in pairs because they have a negative perception about group work from previous experience. It is essential that the advantages of pair programming are explained to them, as well as what measures are taken to prevent one learner from taking a free ride while the other does all the work. It is generally taken for granted that learners know how to work in groups, and that teachers only need to set assignments and facilitate the process. This assumption has proven to be wrong (Chiriac 2014). To coordinate the efforts of the pair members, learners need to be taught exactly what is expected of them within the roles of navigator and driver. They need to know how to act in each role, how to take up the responsibility, to share roles, set pair goals, communicate with each other, and resolve conflict (McWhaw *et al.* 2003).

➜　　*Be prepared*

The teacher/facilitator should be thoroughly prepared by designing and structuring pair activities carefully, and setting specific goals for pairs to achieve the necessary objectives. The planning of specific assignments, which could enhance programming skills because of their problem-solving nature and application of higher levels of thinking skills, is preferable. Always keep the outcomes in mind and never implement pair programming for the sake of pair programming. Therefore, goals set for the pair must correlate with the objectives that the learners need to achieve. Learners must be informed about how and when assessment will take place and what the criteria for assessment will be.

Carefully plan what measures need to be put in place in order to promote positive interdependence and individual accountability in learners.

Ensure that sufficient time is available for learners to complete the task. A timeframe serves as motivation and creates a sense of urgency in the pair, thus promoting an active learning environment.

The teacher must assign the pairs in advance, whether it is a random assignment or not. Keep record of the allocation of partners and see to it that every learner in the class gets the opportunity to work with every other learner. It is preferable that members of the pairs change frequently to give learners the opportunity to work with different personality types and skills levels. The teacher also needs to decide on the right time to rotate the roles in the pair.

➡ *Guidance and facilitation of the process: A practical approach*

During facilitation of pair programming the teacher needs to ensure that learners know exactly what they have to do. Go over the specification of the program that they need to write, and give them time to ask any questions they may have. Set a time limit by roughly indicating when an assignment needs to be completed. It is preferable that learners need to complete assignments during class time.

During the pair programming activities, the teacher should be available for consultation, guidance and assessment. Assist learners by asking questions which will lead them to the solution to the problem, rather than by direct answers. Encourage them to seek answers by themselves, praising them when good cooperation occurs. The roles of navigator and driver need to be carefully monitored to ensure that each member performs the role effectively and that they change roles frequently.

Make sure all the students are participating in the activity, giving assistance when needed, making on-the-spot error corrections when communication amongst the pair members are hampered, and making notes on errors that can be discussed after the activity. The facilitator must observe students continuously and give feedback on their cooperative abilities. Help them to understand that there is not only one correct way, algorithm or program solution. When conflict occurs which learners cannot resolve on their own, the teacher needs to assist and guide them to resolve it. It is not preferable to split pair members before they have learned to resolve the conflict.

General errors which are spotted during pair programming can be dealt with at the end of the assignment. It is important that a specific time allocation be provided at the end for the teacher to reflect on problems which learners had and solutions that learners found. It serves as a valuable learning opportunity, since everyone has already been involved in thinking and reasoning about the relevant problems. Frequently learners discover that there in fact was a shorter method to the solution of the problem and they thus gain better insight and understanding. Teachers have also found that during these discussions learners show more willingness to share their experiences and solution with the class. During the time allocated, the opportunity can also be created for students to demonstrate their work in front of the class. To strengthen positive interdependence, the class can award a mark to the pair for the demonstration of their program.

➡ *Assessment*

Assessment of pair programming implies that the outcomes of the process, as well as the process itself should be assessed. Each individual should be assessed on his or her cognitive and cooperative skills.

Self-, peer-, teacher-, class- and individual assessment can form part of the assessment process of pair programming. Members of the pair assess each other's contribution to the success of the outcome, as well as their own contribution. The teacher can assess the pair on the outcome of the assignment, as well as on the work done by the pair. An individual test on the outcomes of the pair assignment is an important indicator of how well the pair functioned, ensuring that each member of the pair contributes equally to the completion of the assignment. The demonstration of the pair's work in front of the class can be assessed by fellow learners. All the assessment can be done on a rubric (see Tables 6.3 and 6.4 as examples of specific outcomes that could be assessed in a short time during classes). Table 6.5 is an example of the possible scores of learners when doing pair programming. Note that except for the individual mark, all the other marks can be assigned during pair programming in the class.

The self-, peer-, class- and facilitator-assessment mark can be quantified as a mark that will count towards the learners' pair mark. To achieve a sense of responsibility to each other, the average of the individual test scores of the pair could also count towards the pair mark. The following is an example of a possible way in which the scores for pair programming could be implemented (note that each member of the pair scores a different mark):

*Table 6.3    An example of an assessment rubric: Peer and self*

NAME AND SURNAME: Self ________________________________________________

NAME AND SURNAME: Peer __________________________________________

Scale:

1: Not at all

2: To a lesser extent

3: To a large extent

4: Totally

Evaluate yourself and your peer on the following categories:

| Knowledge and skills on | Self | | | | Peer | | | |
|---|---|---|---|---|---|---|---|---|
| 1. Screen layout development | 1 | 2 | 3 | 4 | 1 | 2 | 3 | 4 |
| 2. Defining of variables | 1 | 2 | 3 | 4 | 1 | 2 | 3 | 4 |
| 3. Algorithm development | 1 | 2 | 3 | 4 | 1 | 2 | 3 | 4 |
| 4. Program syntax | 1 | 2 | 3 | 4 | 1 | 2 | 3 | 4 |
| 5. Debugging | 1 | 2 | 3 | 4 | 1 | 2 | 3 | 4 |
| 6. The achievement of desired outcomes | 1 | 2 | 3 | 4 | 1 | 2 | 3 | 4 |
| Criteria on cooperation | | | | | | | | |
| 7. Listening skills | 1 | 2 | 3 | 4 | 1 | 2 | 3 | 4 |
| 8 Interpersonal communication and skills | 1 | 2 | 3 | 4 | 1 | 2 | 3 | 4 |
| 9. General cooperation | 1 | 2 | 3 | 4 | 1 | 2 | 3 | 4 |
| 10. Fulfillment of roles as driver and navigator | 1 | 2 | 3 | 4 | 1 | 2 | 3 | 4 |
| TOTAL 40/4 (Mark out of 10) | | | | | | | | |

*Table 6.4    Example of a rubric for teacher assessment*

Grade: _______________________________

Scale:

1: Not achieved

2: Achieved to a lesser extent

3: Achieved to a large extent

4: Totally achieved

| Name of learner | 1. Screen layout | | | | 2. Definition of variables | | | | 3. Program syntax | | | | 4. Correctness | | | | 5. Any other outcomes | | | | 6. Cooperation | | | | Total |
|---|---|---|---|---|---|---|---|---|---|---|---|---|---|---|---|---|---|---|---|---|---|---|---|---|---|
| | 1 | 2 | 3 | 4 | 1 | 2 | 3 | 4 | 1 | 2 | 3 | 4 | 1 | 2 | 3 | 4 | 1 | 2 | 3 | 4 | 1 | 2 | 3 | 4 | |
| | 1 | 2 | 3 | 4 | 1 | 2 | 3 | 4 | 1 | 2 | 3 | 4 | 1 | 2 | 3 | 4 | 1 | 2 | 3 | 4 | 1 | 2 | 3 | 4 | |
| | 1 | 2 | 3 | 4 | 1 | 2 | 3 | 4 | 1 | 2 | 3 | 4 | 1 | 2 | 3 | 4 | 1 | 2 | 3 | 4 | 1 | 2 | 3 | 4 | |
| | 1 | 2 | 3 | 4 | 1 | 2 | 3 | 4 | 1 | 2 | 3 | 4 | 1 | 2 | 3 | 4 | 1 | 2 | 3 | 4 | 1 | 2 | 3 | 4 | |
| | 1 | 2 | 3 | 4 | 1 | 2 | 3 | 4 | 1 | 2 | 3 | 4 | 1 | 2 | 3 | 4 | 1 | 2 | 3 | 4 | 1 | 2 | 3 | 4 | |

*Table 6.5    Example of an assessment of one pair*

| Name of learner | Self assessment (10) | Peer assessment (10) | Facilitator assessment (10) | Individual test (10) | Average individual test (10) | Bonus points | Class presentation (10) | Pair mark (50) |
|---|---|---|---|---|---|---|---|---|
| Alrischa Bana | 8 | 7 | 7 | 8 | 6.5 | - | 6 | 34.5 |
| Thabo Mbuli | 7 | 5 | 7 | 5 | 6.5 | - | 6 | 31.5 |

To foster individual accountability and positive interdependence amongst members of the pair, they could, for example, be rewarded with bonus points if both members cooperate in completion of the program, score above a certain average on the individual evaluation, or complete the program correctly within a given time frame. Individual accountability can also be fostered by randomly selecting one of the members of the pair to demonstrate and explain their program to the class or facilitator. This creates a feeling of commitment to the task and prevents free-riding. The class members could also allocate a mark for their presentation. Class presentations work well when all the pairs receive different programming assignments with similar outcomes. If assessment works well, there will be no competition between team members and blame for problems will never be placed on one partner (Williams and Kessler 2000).

Assessment should be done after completion of each assignment and the teacher should give enough time to each student to complete the self-assessment, as well as the peer assessment rubric. The rubric will help the students to identify their own mistakes, evaluate their progress, and clearly see which of their skills need improvement.

➜ *Create the opportunity for group processing*

Feedback and reflection after assessment is very important. Specific time needs to be set aside for feedback to improve the performance of their assigned tasks and responsibilities, to reflect on their work, and to learn from mistakes made. Depending on the time available, learners can do this in the form of a journal, or simply discuss this with each other. Initially it will be necessary for the teacher to structure the reflection with the following questions:

▷ What worked well?

▷ What did not work well?

▷ What have I learned from you that I can use next time?

▷ What should we change next time?

Later-stage learners will be able to structure and broaden this discussion by themselves, to give feedback to each other about where gaps exist and where objectives have not been fully reached.

When the teacher gives feedback on pair programming assignments, the learners are aware of which cognitive outcomes they still have to master and more attention can be given to those.

Feedback from the individual assessment must be given to the specific member, as well as to the pair. General feedback on how well each pair has functioned, as well as on the achievement of the necessary outcome must also be done by the teacher. The teacher can also extend the feedback into a full-class discussion, examine errors that students made while working in pairs, or discuss general programming problems that they may have experienced.

## 6.6.3 Responsibility of team members

Apart from working correctly as driver or navigator, sharing resources and taking up their individual responsibility, members of the pair should provide each other with efficient and effective assistance. Teaching and explaining one's knowledge to others increases the degree to which both members of the pair process and understand information, engage on higher levels of reasoning, and increase the commitment to achieve the goal. Therefore, it is the responsibility of each member of the pair to listen carefully and critically to the explanations of their peer and provide each other with feedback in order to improve their performance. When challenging each other's conclusions and reasoning, it motivates them to learn and promotes curiosity and greater insight into the problem. It is their responsibility to encourage each other to achieve the mutual goal, explore different options and think critically in order to solve the problem (Johnson and Johnson 2009a).

### 6.6.4  Reaction from students working in pairs

A number of studies have been done on the perception of students working in pairs. Initially, students' reaction to pair programming can be negative because they do not know what to expect and some students will always prefer to work alone. However, after working in pairs, their perception normally changes and most of them prefer working in pairs rather than alone. According to Van Niekerk (2018), who applied cooperative pair problem-solving as a teaching-learning strategy, some of these challenges can be addressed.

### 6.6.5  The benefits of pair programming

From research over the years, a number of benefits of pair programming were identified:

- it improves a student's performance on programming assignments and examinations (Bevan, Werner and McDowell 2002; Nagappan *et al.* 2003; Venkatesan and Annamalali 2010);
- it results in higher quality programs and fewer errors in the end product (McDowell, Hanks and Werner 2003; Jensen 2005; Venkatesan and Annamalali 2010; Faja 2014);
- it decreases time to complete programs (Williams and Upchurch 2001; Chaparro *et al.* 2005);
- it fosters greater understanding of the programming process (DeClue 2003; Howard 2006);
- it increases enjoyment of programming and improves course completion rates and retention  (McDowell *et al.* 2003);
- it decreases students' dependence on teaching staff;
- it results in more focused, motivated learners (Jensen 2005);
- it results in more satisfaction and less frustration (Chaparro *et al.* 2005; Venkatesan and Annamalali 2010);
- it improves communication and confidence (Williams *et al.* 2000; Venkatesan and Annamalali 2010);
- it leads to improved comprehension and learning (Williams and Kessler 2003; Venkatesan and Annamalali 2010); and
- it enhances teamwork and social skills (Williams and Kessler 2003; Edwards, Stewart and Ferati 2010).

### 6.6.6  Limitations of pair programming

Although the literature shows a convincing number of advantages in favour of pair programming, there are certain limitations that a teacher needs to be aware of. If pair programming is implemented correctly, these limitations could be reduced to the minimum. The problems experienced with pair programming are normally limited to:

- pair incompatibility, especially when the pairs are not rotated frequently;

- schedule-related issues when pair programming is not performed in a scheduled classroom environment (Bevan, Werner and McDowell 2002; Howard 2006); and

- unequal participation by the individuals in a pair when individual accountability or positive interdependence is not enforced.

Pair programming outside the scheduled classroom environment tends to have more limitations. It is more difficult to ensure that the five elements of cooperative learning are still implemented. The individual efforts as well as the group collaboration cannot always be measured or controlled and as a result a member of the pair could easily do all the work. The roles of driver and navigator and the rotation of roles, communication and conflict handling can also not be easily monitored. Furthermore, if there is no time limitation on the completion of the program, pairs could be less focused. However, pair programming in an online environment can be structured in a way to avoid all these limitations and to model a classroom environment as discussed in this chapter. Technology-supported cooperative learning in an online environment can be very successful, provided that the elements of cooperative learning are still built into the online environment.

## ACTIVITY 6.3

(a) Explain in detail **_all the planning_** that an IT teacher should perform to implement pair programming in a Grade 10 IT class with specific reference to how the key elements for cooperative learning should be incorporated into the implementation, **_OR_**

Explain in detail **_all the planning_** that a CAT teacher should perform to implement cooperative learning or pair problem-solving in a practical CAT lesson of your choice.

(b) Design a complete pair programming lesson for a Grade 10 class on a topic of your choice, **_OR_**

Design a cooperative learning lesson for a practical CAT class on a topic of your choice.

## 6.7   CONCLUSION

We believe that group work in the IT and CAT class could enhance learners' understanding of difficult concepts and improve social skills, while learning to work effectively with others in a team or group. It is the responsibility of the IT and CAT teacher to effectively implement group work in their classes.

## ACKNOWLEDGEMENT

We based part of this chapter on research financially supported by the National Research Foundation (NRF) in South Africa. Any opinions, findings, conclusions or recommendations expressed in this chapter are those of the authors and the NRF does not accept any liability in regard thereto.

## REFERENCES

Agrawal, M., Joshi, N. and Purohit, N. 2020. Cooperative Communications Framework for Industrial Applications. (In *Advances in VLSI, Communication, and Signal Processing.* Singapore: Springer, pp. 171-179.) https://doi.org/10.1007/978-981-32-9775-3_17

Alfares, N. 2017. Benefits and difficulties of learning in group work in EFL classes in Saudi Arabia. *English Language Teaching*, 10(7):247-256. https://doi.org/10.5539/elt.v10n7p247

Barkley, E.F., Cross, P.K. and Major, C.H. 2014. *Collaborative learning techniques. A Handbook for college faculty.* Hoboken, NJ: John Wiley & Sons.

Bevan, J., Werner, L. and McDowell, C. 2002. Guidelines for the use of pair programming in a freshman programming class. Presented at the Conference on Software Engineering Education and Training, Kentucky.

Bipp, T., Lepper, A. and Schmedding, D. 2007. Pair programming in software development teams: an empirical study of its benefits. *Information and Software Technology.* https://doi.org/10.1016/j.infsof.2007.05.006

Bolton, A., Goosen, L and Kritzinger, E. 2022. *Impact of Digital Transformation via Unified Communication and Collaboration Technologies: Productivity and Innovation at a Global Enterprise.* https://doi.org/10.4018/978-1-7998-9179-6.ch014

Buchs, C. and Butera, F. 2015. Cooperative learning and social skills development. (In R.Gilies, ed. *Collaborative Learning: Developments in Research and Practice.* New York: Nova Science.)

Chaparro, E.A., Aybala, Y., Romero, P. and Bryant, S. 2005. *Factors affecting the perceived effectiveness of pair programming in higher education.* 17th Workshop of Psychology of Pair Programming Interest Group, Sussex University, June, pp. 5-18.

Chiriac, E.A. 2014. Group work as an incentive for learning – students' experiences of group work. *Frontiers in Psychology*, 5:558. https://doi.org/10.3389/fpsyg.2014.00558

DeClue, T. 2003. Pair programming and pair trading: Effects on learning and motivation in a CS2 course. *The Journal of Computing in Small Colleges*, 18(5):49-56.

Du Toit, A. 2019. Constructive congruencies in self-directed learning and entrepreneurship education. (In: E. Mentz, J. de Beer and R. Bailey, eds. *Self-Directed Learning for the 21st Century: Implications for Higher Education.* Cape Town: Aosis, pp. 313-340.) https://doi.org/10.4102/aosis.2019.BK134.10

Edwards, R.L., Stewart, J.K. and Ferati, M. 2010. Assessing the effectiveness of distributed pair programming for an online informatics curriculum. *ACM Inroads*, 1(1):48-54. https://doi.org/10.1145/1721933.1721951

Faja, S. 2014. Evaluating effectiveness of pair programming as a teaching tool in programming courses. *Information Systems Education Journal*, 12(6):36-45.

Forsell, J., Frykedal, K.F. and Chiriac, E.H. 2021. Teachers' perceived challenges in group work assessment. *Cogent Education*, 8(1). https://doi.org/10.1080/2331186X.2021.1886474

Garcia, M.B. 2021. Cooperative learning in computer programming: A quasi-experimental evaluation of Jigsaw teaching strategy with novice programmers. *Education and Information Technologies*, 26:4839-4856. https://doi.org/10.1007/s10639-021-10502-6

Geldenhuys, E.J. 2012. Sosiale vaardighede vir paarprogrammering. M.Ed.-verhandeling. Noordwes-Universiteit, Potchefstroom.

Gillies, R.M. 2003. Structuring cooperative group work in classrooms. *International Journal of Educational Research*, 39(1-2):35-49. https://doi.org/10.1016/S0883-0355(03)00072-7

Gillies, R.M. 2016. Cooperative Learning: Review of research and practice. *Australian Journal of Teacher Education*, 41(3). https://doi.org/10.14221/ajte.2016v41n3.3

Gillies, R.M. 2019. Promoting academically productive student dialogue during collaborative learning. *International Journal of Educational Research*, 97:200-209. https://doi.org/10.1016/j.ijer.2017.07.014

Goosen, L. and Mentz, E. 2007. "United we stand, divided we fall": Learning from experiences of group work in Information Technology. (In *Proceedings of the 2007 Computer Science and Information Technology Education Conference*, 16-18 November, Hotel La

Plantation, Mauritius. Santa Rosa: Informing Science Institute, pp. 255-267.)

Hahn, J.H. 2008. Paarassessering teenoor individuele assessering in rekenaarprogrammering. M.Ed.-verhandeling, Noordwes-Universiteit, Potchefstroom.

Howard, E.V. 2006. Attitudes on using pair-programmming. *Journal of Educational Technology Systems*, 35(1):89-103. https://doi.org/10.2190/5K87-58W8-G07M-2811

Jensen, R.W. 2005. A pair programming experience. *Overload*, 65:22-25.

Johnson, D.W. and Johnson, R.T. 2005. Essential components of peace education. *Theory Into Practice*, 44(4):280-292. https://doi.org/10.1207/s15430421tip4404_2

Johnson, D.W. and Johnson, R.T. 2009a. *Joining together: Group theory and group skills*, 10th ed. Upper Saddle River, NJ: Pearson.

Johnson, D.W. and Johnson, R.T. 2009b. An educational psychology success story: Social interdependence theory and cooperative learning. *Educational Researcher*, 38(5):365-379. https://doi.org/10.3102/0013189X09339057

Johnson, D.W. and Johnson, R.T. 2018. Cooperative learning: The foundation for active learning. (In S.M. Brito, ed. *Active learning: Beyond the Future*. London: IntechOpen.) https://doi.org/10.5772/intechopen.81086

Johnson, D.W. and Johnson, R.T. 2019. The impact of cooperative learning on self-directed learning. (In E. Mentz, J. de Beer and R. Bailey, eds. *Self-Directed Learning for the 21st Century: Implications for Higher Education*. NWU Self-Directed Learning Series Volume 1. Cape Town: Aosis, pp. 37-66.) https://doi.org/10.4102/aosis.2019.BK134.02

Johnson, D.W., Johnson, R.T. and Holubec, E.J. 2007. *The nuts & bolts of cooperative learning*. Edina, MN: Interaction Book Company.

Johnson, D.W., Johnson, R.T. and Holubec, E.J. 2008. *Cooperation in the classroom*. Edina, MN: Interaction Book Company.

Johnson, D.W., Johnson, R.T., Roseth, C. and Shin, T.S. 2014. The relationship between motivation and achievement in interdependent situations. Goal structures, motivation, and achievement. *Journal of Applied Social Psychology*, 44(9):622-633. https://doi.org/10.1111/jasp.12280

Johnson, D.W., Johnson, R.T. and Stanne, N.W. 2000. *Cooperative learning methods: A meta-analysis*. https://bit.ly/3EDGWR4

Katira, N., Williams, L., Wiebe, E., Miller, C., Balik, S. and Gehringer, E. 2004. On understanding compatibility of student pair programmers. Technical symposium on Computer Science education. (In *Proceedings of the 35th SIGCSE Technical Symposium on Computer Science Education*, 3-7 March, Norfolk, Virginia, USA. NY: ACM, pp. 7-11.) https://doi.org/10.1145/971300.971307

Kishore, K. 2012. *Cooperative learning*. India: APH Publishing Corporation.

Kristiansen, S.D., Burner, T. and Johnsen, B.H. 2019. Face-to-face promotive interaction leading to successful cooperative learning: A review study. *Cogent Education*, 6. https://doi.org/10.1080/2331186X.2019.1674067

Laal, M., Geranpaye, L. and Daemi, M. 2013. Individual accountability in collaborative learning. *Procedia: Social and Behavioral Sciences*, 93:286-289. https://doi.org/10.1016/j.sbspro.2013.09.191

McDowell, C., Hanks, B. and Werner, L. 2003. Experimenting with pair programming in the classroom. (In *Proceedings of the 8th Annual Conference on Innovation and Technology in Computer Science Education*, 30 June–2 July, Thessaloniki, Greece. NY: ACM, pp. 60-64.) https://doi.org/10.1145/961511.961531

McDowell, C., Werner, L., Bullock, H. and Fernald, J. 2003. The impact of pair programming on student performance, perception and persistence. (In *Proceedings of the 25th International conference on Software Engineering*. 3-10 May, The Hilton Portland Hotel, Portland, Oregon. NY: ACM, pp. 602-607.) https://doi.org/10.1109/ICSE.2003.1201243

McKinney, D. and Denton, L.F. 2005. Affective assessment of team skills in agile CS1 labs: The good, the bad, and the ugly. (In *Proceedings of the 36th SIGCSE Technical Symposium on Computer Science Education*, 22-27 February, St. Louis, Missouri, USA. NY: ACM, pp. 465-469.) https://doi.org/10.1145/1047124.1047494

McWhaw, K., Schackenber, H., Sclater, J. and Abrami, P.C. 2003. From co-operation to collaboration: Helping students become collaborative learners. (In R.M. Gilles and A.F. Ashman, eds. *Co-operative Learning: The social and intellectual outcomes of learning in groups*. London: Routledge Falmer, pp. 69-84.)

Meijer, H., Hoekstra, R., Brouwer, J. and Strijbos, J. 2020. Unfolding collaborative learning assessment literacy: a reflection on current assessment methods in higher education. *Assessment & evaluation in higher education*, 45(8):1222-1240. https://doi.org/10.1080/02602938.2020.1729696

Mentz, E. 2011. 'n Sosiaalkonstruktiwistiese benadering tot die aanleer van programmeringsvaardighede: Implikasiesvir die praktyk. Intreerede nr. 241, Noordwes-Universiteit, Potchefstroom.

Mentz, E. and Goosen, L. 2007. Are groups working in the Information Technology class? *South African Journal of Education*, 27(2):329-343.

Mentz, E., Van der Walt, J. and Goosen, L. 2008. The effect of incorporating cooperative learning principles in pair programming for student teachers. *Computer Science Education*, 18(4):247-260. https://doi.org/10.1080/089 93400802461396

Mentz, E. and Van Zyl, S. 2016. Introducing cooperative learning: students' attitudes towards learning and the implications for self-directed learning. *Journal of Education*, 64:79-109. https://doi.org/10.17159/i64a04

Millis, B.J. and Cottell P.J. Jr. 1998. *Cooperative learning for higher education faculty.* Phoenix, AZ: American Council on Education and The Oryx Press.

Nagappan, N., Williams, L., Ferzli, M., Wiebe, E., Yang, K., Miller, C. and Balik, S. 2003. Improving the CS1 experience with pair programming. (In *Proceedings of the 34th SIGSCE Technical Symposium on Computer Science Education*, 19-23 February, Reno, Nevada, USA. NY: ACM, pp. 359-362.) https://doi. org/10.1145/792548.612006

Nhan, H. and Nhan, T.A. 2019. Different grouping strategies for cooperative learning in English majored seniors and juniors at Can Tho University, Vietnam. *Education Sciences*, 9(1):59. https://doi.org/10.3390/educsci9010059

Nipp, M.B. and Palenque, S.M. 2017. Strategies for successful group work. *Journal of Instructional Research*, 6:42-45. https://doi.org/10.9743/JIR.2017.7

Nuutila, E., Törmä, S. and Malmi, L. 2005. PBL and computer programming: The seven steps method with adaptations. *Computer Science Education*, 15(2):123-142. https://doi.org/10.1080/08993400500150788

Panitz, T. 1997. Collaborative versus cooperative learning: Comparing the two definitions helps understand the nature of interactive learning. *Cooperative Learning and College Teaching*, 8(2).

Panitz, T. 2000. Using cooperative learning 100% of the time in mathematics classes establishes a student-centred interactive learning environment. https://bit.ly/38elp5m

Patesan, M., Balagiu, A. and Zechia, D. 2016. The benefits of cooperative learning. *International Conference Knowledge-based Organization*, 22(2). https://doi.org/ 10.1515/kbo-2016-0082

Pollock, L. and Jochen, M. 2001. Making parallel programming accessible to inexperienced programmers through cooperative learning. (In *Proceedings of the 32nd SIGCSE Technical Symposium on Computer Science Education*, 21-25 February, Charlotte, NC, USA. NY: ACM, pp. 224-228.) https://doi.org/10.1145/366413.364589

Raveh, O. and Meir, R. 2020. PAC guarantees for cooperative multi-agent reinforcement learning with restricted communication. (In *Proceedings of the 31st International Conference on Algorithmic Learning Theory on Machine Learning Research*, 99:1-42.)

Samary, M.M. and Ochoa, S.F. 2014. Improving teamwork in students software projects. (In *Proceedings of the IEEE 27th Conference on Software Engineering Education and Training (CSEE&T)*, pp. 99-108.) https://doi.org/10.1109/ CSEET.2014.6816787

Sedano, T., Ralph, P. and Peraire, C. 2016. Practice and perception of team code ownership. (In *Proceedings of the 20th International Conference on Evaluation and Assessment in Software Engineering*, Article 36, pp. 1-6.) https://doi.org/10.1145/2915970.2916002

Smarkusky, D., Dempsey, R., Ludka, J. and De Quillettes, R. 2005. Enhancing team knowledge: Instruction vs. experience. (In *Proceedings of the 36th SIGCSE Technical Symposium on Computer Science Education*, 22-27 February, St. Louis, Missouri, USA. NY: ACM, pp. 460-464.) https://doi.org/10.1145/1047124.1047493

Smite, D., Mikalsen, M., Moe, N.B., Stray, V. and Klotins, E. 2021. From collaboration to solitude and back: Remote pair programming during COVID-19. (In P. Gregory, C. Lassenius, X. Wang and P. Kruchten, eds. *Agile processes in software engineering and extreme programming.* Springer.) https://doi.org/10.1007/978-3-030-78098-2_1

Sudweeks, F. 2003. Promoting cooperation and collaboration in a web-based learning environment. (In *Proceedings of the Informing Science and Information Technology Education Joint Conference*, 24-27 June, Pori, Finland. USA: The Informing Science Institute, pp. 1439-1446.) https://doi.org/10.28945/2723

Tadesse, T., Gillies, R.M. and Manathunga, C. 2020. Shifting the instructional paradigm in higher education classrooms in Ethiopia: What happens when we use cooperative learning pedagogies more seriously? *International Journal of Educational Research*, 99 (Article 101509). https://doi.org/10.1016/j.ijer.20 19.101509

Terwel, J. 2003. Co-operative learning in secondary education: A curriculum perspective. (In R.M. Gillies and A.F. Ashman, eds. *Co-operative learning: the social and intellectual outcomes of learning in groups.* London: Routledge Falmer, pp. 54-68.)

Tran, V.D. 2013. Theoretical perspectives underlying the application of cooperative learning in classrooms. *International Journal of Higher Education*, 2(4):111-115. https://doi.org/10.5430/ijhe.v2n4p101

Tsan, J., Vandenberg, J., Zakaria, Z., Wiggins, J.B., Webber, A.R., Bradbury, A., Lynch, C., Wiebe, E. and Boyer, K.E. 2020. A comparison of two pair programming configurations for upper elementary students. (In *Proceedings of the 51st ACM Technical symposium on Computer Science Education*, pp. 346-352.) https://doi.org/10.1145/3328778.3366941

Tsompanoudi, D., Satratzemi, M. and Xinogalos, S. 2015. Distributed pair programming using collaboration scripts: an educational system and initial results. *Informatics in Education*, 14(2):291-314. https://doi.org/10.15388/infedu.2015.17

Van Niekerk, W.M.K. 2018. Cooperative pair problem solving: a teaching-learning strategy for tutorials in mechanical engineering thermodynamics. Ph.D. thesis, North-West University, Potchefstroom.

Veenman, S., VanBenthum, N., Bootsma, D., VanDieren, J. and Van der Kemp, N. 2002. Cooperative learning and teacher education. *Teaching and Teacher Education*, 18:87-103. https://doi.org/10.1016/S0742-051X(01)00052-X

Venkatesan, V. and Annamalai, S. 2010. Adoption of pair programming in the academic environment with different degree of complexity in students perspective: an empirical study. *International Journal of Engineering Science and Technology*, 2(9):4791-4800.

Werner, L.L., Denner, J. and Bean, S. 2004. Pair programming strategies for Middle School girls. (In *Proceedings of the 7th IASTED International Conference Computer and Advance Technology in Education*, 16-18 August, Kauai, Hawaii. USA: ACTA Press, pp. 161-166.)

Williams, L.A. and Kessler, R.R. 2000. The effects of "pair-pressure" and "pair-learning" on software engineering education. (In *Proceedings of the 13th Conference on Software Engineering Education & Training*, 6-8 March, Austin, Texas. USA: IEEE Computer Society Press, pp. 59-65.)

Williams, L. and Kessler, R. 2003. *Pair programming illustrated*. Boston, Massachusetts: Addison Wesley.

Williams, L. and Upchurch, R. 2001. In support of student pair programming. (In *Proceedings of the 32nd SIGCSE Technical Symposium on Computer Science Education*, 21-25 February, Charlotte, NC, USA. NY: ACM, pp. 327-331.) https://doi.org/10.1145/366413.364614

Whatley, J., Bell, F., Shaylor, J., Zaitseva, E. and Zakrzewska, D. 2005. AB-Collaboration across borders: Peer evaluation for collaborative learning. (In *Proceedings of the Informing Science and Information Technology Education Joint Conference*, 16-19 June, Flagstaff, USA: The Informing Science Institute, pp. 33-48.)

Yerion, K.A. and Rinehart, J.A. 1995. Guidelines for collaborative learning in Computer Science. *SIGCSE Bulletin*, 27(4):29-34. https://doi.org/10.1145/216511.216529

# CHAPTER 7

# Teaching and learning programming

Marietjie Havenga

# OBJECTIVES

**After completing this chapter, you should be able to:**

➲ *discuss and apply various knowledge, skills and strategies to scaffold the learning of programming; and*

➲ *explain programming skills to learners and enable them to understand and implement these concepts successfully when planning and writing their own programs.*

## 7.1    INTRODUCTION

The learning of computer programming is difficult and therefore teachers are required to support learners. This implies that the teacher needs to use various skills, strategies and activities to scaffold the learning of programming. The purpose of this chapter is to provide guidelines in teaching computer programming.

## 7.2    WAYS TO SUPPORT THE LEARNER IN PLANNING AND TESTING PROGRAMMING SOLUTIONS

Many learners are very excited to begin working on the computer, and want to develop programs by starting to code immediately. However, it is important that they should plan a program and ensure the logic is correct before starting to code. Algorithms and trace tables are used to direct programming logic and evaluate the correctness thereof.

### Algorithms

An algorithm is a set of rules for solving a problem in a finite number of steps. The writing of algorithms should be done *before* learners begin with the programming on computers. Teachers may even require learners to show them their correct algorithm before starting to implement this in a high-level programming language. The value of algorithms is to ensure that learners plan in detail and reflect on their efforts, especially Grade 10 learners with no previous experience of problem-solving activities!

### Trace tables

A trace table is used to *test* an algorithm. The trace table represents variable(s) in various columns to indicate a change in such variables as a result of the assignment of values or calculations, for example. The value of using a trace table is to oblige learners to check the logic of their planning and algorithms to ensure the successful execution of their programs.

## ACTIVITY 7.1

**Design an assignment for Grade 10 learners where they are required to write an algorithm and design a trace table before starting to code the program. Provide a memorandum regarding how you will assess the assignment.**

## 7.3    HOW TO TEACH NEW PROGRAMMING CONCEPTS

Learners' understanding of programming concepts can be supported by using various teaching strategies. These strategies depend on the specific concept learners need to understand, as well as the background of the learners, and the preferences of the individual teacher. In the following section, some guidelines for the teacher in this regard will be discussed.

## 7.3.1 Link with real-life experiences

Learners will understand difficult programming concepts better if it can be linked to known real-life experiences. Teachers should be creative and think about ways in which a programming concept can be linked to the knowledge of the learner from their everyday life. This subsection will offer some examples that can be used for the teaching of certain concepts. The ultimate aim is that IT teachers build themselves a database of examples from the life experiences of their learners which can clarify difficult programming concepts. Teachers should also take into account the cultural differences of their learners. In an IT class in a deep rural area, learners will have a different frame of reference, and examples used in an upper class urban school will most probably not be suitable. A few examples from the real-life experiences of learners will be discussed.

### A)  Conceptual understanding of variables

To enable a learner to understand the concept "variable", the learner is required to open the "Contacts" on his/her cell phone. When opening a specific person's name, e.g. Peter, his cell phone number is displayed. You can also overwrite a number when it has been changed (overwrite the value of the variable) (see Figure 7.1).

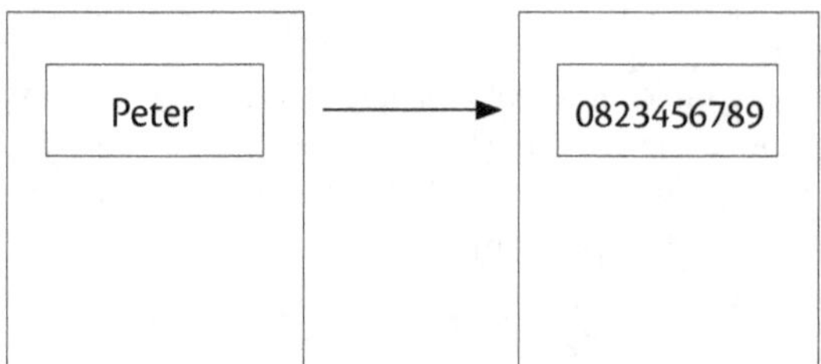


*Figure 7.1     Conceptual understanding of variables*

### B)  Understanding the assignment of values

With reference to problem-solving in Chapter 5, one important aspect is the representation of the problem. The following is an example to represent the understanding of how to increment a value. For example: In this program segment you want to determine the amount of money collected:

$$\textbf{rTotalAmound = rTotalAmount + rAmount}$$

To explain why a specific variable must be incremented refers in your explanation to a cash box (Figure 7.2). You use a cash box as a temporary store for the tuck shop's money. Initially there is no money in the cash box, however, after each day's purchases you add that day's amount to the previous amount. You may do banking at the end of each week. The total amount for one week is determined on Fridays.

*Figure 7.2      Example of a cash box*

## C)   Representation of *local* and *non-local* variables

When declaring variables, learners must decide on its scope. The scope of a variable is determined by the inclusion of so-called block structures (**begin ... end** in Delphi) and the position in a program where it is declared. Local variables are declared within a block structure and have only visibility in the block where it is declared. To enable learners to understand the difference between local and non-local variables a real-life example can be used. In the classroom the teacher has his/her own stationery and it is only used by the specific teacher. This stationery can be seen as belonging only to one teacher in one class (local). A copy machine in the secretary's office is shared by all teachers in the school (non-local). Non-local variables of a unit or program are visible within that section and all methods declared in this program/unit have access to these variables.

## D)   Conceptual understanding of arrays

The use of arrays is difficult for learners to grasp, therefore teachers need to use examples to explain it. Discuss the tables in your class as a real-life example to explain arrays (or matrices). This can be represented as in Figure 7.3.

There are five rows in your class and each row has eight learners:

| Number of learner in each row | | | | | | | |
|---|---|---|---|---|---|---|---|
| **1** | 1 | 2 | 3 | 4 | 5 | 6 | 7 | 8 |
| **2** | | | | | | | | |
| **3** | | | | | | | | |
| **4** | | | | X | | | | |
| **5** | | | | | | | | |

(Row label: **Rows**)

*Figure 7.3      Conceptual understanding of arrays*

Each learner is required to determine his or her position in the class. Upon the teacher's question, he or she needs to mention his or her position in class. For example, the learner's position marked with an "x" above is in Row 4, Table 5, or Position[4,5].

The diagram above can be linked to two-dimensional arrays or matrices as follows (remember that the presentation of a matrix may also start in Row 0, however, it enhances conceptual understanding when referring to "Row 1" as the first row) (Figure 7.4).

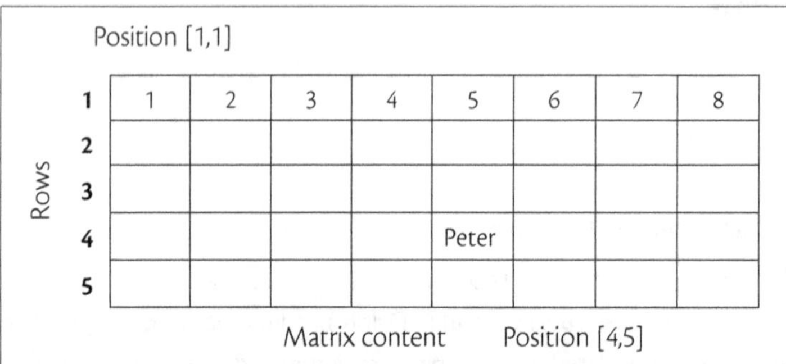


Figure 7.4     *Position of the name 'Peter' in a matrix*

The name 'Peter' is shown in row 4, column 5.

### E)   Conceptual understanding of classes and objects

As the object-oriented programming approach is currently used, learners need to understand the basics thereof and understand *why* classes and objects are required. A class and an object can be explained in terms of the building of houses (Figure 7.5). A class is similar to the *architectural design, template* or *pattern* of a new house. This is an abstract representation of the real world – it is only a **two-dimensional picture**.

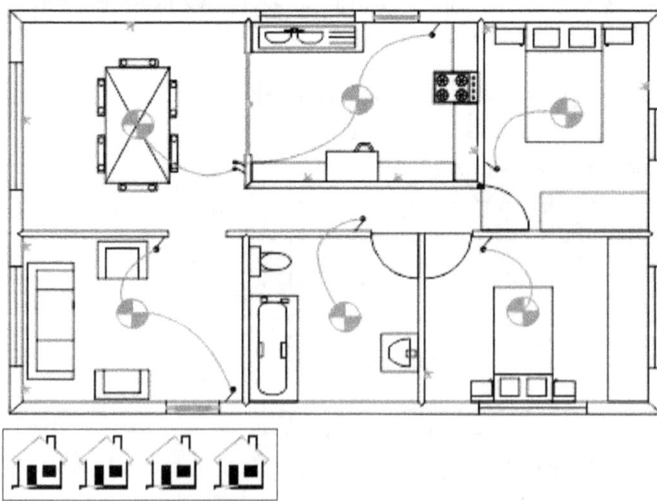

Figure 7.5     *Representation of classes and objects*

An object is an *instantiation* of a class. In this example, **houses are objects (three-dimensional 'instances')** which are built *based* on the architectural design.

A house has properties and methods. The type, colour and size of a house indicate its properties.

### F)   Use the World Wide Web

Various examples of how to teach basic computer concepts can be found on the internet. The *Computer Science Unplugged* website is one example of such a website where examples of how to teach computer programming are included. These websites can provide teachers with valuable ideas and support in order to explain difficult programming concepts to learners. Also watch Mr Long's YouTube videos on Delphi programming.

## 7.3.2  Visual representations

The teacher may use various visual representations to explain concepts/principles to learners. Some examples are included:

### A)   Visual representation of the *if* statement

Teachers may use one-way, two-way and/or multiple selectors to indicate the use of *if/if…then* statements.

---

**Example of a one-way selection**

Assume in this example there is only **one** way forward on a narrow path high in the mountains. The vehicle therefore moves forward. The algorithm for this selection is: ***if… then …***

**Example of a two-way selection**

The driver can select to drive in any **one** of the two directions. Note that it is not possible to drive in both directions at the same time. The algorithm for this selection is: ***if… then … else***

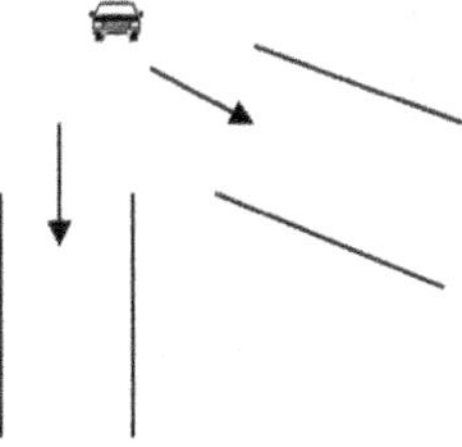

---

Figure 7.6     *Visual representation of the 'if' statement*

**Example of a multiple selector construct**

A multiple selector construct is used when a statement can have a number of possible execution paths (more than two available paths). The driver may select to drive in any **one** of the many directions, depending on the selector statement. This can be used to explain the *case* (Delphi):

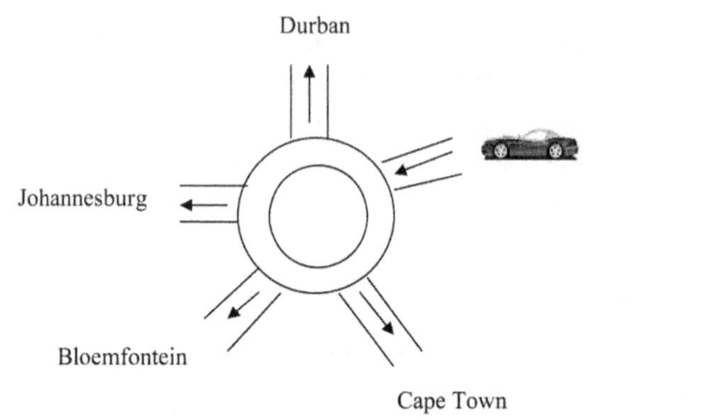


Figure 7.7    *Visual representation of a multiple selector construct*

## B)   Visual explanation of the swapping of data

The teacher may use *Excel* to explain the principle of the swapping of data. The swapping of data is essential when elements are sorted in a list (array). In this example, column A should be alphabetically ordered, therefore Ann should be the first name:

|   | A | B |
|---|---|---|
| 1 |   | **Test1** |
| 2 |   | [25] |
| 3 | Peter | 12 |
| 4 | Ann | 21 |

When sorting the data manually by copying Ann from row 4 to row 3, the name Peter is overwritten:

|   | A | B |
|---|---|---|
| 1 |   | **Test1** |
| 2 |   | [25] |
| 3 | Ann | 21 |
| 4 | Ann | 21 |

To solve the problem do the following steps:

1.  *cut* the data of the first name, "Peter", in row 3 and *paste* it into another row, e.g. into row 7

2.  *cut* Ann's data in row 4 and *paste* it into row 3

3.  *cut* Peter's data in row 7 and *paste* it into row 4

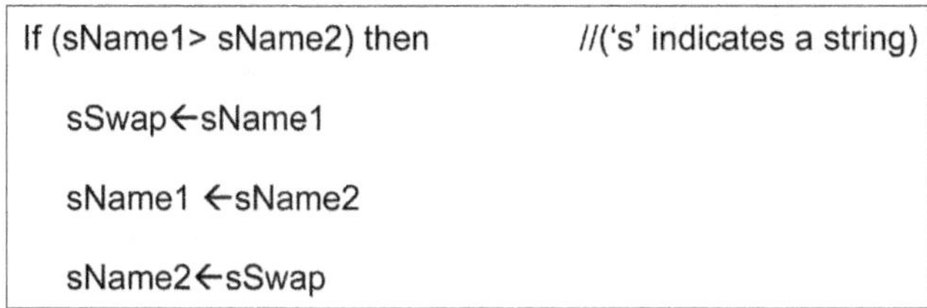

The same principle can now be applied in a program by using the following algorithm to swap two names:

```
If (sName1> sName2) then          //('s' indicates a string)

    sSwap←sName1

    sName1 ←sName2

    sName2←sSwap
```

You can also use the following diagram to explain the swapping of names:

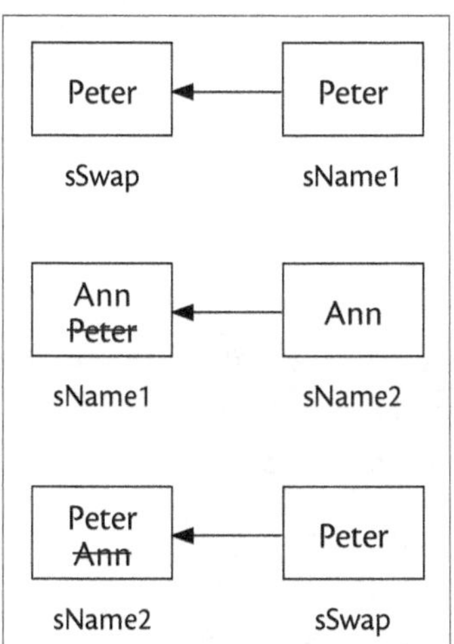


Figure 7.8    *Visual representations of the swapping of two names*

## C)  Visual representation of Boolean operators

Learners need to distinguish between various Boolean operators. These operators are used, for example, in combination with iteration and/or decision statements. The purpose thereof is to control the execution of e.g. *while* and *repeat* loops. Examples of Boolean operators are: ***And, Or, Not***. Both decisions should be **true** when using the ***And*** operator to execute the loop. In the case of the *Or* operator, only one decision should be **true** to execute the loop. Make use of the following diagram to explain the logic of these operators to learners:

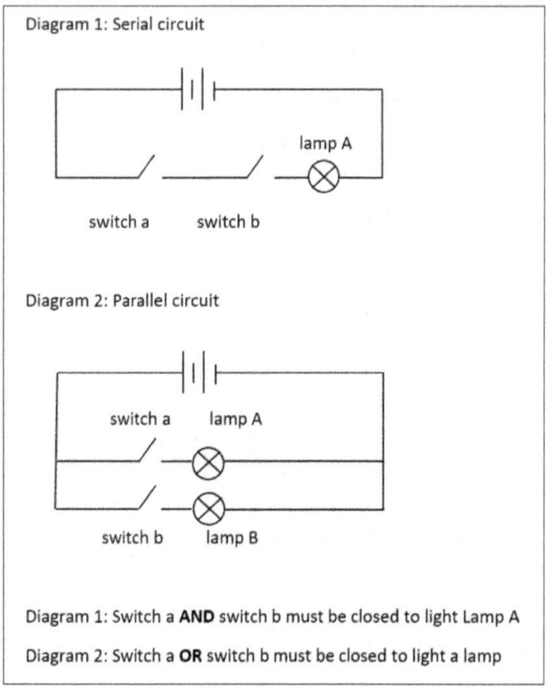


*Figure 7.9    Visual representation of the Boolean operators* And *and* Or

## D)  Visual explanation of methods

Learners may experience problems in understanding what methods are, why they are required, and how parameters are passed. A method is a program section or segment that performs specific operations one or more times. Some methods may require data in the form of parameters.

## *Parameters and parameter passing*

Learners need to distinguish between the following types of parameters:  formal and actual parameters. A teacher asks a learner to take an envelope with one document inside to another teacher. Upon receiving of the envelope, the second teacher changes the document and decide to either keep it or return it within the envelope ("return a value") to the first teacher. Each envelope only contains one document (note that the name of the "receiving" teacher is on the envelope.)

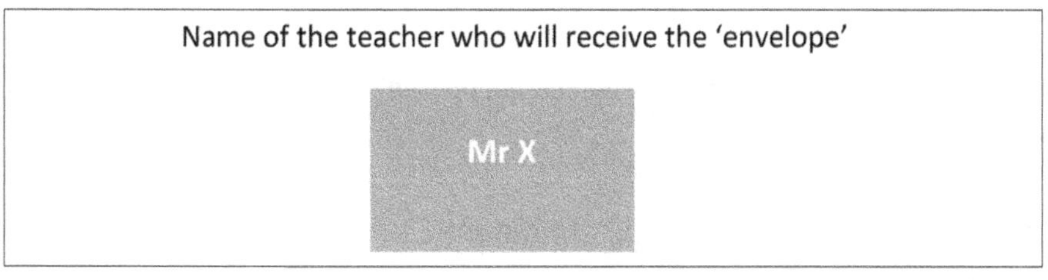



**Parameter passing**

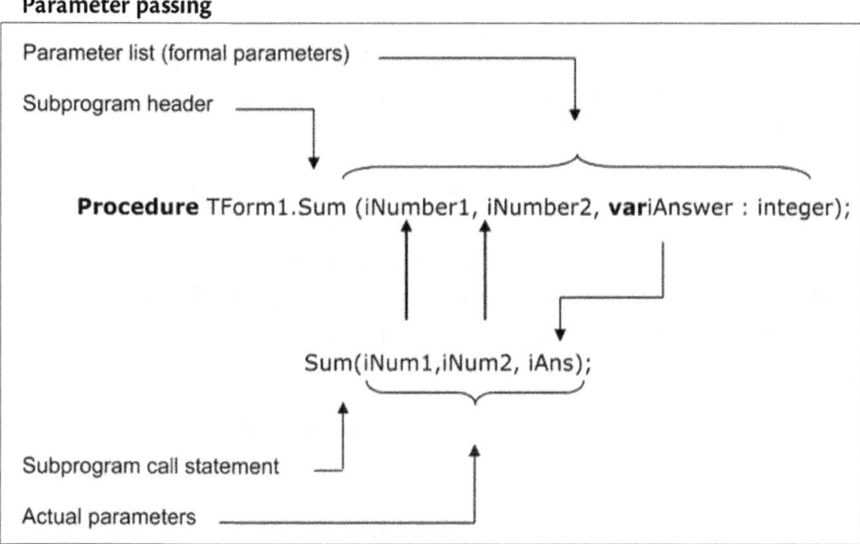



*Figure 7.10    Visual representation of the passing of parameters*

Remember to explain to learners that they should distinguish between two ways of using the "var". The "var" is used to (1) declare variables, and (2) to ensure that a parameter(s) is transferred back to the calling statement!

Emphasise that the actual and formal parameters should match regarding their (1) **order**, (2) **number** and (3) **type**.

## ACTIVITY 7.2

**Search on the internet for a YouTube video that, according to you, is a good example of explaining parameter passing. Study this video and motivate whether you will use it in your class.**

### 7.3.3  Role playing

Learners may use role playing to simulate how various sorting algorithms can be used, e.g. the use of bubble sort or selection sort.

### 7.3.4  Create a need to use a specific statement

When a new programming concept or statement is introduced to learners it can be useful not to explain it but rather ask the learners to solve a programming problem and let them discover that a specific programming statement is required that they do not have prior knowledge about. It creates the desire to explore and find new ways to solve a problem. An example where teachers can apply this strategy is the following:

Ask a learner to type seven marks for each of his/her subjects and determine the average of these subjects. This implies that a learner is required to repeat the following: display a message and insert a variable *seven* times. There needs to be a way to manage this repetition of statements. What is the implication when determining the average of each learner's seven marks for 200 learners? The purpose of this is to create a requirement to use specific statements to repeat some messages and/ or statements many times.

Sometimes there is a need to use flags (true or false values) in a program to stop a loop to continue execution. It can be explained as follows: When an athlete runs inside the track, a white flag is displayed and when the athlete crosses the track, a red flag is displayed. The red flag indicates that the athlete is disqualified and must stop running (Figure 7.11).

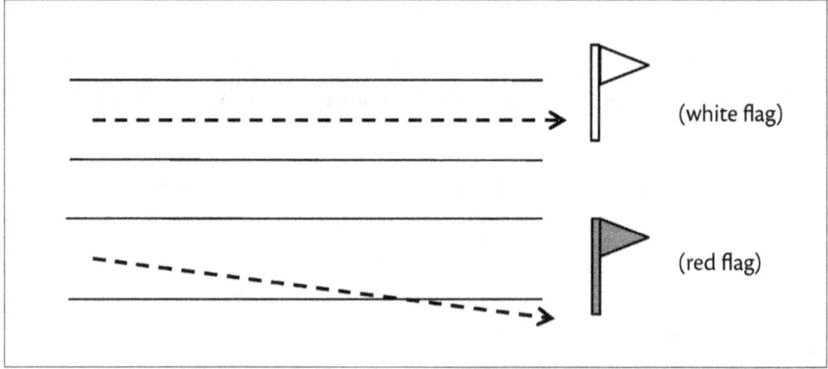


Figure 7.11    *Visual representation of the use of flags in logical-controlled iterative statements*

## ACTIVITY 7.3

**Discuss how you will explain to learners to distinguish between (a) counter-controlled iterative, and (b) logical-controlled iterative statements with reference to the use of flags (use your own examples).**

## 7.4 HOW TO FIND ERRORS AND SOLVE PROGRAMMING PROBLEMS

When learners are programming an assignment or test, most of their time is used to find errors and/ or to debug a program. The teacher needs to scaffold learners in this process.

### 7.4.1 Scaffolding the search for errors

When learners iteratively search for errors or they are unable to interpret error messages, it may result in a negative approach towards programming. The teacher may scaffold this process by showing on a program how to identify and interpret error messages. For example, when a learner does not include a semicolon after a programming statement, the cursor does not always show the exact position where the error occurs. The learner needs to deliberately check various programming statements where the semicolon is probably omitted.

### 7.4.2 Support the learners in identifying errors

The teacher is required to support learners in how to identify and correct programming errors themselves. This can be done by using various guidelines:

*Some guidelines:*

- ▶ Explain good programming techniques to learners such as:
  - the use of descriptive variables;
  - indentation;
  - program documentation;
  - the use of exception handling, e.g. *Try … except* statements; and
  - explain *readability* (well-structured, readable programs), *reliability* (reliable performance: type checking, exception handling).
- ▶ Learners need to plan the program, write an algorithm and test the algorithm with a trace table *before* starting with the programming. This will minimise logical errors.

- Give examples and discuss various types of errors with learners, e.g. (1) runtime errors, (2) syntax errors, and (3) logical errors.
- Discuss the integrated debugger and (depending on the IDE in use) refer to:
  - compilation;
  - insertion of breakpoints;
  - trace the program's output; and
  - use "watches" to evaluate variables in the memory of the computer.
- Select those error messages that are mostly shown on learners' computer screens. Discuss each error with the class and also ask learners to indicate how the problem should be solved.
- The use of pair programming may assist learners to support each other on how to interpret errors and solve problems.

## ACTIVITY 7.4

1. **Decribe to learners how you will explain the concept of an array and a flag.**
2. **Discuss the value of a trace table to test an algorithm before coding the program.**
3. **Describe how you will explain error detection and error correction to learners by referring to**
   (1) **type checking;**
   (2) **exception handling;**
   (3) **readability and reliability of programming performance; and**
   (4) **the different types of errors (runtime, syntax and logical errors).**

### 7.4.3  Role of evaluation and test data

Some additional techniques can be used to enhance program evaluation. The following techniques should be discussed in detail with all learners:

- the effective selection and use of test data for a specific program;
- give learners more than one solution for a programming problem; they are required to select the best solution, depending on specific criteria;
- ask learners to evaluate one another's program; they are required to give written feedback to their peers;
- guide students to develop a reflective approach towards the programming solution (see Chapter 5);

▸  ask learners to explain the reasoning that underlies the solving of a specific computer program; and

▸  teach a diagnostic approach to correct flaws and errors in programming.

## 7.5  TEACHING AND LEARNING OF ROBOTICS IN EDUCATION

Educational robotics focuses on the application of digital and physical robots to support learner cooperation and essential skill development for requirements of the Fourth-Industrial Revolution (4IR). The idea of robotics was initiated by Seymour Papert (Papert 1980). He developed the programming language LOGO to control the movement of a turtle on the computer. Since then, various environments for programming digital (online robotics platforms) and physical robots have been developed. Some examples of hardware used for programming robotics are Arduino, Micro:bit, Raspberry Pi, Lego Mindstorms EV3 and Lego Mindstorms Robot Inventor, while some software environments are Scratch, IDE-Arduino, Coder Z and TinkerCad (Figure 7.12).

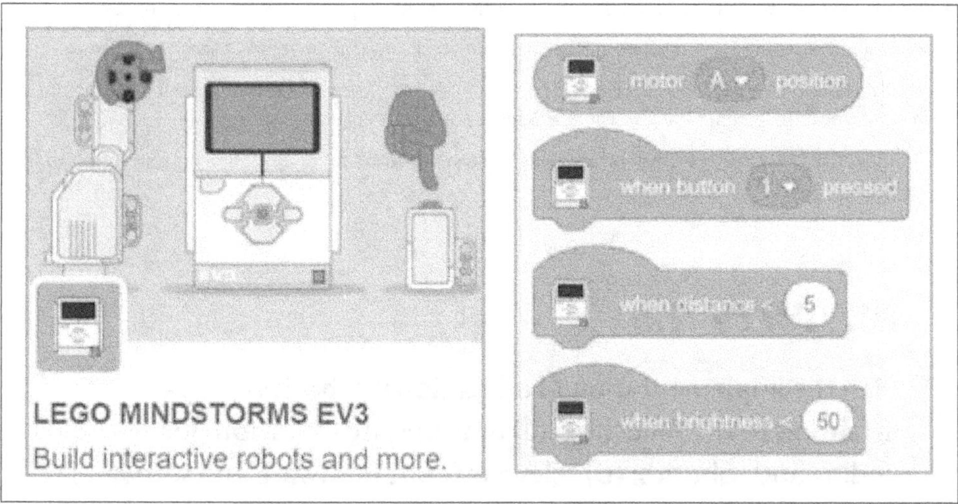


*Figure 7.12*    *Representation of Scratch LEGO Mindstorms environment*

Educational robotics (ER) can support active and responsible learning and develop essential knowledge and self-directed learning skills. Robotics provide a concrete environment to develop computational thinking (CT). CT is based on computer science and involves skills such as abstract thinking, breaking a problem down into simpler parts, algorithmic thinking and pattern recognition (Wing, 2006) (see Chapter 5). We therefore need to discuss how robotics can be incorporated in the teaching and learning of programming.

Robotics is primarily applied to address open-ended problems in groups. It is, therefore, important to incorporate the principles of cooperative learning and problem-based learning in educational robotics (Chapter 6). To plan activities involved in robotics, the following must be kept in mind (Ronsivalle *et al.* 2018):

- ▶ Understand the problem that has to be solved;
- ▶ Make a mental representation of robot movements;
- ▶ Categorise the problem (based on Bloom's taxonomy);
- ▶ Plan the robot programming and other associated activities;
- ▶ Continuously reflect on your thinking; and
- ▶ Evaluate the solution (program and robot movement).

Some practical suggestions to implement robotics in schools are the following:

- ▶ Determine whether a class is available to be used as a robotics laboratory or use the school's computer laboratory;
- ▶ Plan what robot activities must be done and first try it yourself;
- ▶ Gradually introduce the topic of robotics (Ronsivalle et al., 2018), by starting with simple tasks and escalate difficulty of problems;
- ▶ Learners should work in small groups. Apply the principles of cooperative learning (see Chapter 6);
- ▶ Keep good programming principles and the purpose of educational robotics in mind;
- ▶ Apply problem-based steps where learners have to brainstorm, formulate their own learning goals, do research, plan the programming activities and reflect on their thinking;
- ▶ If funds are limited to buy expensive hardware, you can use digital robot environments that are available online for free.

## ACTIVITY 7.5

**Plan the implementation of educational robotics and pay attention to the following: (a) appropriate classroom for coding and robotics; (b) relevant robot hardware and software; (c) computational thinking; and (d) a complete lesson plan (Chapter 2) on robotics for learners in your class and include active teaching-learning strategies.**

## 7.6    CONCLUSION

The teaching of computer programming should not only focus on programming content but also on the effective teaching thereof. The purpose of this chapter was to explain various ways how to teach programming concepts and skills to learners and enable them to understand and implement these successfully in their programs. In addition, some aspects related to educational robotics were outlined.

## REFERENCES


Papert, S. 1980. *Mindstorms, Children, Computers, and Powerful Ideas*. New York: Basic Books.

Ronsivalle, G.B., Boldi, A., Gusella, V., Inama, C. and Carta, S. 2018. How to Implement Educational Robotics' Programs in Italian Schools: A Brief Guideline According to an Instructional Design Point of View. *Technology, Knowledge and Learning*, 24:227-245. https://doi.org/10.1007/s10758-018-9389-5

Wing, J.M. 2006. Computational thinking. *Communications of the ACM*, 49(3):33-35. https://doi.org/10.1145/1118178.1118215

# CHAPTER 8

# Teaching and learning theoretical content

**Leila Goosen**

# OBJECTIVES

**After completing this chapter, you should be able to:**

- discuss the role of learners' contexts in planning to teach IT and/or CAT theoretical content;

- discuss the use of direct instruction in the context of teaching and learning theoretical content;

- using your own practical examples, explain how problem-based learning could be applied in the teaching and learning of theoretical content;

- use your own practical examples to explain how theoretical content could be learned cooperatively, including references to numbered groups, TGT, STAD, Jigsaw II and/or group investigation; and

- give your opinion on some of the pitfalls in teaching theoretical content.

## 8.1    INTRODUCTION

The subjects Computer Applications Technology (CAT) and Information Technology (IT) are embedded in an ever-expanding field that is characterised by a combination of theory, practice, knowledge and skills (Goosen 2004). Within such a context, pedagogical innovation is necessary for continued success. Because of this, pedagogical approaches are in considerable flux as teachers and researchers in the field define and assess current teaching practices and introduce alternative approaches to instruction. In this field context, the teaching and learning of the theoretical content components of IT and CAT requires teachers to once more think creatively and innovatively regarding strategies and methods that enhance meaningful learning.

In teaching, it is not only important what the learner knows, but also how this knowledge is assembled and represented. For learners to really gain from learning, knowledge should be constructed actively and not merely be received in a passive way. It needs to be emphasised that classroom instruction is effective only to the extent that it purposefully makes possible and facilitates relevant and meaningful learning with comprehension.

This chapter should equip you with the necessary knowledge, skills and attitudes to teach theoretical content in ways that enable learners to acquire what they need to apply in IT and/or CAT classrooms. This will be accomplished by presenting examples of teaching strategies and methods that can be used for teaching the theory components of IT and CAT. The use of direct instruction, problem-based learning, as well as various cooperative options for the effective teaching of the theory components of these subjects are discussed and illustrated with practical examples.

## 8.2    THE THEORY COMPONENTS IN IT AND CAT CURRICULA

When looking at the topics to be covered in the IT and CAT curricula, it is clear that around 60 percent of the weighting in terms of content volume in each subject is allocated to Solution Development. The remaining 40 percent represents topics which all have theoretical content aspects – Systems, Network/Communication and Internet Technologies, (Data and) Information Management and Social Implications. This chapter will guide you in understanding how to present the theoretical content in the CAT and IT curricula effectively. Generally speaking, it could too easily be said that learners simply need to memorise this information and that teachers should not spend much time on theoretical work in class. Although time constraints and the level of difficulty of the content related to Solution Development often require that teachers spend more time on this topic, this is no excuse for teachers to not pay attention to theoretical content. If learners listen to teachers' direct instruction on theoretical work, or have to study theoretical work on their own without becoming engaged in the learning process, it is unlikely that this knowledge will be interesting and valuable to learners. Therefore, it is necessary for teachers to understand what makes the learning of a specific topic easy or difficult and to adapt teaching strategies accordingly.

## 8.3  CONSIDERING LEARNERS WHEN PLANNING TO TEACH IT AND CAT THEORETICAL CONTENT

The teaching and learning of the content of IT and/or CAT depends on multiple factors, such as the social contexts of the schools and learners, the amount and quality of your experience, your professional knowledge on curriculum and instruction, and your own personal theories about effective teaching and learning practices for these subjects. As a teacher, you need to establish the appropriateness of specific content for your learners, "rate the suitability of new materials in terms of what" your learners could possibly do, and go with what you think is ideal and what your learners need (Goosen 2004:97). In this way, you provide an important reality check of what is thought to be suitable in terms of the curriculum and what you believe is appropriate in terms of your day-to-day interaction with learners. As a teacher, you need to make sure that the related specific aims are met, as required in policy statements for IT and CAT respectively. You also need to pay attention to how the learning programme is organised and the level of and extent to which ideas and topics are presented in various grades.

A perspective that stresses the importance of the relatedness of knowledge must be adopted. Acknowledgement must be given to the fact that learners (especially in IT and CAT classes) bring certain skills, knowledge and ideas with them to the class and that this background will determine how they come to understand new knowledge. The assumption here is that knowledge is more accessible, and thus is more likely to be transferred to new situations, when it is a central and integral part of a learner's cognitive structure.

The learning of IT and CAT definitely happens within the context of the computer knowledge that the learner acquires in his immediate environment outside school – at home, in the internet café, etc. Through an active learning process, where there is interaction between learners and new knowledge, learners receive the opportunity to give meaning to new knowledge, to connect it with their existing knowledge and to test their understanding thereof against other meanings, while they are exposed to a variety of views.

Thus, as mentioned in Chapter 2, any lesson must begin with an evaluation of what the learners already know and understand, and from there on one can continue to build a specific lesson series aimed at achieving the desired effects.

From the first opportunity in Grade 10 where you as teacher and the learners come together, you can start setting up a profile of each learner in terms of general computer knowledge and skills, as well as specific areas in which learners already possess certain knowledge and skills. This will enable you to understand how to deal with learners' thinking, learners' multiple approaches to problems, and the misconceptions that learners might have as they face different ideas (Goosen 2004).

Learners might gain from listing the factors that prevent them from doing well or improving their achievement, in IT and/or CAT, and then making suggestions about what they can do about these problems themselves. Great improvement in attitude, attendance, completion of assignments, and willingness to participate in class could be gained if the lesson is carefully planned to adhere to learners' needs and interest.

Planning of a theoretical lesson is of great importance to ensure that learners all take part in the learning experience and become actively involved in the learning process. It is important that the planning includes the specific teaching strategies that are applicable for the lesson objectives that the learners need to achieve. The teacher also needs to ensure that learners have applicable and sufficient resources to enable them to complete the tasks and achieve these aims.

## 8.4 TEACHING STRATEGIES AND METHODS FOR LEARNING THEORETICAL CONTENT

A selection of different teaching strategies and methods for learning theoretical content in IT and CAT are mentioned by researchers such as Ghaith (2004), Liu *et al.* (2005) and Van Wyk (2011). According to Sharan (2010:303), some of these "emphasise mastery of knowledge and motivation" within a cooperative learning environment, such as Jigsaw (II) and Student Teams Achievement Division (STAD), or Group Investigation and Teams-Games-Tournaments (TGT). The purpose of this chapter is not to discuss all possible strategies for the teaching of all possible theoretical content in IT and CAT, but rather to offer some examples to stimulate your own creativity in designing effective learning experiences for learners.

### 8.4.1 Using direct instruction when teaching and learning theoretical content

When learners work on their own in non-directive, hands-on teaching programmes, it can happen that they are not successful in the discovery of all the required knowledge and skills. It may be necessary for the teacher to provide structure and mediated guidance. Structuring learning content ensures that the learner receives the basic information in a useful order, while the mediation of the teacher ensures that the learner connects the presented information with relevant existing knowledge. An exploration phase ought to be included before the phase of verbalisation and concept formation, and the material to be learned needs to be connected to, and contribute to, the integral thought processes of the learner.

The teacher should provide learners with instructional support, especially when they are learning difficult tasks. Such support or scaffolds could include providing learners with "prompts for steps they might use" (Rosenshine 2010:22). The provision of scaffolding is considered to be a form of guided practice, which should include sequencing the learning material in such a way as to minimise possible confusion of leaners. Only small sections of new learning material should be selected together with structured experiential learning that provide learners with opportunities to exercise and reinforce recently acquired skills and knowledge. In order for learners to sufficiently practise their newly acquired skills to an acceptable level of mastery, they should be provided with substantial amounts of time to explore and apply the ideas and principles they learn in class (Goosen 2004).

As mentioned in Chapter 2, it is recommended that direct instruction as a teaching strategy is avoided as far as possible, since direct instruction is a teacher-centred strategy that, in itself, requires no or very little activity and involvement of the learners.

## 8.4.2 Using problem-based learning for teaching theoretical content

One approach to the teaching and learning of the theoretical content of IT and CAT is that of problem-based learning. According to the 'father of problem-solving' (Polya 1981), learners need to find pleasure in the learning activity, be interested in the learning material, and therefore it is necessary that they discover as much as possible of the learning content themselves. Klahr and Nigam (2004:661) refer to the premise that learners who are empowered to discover a general concept on their own, even if careful hints from the teacher may be needed, "are more likely to apply and extend that knowledge" than learners who only receive direct instruction.

Saputra, Joyoatmojo, Wardani and Sangka (2019) examined the effectiveness of problem-based learning (PBL) when used together with the Jigsaw model (see section 8.4.3.4) in developing students' critical thinking skills.

To use problem-based learning effectively, more should be done than just presenting learners with problems. The aim of the problem-solving should be explicitly stated, and learners should also receive proper instruction in the strategies that can be used to solve problems (Goosen 2004). This necessitates teachers developing learner-friendly, reliable working methods that can be used in the classroom. The role of the teacher will be to facilitate the learning of learners who are actively involved in their own learning.

The problem(s) used in a problem-based approach should be as meaningful and relevant as possible from the learner's perspective, but should also display certain characteristics. Problems suitable for problem-based learning are aimed at attaining relevant specific outcomes that:

- relate to the real world;
- motivate learners to solve the problem;
- require decision-making or judgements;
- are multi-page and multi-stage;
- are normally designed for group-solving;
- pose open-ended initial questions that encourage discussion; and
- incorporate higher order thinking.

In problem-based learning, it is critical to clearly indicate to learners how they will be assessed (Belland, French and Ertmer 2009). One of the well-acknowledged issues that learners report in problem-based learning is that they are unsure of how much they need to know, how far to explore their problems, and when they can reasonably stop learning (Goosen 2004). This difficulty can be addressed by using a carefully crafted set of assessment requirements. It is especially important with theoretical content that learners should grasp that the teacher continually assesses the learners' understanding throughout the lesson. In general, planning should specifically include the desired lesson objectives, as well as the procedures used to determine to what extent these have been reached. At the end of a unit, for closure and consolidation of the topic, a typical test can be given to the learners to be discussed amongst themselves in order to work out the best solutions.

Although problem-based learning is generally exercised in groups solving complex problems, as discussed in section 8.4.3, it can in certain circumstances be expected of a learner to individually solve a problem, especially where rather basic problem statements are used as a starting point in this approach.

Once learners are at ease with the approach of solving problems, the notion of sequence problems can be introduced. The process used to explore sequence problems starts with a relatively long stage in which the learner gradually specifies and comes to know the specifics of independent situations. As the confidence of the learner increases with each situation, a feeling of underlying sameness develops between the different situations. Gradually the learner becomes able to articulate this sameness, and (s)he starts to understand the concepts grounding it. Lastly, there is a phase were the generalisation is tested and verified. The role of the teacher during the solving of sequence problems is to support the learners to become aware of the underlying sameness between the situations and to eventually support them to articulate it.

The following are two examples of problems that can be adapted according to the level of difficulty intended for a specific group of learners.

### 8.4.2.1  Example 1

Design a diagram for the QUICKMESSAGE franchise for a local area network between two buildings not more than 120 m apart. The following requirements should be addressed:

- three users and four users in the two buildings respectively;
- communication medium;
- connecting devices; and
- transmission methods and topology to be used in a building.

Motivate you decisions regarding the devices, topology and cabling that you suggest should be used. You must submit a report including at least your analysis of the problem, diagrams of the prototype and the network, and your reasons or motivation for the design you suggest.

A solution for the problem could include the following:

- analysis of the problem;
- two buildings linked with each other;
- one building has three users and the other four;

- types of cables – probably twisted pair (or wireless communication, depending on the budget);

- connecting devices, e.g. router;

- ethernet – 1000BaseT, low cost twisted pair copper cable (UTP) (or wireless equivalent); and

- bus topology / star topology.

## Design a prototype

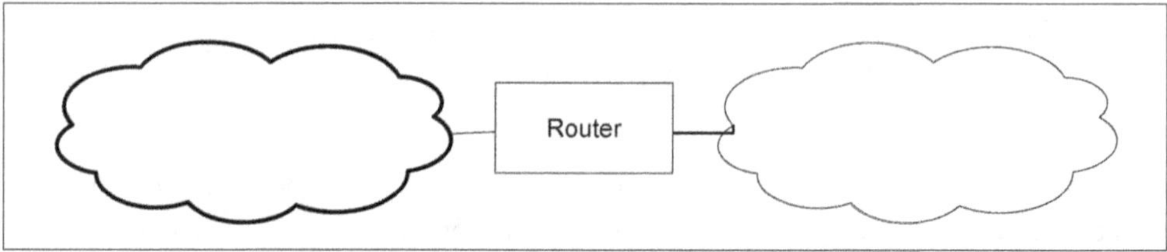



## Design of the network

Design the network and include the basic requirements:

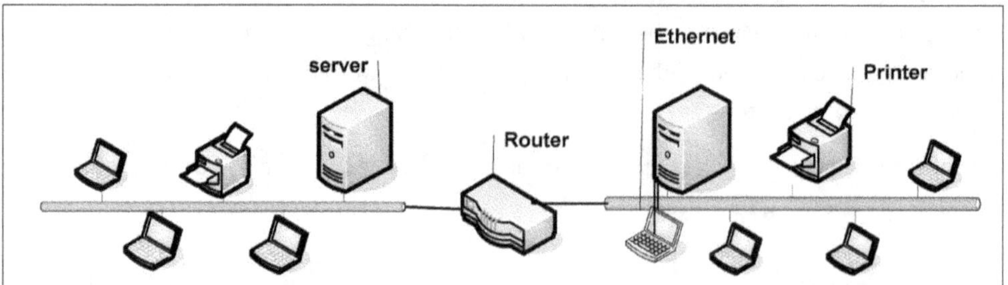



Reasons:

- motivation must be in accordance with design;

- router performs some of the functions such as filtering and forwarding and has built-in intelligence to direct packets to specific networks;

- according to the IEEE ethernet standards, twisted pair cables can be used; and

- a bus topology consists of cable from one PC to the next. A terminator is connected to each end.

### 8.4.2.2 Example 2

A computer virus is a program which intentionally makes copies of itself and may contain destructive code. Discuss viruses from an ethical perspective and refer to the following:

- types of viruses;

- your ethical perspective on viruses – also refer to virus-writing tutorials and hacker and cracker clubs on the internet;

- precautions; and

▷ provide the addresses of at least three websites that you obtained your information from.
   (Some requirements regarding the format of the report can also be given.)

A solution for the problem could include the following:

▷ Analysis of the problem
  – Discuss viruses from an ethical perspective and refer to type, precautions, virus-writing tutorials and hacker and cracker clubs.

▷ Types of viruses
  – Boot sector virus, executable virus, polymorphic virus and a macro-virus (a Trojan horse is not a virus but only a carrier of a virus). Elaborate on each type of virus.

▷ Your ethical perspective on viruses
  – (Complete on your own)

▷ Discussion of precautions such as:
  – always scan all freeware and shareware before using it;
  – scan all internet downloads before installing or running;
  – scan flash disks regularly;
  – never use pirate software;
  – scan attached programs to email before running; and
  – back-up your data regularly.

## 8.4.3  Learning theoretical content cooperatively

Before studying the following examples, it would be wise to review Chapter 6 on cooperative learning to ensure that the correct principles are applied when teaching and learning are done in groups.

### 8.4.3.1  *An example of the application of numbered groups when raising learners' awareness of new trends and developments*

Using numbered groups is an example of peer tuition, and provides an easy way to enhance learner involvement in lessons. Policy documents of the South African National Department of Basic Education (DBE) for CAT (DBE 2011a:15) and IT (DBE 2011b:16) note that learners should be taught to "be aware of new trends and developments". The teacher prepares learners ahead of time by indicating that new trends and developments will be studied, and asks them to study relevant literature, and, for example, to bring magazines to class. On the day of the discussion, the learners within a group are numbered. The teacher uses a list of questions that (s)he has prepared beforehand and then poses one question or topic at a time for the learners to discuss. After some time, the teacher chooses a number. The learner with that number in each group has to make a contribution to answer the question, either verbally or written. Everyone in the group must be able to give the answer, representing the group response, and thus everyone must understand, since they do not know who will be asked.

### 8.4.3.2   An example of the application of the Teams Games Tournaments model for learning to use Boolean conditions in relation to advanced search techniques

The Teams Games Tournaments model is best used to teach well-defined material with single, correct answers. The purpose of the study by Kamaruddin and Yusoff (2019) was to investigate the effectiveness of the TGT and Jigsaw (see section 8.4.3.4) cooperative learning models towards developing learners' social skills, while Sa'adah (2017) implemented TGT as cooperative learning model to improve learners' interest and learning outcomes, and Syaifuddin, Nurlela and Prasetya (2020) looked at the effect of TGT as cooperative learning model and learning motivation on student learning outcomes. The TGT process progresses through the following phases:

▸ **A new concept is presented**

In Grades 11 and 12, CAT learners design basic queries using "and", "or" and "not" as part of Database Solution Development (DBE 2011a:33, 40), while Grade 10 IT learners, also as part of Solution Development, implement "Boolean logic/operators (and, or, not) … using an Introductory Graphical Programming Tool" (DBE 2011b:23). The use of Boolean conditions in relation to advanced search techniques for finding information can be explained using direct instruction in presentations by the teacher in a conventional classroom set-up (Liu *et al.* 2005; Van Wyk 2011). During guided practice, learners work through examples individually to show comprehension of handling.

▸ **Learners form heterogeneous study teams for practice (Games)**

Following the individual practice, learners are divided into heterogeneous study teams "comprising three or four members each" (Liu *et al.* 2005), who study together during an additional practice session. Within the study team, each learner has the opportunity to participate in team learning activities that illustrate the use of the Boolean conditions in advanced search techniques, with immediate feedback from other team members. Each team receives "worksheets reviewing the material covered that week" (Wodarski, Wodarski and Parris 2004:109). Peer tutoring is encouraged while learners are working together in pairs within the teams to solve the problems, explaining the answers to each other, and comparing their work with the answer sheets. In these teams, learners can also play instructional games provided, which are usually short-answer questions designed to assess and reinforce the material taught in class. Finally, each team member is also responsible for ensuring that all team members understand the procedures and can implement these.

▸ **Participation in academic tournaments**

Learners who are of comparable achievement levels are divided into new groups of three learners each for the weekly academic tournament activities they will take part in (Wodarski *et al.* 2004). In these tournaments, teams compete "with members of other teams to contribute points" during the competition for their initial group (Van Wyk 2011:185). Each tournament group receives a pack of cards with search criteria in word/sentence format that needs to be written in terms of Boolean conditions, on the one side, and the answer on the back. The cards are shuffled and the game continues according to the following rules:

- The three players act as the card man, the first challenger and the second challenger. Each player writes down the required condition(s) for the top card of the deck. The card man has to give his answer first. The challengers can let the opportunity pass if they agree with the card man, or they can challenge the card man if they believe the given answer to be wrong.

- The card is turned over to reveal the correct answer on the back. If the card man's answer was correct (s)he receives the card. If one of the challengers challenged the correct answer with a wrong one, the challenger loses one of her/his cards, which is placed underneath the playing deck. However, if the card man was wrong, and one of the challengers was correct, then that challenger receives the card.

- The first challenger now becomes the card man, the second challenger the first, and the previous card man the second challenger (the roles rotate within the group).The next condition(s) is/are written down, and so on, until the group's pack of cards is finished.

- Each player's cards are counted and 120 points are divided between the group members: If they all have different numbers, the "top scorer at each tournament table brings sixty points to his or her" original team (Van Wyk 2011:185), second place 40 points, and third place 20 points; if they all have the same number of cards, each one receives 40 points; if there are two winners, each receives 50 and the loser 20 points; if there is a winner and the other two are equal, they each receive 30 and the winner 60 points. After calculating the points in the group, the players return to their original study teams, where their team score is computed by adding each player's points "to those earned by other members of" that learner's team (Wodarski *et al.* 2004:109).

▸ **Finally, the winning group is acknowledged.**

### 8.4.3.3  *The Student Teams Achievement Division (STAD) model*

The Student Teams Achievement Division (STAD) model was developed for those teachers who were uncomfortable with awarding marks on the basis of the group performance in the TGT model, and therefore has the same basis as the latter model, as explained in the previous section.

Recently, the study by Sholikhah, Raharjo and Suhandini (2020) aimed to determine the abilities of students in terms of critical thinking skills before and after the implementation of the STAD learning model. The research by Zubaidah, Mahanal, Ramadhan, Tendrita and Ismirawati (2018:75) was a quasi-experiment with the aim of empowering the critical and creative thinking skills of students through the STAD learning model. The study by Nazari, Tabatabaei and Heidari Shahreza (2021:191) "investigated the impact of cooperative learning on" high school "learners' critical thinking and motivation".

Earlier, Li and Luo (2010) specifically found that the STAD model was suitable for teaching computer-related content. As a first step, learners listen to the teacher introducing and explaining the study material on the content, following which they return to their respective heterogeneous groups of four members to work together cooperatively on completing a set of worksheets and/or exercises on the lesson (Ghaith 2004). However, after learners have studied together in their groups, the third step in the TGT model (participation in the "tournament") is replaced by a normal individual achievement test on the material that all learners participate in. Bonus points/certificates can be earned for their groups by those group members whose individual scores improve by a predetermined amount from their own past averages. Finally, the highest scoring learners and group(s) receive rewards such as, for example, recognition in a weekly class newsletter, acknowledging their team achievements.

### 8.4.3.4  *An example of the application of the Jigsaw II model for studying e-communication*

Although Garcia (2021) provided a quasi-experimental evaluation of the Jigsaw teaching cooperative learning model with novice programmers, the Jigsaw II model can also be used for learning factual knowledge. The purpose of the study by Kim and Park (2019:36) was to carry out a preliminary experimental study with a "control group to confirm the effects of" using the jigsaw model together with flipped learning. One of the main reasons why the form of task specialisation used in Jigsaw was developed was to promote mutual interdependence between different group members. This is achieved by dividing learners into study groups, where each group member receives a part of the information. In order to obtain all the information, learners have to work together in the study group.

▸ **Introduction to Jigsaw II**

The first time the method is used, the teacher will have to explain the working of the method to the learners. In the Jigsaw method, learners study material on one of a number of concepts. The rules during group activities are given to the learners: no learner is permitted to leave the group area before the assignment is finished, each group member is responsible for ensuring that everybody understands and will be able to complete the assignment successfully, and if there is a learner who has trouble understanding the assignment, the group members must be asked for help first, before calling the teacher.

▸ **Division into study groups**

Basic concepts in terms of electronic communication, such as a description of e-communication, an overview of applications/tools that facilitate e-communication, and an introduction to communication styles and the responsible use of the internet, email and netiquette, are studied (DBE 2011a:15; 2011b). The learning material is divided so that each of the concepts is distributed between the different members in the home/study groups – each of the group members get the opportunity to focus on mastering one specific part of the learning material "to be read and learned" through the assignment of an expert concept and a set of guiding questions (Chan 2004:93).

▸ **Meeting in expert groups for discussion**

Upon finishing reading the appropriate section in their textbooks, learners from different study groups who are responsible for studying the same concept from the learning materials then "separate from their own groups" to meet in so-called "expert groups" (Sahin 2010:778). Here, they discuss and share information on what the learning materials contain on their concepts with members of other groups. They make plans about how they can explain the subject to their home group members, e.g. by preparing notes on their expert concept and working out the best answers to each question from a range of sources provided.

▸ **Experts report back to teach their study groups**

When the "experts" have mastered a clear understanding of their concepts, they return to their own study group to report on "what they have discussed in the expert group" (Chan 2004:93). It is the responsibility of each expert learner to ensure that this information is transferred by explaining their speciality concept to the other members of their original study groups with the help of the notes and answers they have prepared (Sahin 2010). After this, it is important to assist all learners within the group in studying to become familiarised with all the concepts in the learning materials and ensuring that they all understand each of the concepts.

▸ **Assessment and group recognition**

In the end, teachers can work with individual learners, a specific group, or the class as a whole to consolidate learning and/or to identify any work that must be taught again (Sahin 2010). Testing is performed with each individual group member, to compare their performance with their original average score to determine each individual's improvement, after which the improvement (if any) in the group's average score is calculated (Chan 2004). Because study groups are heterogenic, the group mark is calculated by adding the improvement on the average mark for each study member. Finally, the group that had obtained the largest improvement on their average is given recognition in the form of a reward and/or receives praise as a group.

As learners get more opportunity to use the Jigsaw II model, their ability to identify key concepts and important information from questions on the work sheet should improve. The learners thus develop as independent learners. Studies of forms of Jigsaw, where group rewards were added to the original model, have found positive achievement outcomes.

### 8.4.3.5  *Using group investigation to explore Social Implications*

Group investigation belongs to another set of popular study methods through which cooperative learning can be expanded (Chan 2004). It "is a learning model that emphasizes" students' ability to think "through group activities to investigate specific problems or topics" (Komala, Lestari and Ichsan 2020:9). The study by Sojayapan and Khlaisang (2020:28) "examined the effects on the team learning ability of upper secondary school students" (like those in IT and CAT classrooms) "using a flipped classroom model with" group investigation, while the aim of the study by Zorlu and Sezek (2019:10) "was to investigate the effects of the applications of" the "learning together and group investigation" models "at different intervals on the features of cooperative learning". The study by Arsy, Prasetyo and Subali (2019:75) "aimed to identify the effect of Predict-Observe-Explain (POE)" with the "Group Investigation (GI) model on students' learning achievement and critical thinking skills", whereas the study by Listiana (2020:915) aimed to "determine the difference between the improvement in students' self-regulation skills before and after the implementation of" group investigation integrated with Think Talk Write. The teacher presents the topic of Social Implications in the form of a question. Discussion of this question by the learners happens through a brainstorming session, where further questions come to mind. These questions are consolidated into key subtopics. In this way, group investigation not only involves the learners in researching and studying the learning material, but also in determining what will be studied.

Each learner now attaches her/himself to a group that will study one of the subtopics that interests that particular learner. Each group of learners, for a specific subtopic, now investigates that subtopic together. Within each group, the subtopic can be further subdivided "among group members who complete individual-specific tasks" (Ghaith 2004:282). Group members write a final project report that reflects their findings, and at the end, when the class as a whole reconvenes, each group presents their report (Sharan 2010).

## 8.5    PITFALLS IN TEACHING THEORETICAL CONTENT

Teachers sometimes employ the following coping strategies which ARE NOT effective ways to teach theoretical content:

- teaching as little theory as possible;
- giving theoretical work for self-study without reflecting or providing feedback on the work afterwards;

- avoiding all but the simplest hands-on work;

- using outside experts excessively;

- emphasising managerial aspects of their practice and concentrating on getting through content;

- concentrating on areas in which confidence is highest, while avoiding those subject units that they do not feel comfortable teaching, or those that they do not regard as significant; and

- relying excessively on textbooks and externally produced worksheets to structure their curriculum.

If you find yourself using one or more of these, STOP and carefully reconsider your options – what can you do to improve the situation?

## 8.6    CONCLUSION

Topics related to theoretical content represent around 40 percent of the weighting in terms of content volume in IT and CAT respectively. Therefore, it is important that teachers of IT and/or CAT pay enough attention to teaching strategies that enhance the learning of these topics and foster interest and enthusiasm amongst learners. Careful planning and structuring of these activities result in optimal learning experiences. If learners have to study some theoretical content on their own, the teacher needs to schedule opportunities for feedback and evaluation to determine if the required aims have been achieved.

# ASSIGNMENT 8

**8.1**   Discuss the role of learners' contexts in planning to teach IT and/or CAT theoretical content.

**8.2**   Discuss the use of direct instruction in the context of teaching and learning theoretical content.

**8.3**   Give your own example of a problem that can be used in problem-based learning. Explain the strategies you will use to apply this in an IT and/or CAT class.

**8.4**   Give your own examples of the implementation of two cooperative strategies in the teaching and learning of theoretical content.

**8.5**   Give your opinion on each of the pitfalls mentioned in 8.5.

## REFERENCES

Arsy, H.I., Prasety, A.P. and Subali, B. 2019. Predict-observe-explain strategy with group investigation effect on students' critical thinking skills and learning achievement. *Journal of Primary Education*, 8(4):75-83.

Belland, B.R., French, B.F. and Ertmer, P.A. 2009. Validity and problem-based learning research: A review of instruments used to assess intended learning outcomes. *Interdisciplinary Journal of Problem-based Learning*, 3(1):59-89. https://doi.org/10.7771/1541-5015.1059

Chan, K. 2004. Using 'Jigsaw II' in teacher education programmes. *Hong Kong Teachers' Centre Journal*, 3:91-97.

DBE (see South Africa. Department of Basic Education.)

Garcia, M.B. 2021. Cooperative learning in computer programming: A quasi-experimental evaluation of Jigsaw teaching strategy with novice programmers. *Education and Information Technologies*, 26:4839-4856. https://doi.org/10.1007/s10639-021-10502-6

Ghaith, G. 2004. Correlates of the implementation of the STAD cooperative learning method in the English as a foreign language classroom. *International Journal of Bilingual Education and Bilingualism*, 7(4):279-294. https://doi.org/10.1080/13670050408667813

Goosen, L. 2004. Criteria and guidelines for the selection and implementation of a first programming language in high schools. Ph.D. dissertation, North-West University, Potchefstroom.

Kamaruddin, S. and Yusoff, N.M. 2019. The Effectiveness of Cooperative Learning Model Jigsaw and Team Games Tournament (TGT) towards Social Skills. *Creative Education*, 10(12):2529-2539. https://doi.org/10.4236/ce.2019.1012180

Kim, H.J. and Park, D. 2019. Effects of convergence education by jigsaw model and flipped learning in nursing students. *Journal of Convergence for Information Technology*, 9(3):36-43.

Klahr, D. and Nigam, M. 2004. The equivalence of learning paths in early science instruction: Effects of direct instruction and discovery learning. *Psychological Science*, 15(10):661-667. https://doi.org/10.1111/j.0956-7976.2004.00737.x

Komala, R., Lestari, D. P. and Ichsan, I.Z. 2020. Group investigation model in environmental learning: An effect for students' higher order thinking skills. *Universal Journal of Educational Research*, 8(4A):9-14. https://doi.org/10.13189/ujer.2020.081802

Li, X. and Luo, L. 2010. Probe into STAD cooperative learning based on Moodle. (In *Proceedings of the Second International Workshop on Education Technology and Computer Science*, 6-7 March, Wuhan, China, pp. 424-427.)

Listiana, L. 2020. Enhancing Self-Regulation Skills through Group Investigation Integrated with Think Talk Write. *International Journal of Instruction*, 13(1):915-930. https://doi.org/10.29333/iji.2020.13159a

Liu, C.C., Tao, S.Y., Nee, J.N., Liu, B.J., Chen, G.D., Hsu, C.C. and Horng, J.T. 2005. Supporting activity awareness for teams-games-tournaments with GSM network. (In *Proceedings of the 2005 IEEE International Workshop on Wireless and Mobile Technologies in Education*, 28-30 November, Tokushima, Japan, pp. 238-242.)

Nazari, A., Tabatabaei, O. and Heidari Shahreza, M.A. 2021. Impact of STAD model of Cooperative Learning on Iranian EFL Learners' Critical Thinking and Motivation. *International Journal of Foreign Language Teaching and Research*, 9(38):191-203. https://doi.org/10.52547/JFL.9.38.191

Polya, G. 1981. *Mathematical discovery*. New York: Wiley.

Rosenshine, B. 2010. *Principles of instruction*. Beaumont/St Julien: ImprimerieVillière.

Sa'adah, S.R. 2017. Implementation of Cooperative Learning Model with Teams Games Tournament (TGT) Method to Improve Interests and Learning Outcomes. *Classroom Action Research Journal (CARJO)*, 1(2):65-72. https://doi.org/10.17977/um013v1i22017p065

Sahin, A. 2010. Effects of Jigsaw II technique on academic achievement and attitudes to written expression course. *Educational Research and Reviews*, 5(12):777-787.

Saputra, M.D., Joyoatmojo, S., Wardani, D.K. and Sangka, K.B. 2019. Developing Critical-Thinking Skills through the Collaboration of Jigsaw Model with Problem-Based Learning Model. *International Journal of Instruction*, 12(1):1077-1094. https://doi.org/10.29333/iji.2019.12169a

Sharan, Y. 2010. Cooperative learning for academic and social gains: Valued pedagogy, problematic practice. *European Journal of Education*, 45(2):300-313. https://doi.org/10.1111/j.1465-3435.2010.01430.x

Sholikhah, F., Raharjo, T.J. and Suhandini, P. 2020. The effect of the STAD learning model aided by students worksheet to improve critical thinking skills of students. *Journal of Primary Education*, 9(1):1-6.

Sojayapan, C. and Khlaisang, J. 2020. The effect of a flipped classroom with online group investigation on students' team learning ability. *Kasetsart Journal of Social Sciences*, 41(1):28-33.

South Africa. Department of Basic Education. 2011a. *Curriculum and assessment policy statement Grades 10-12: Computer Applications Technology.* Pretoria: Government Printing Works.

South Africa. Department of Basic Education. 2011b. *Curriculum and assessment policy statement Grades 10-12: Information Technology.* Pretoria: Government Printing Works.

Syaifuddin, T., Nurlela, L. and Prasetya, S.P. 2020. The effect of cooperative learning model type Team Games Tournaments (TGT) and learning motivation on student learning outcomes. *International Joint Conference on Arts and Humanities (IJCAH)*, December. Atlantis Press. https://doi.org/10.2991/assehr.k.201201.235

Van Wyk, M.M. 2011. The effects of teams-games-tournaments on achievement, retention, and attitudes of economics education students. *Journal of Social Sciences*, 26(3):183-193. https://doi.org/10.1080/0971 8923.2011.11892895

Wodarski, J.S., Wodarski, L.A. and Parris, H.N. 2004. Adolescent preventive health and teams-games-tournaments. *Journal of Evidence-Based Social Work*, 1(1):101-124. https://doi.org/10.1300/J394v01n01_06

Zorlu, F. and Sezek, F. 2019. Students' Opinions about the Effect of the Application of Learning Together and Group Investigation Methods at Different Intervals on the Features of Cooperative Learning Model. *Malaysian Online Journal of Educational Sciences*, 7(2):10-24.

Zubaidah, S., Mahanal, S., Ramadhan, F., Tendrita, M. and Ismirawati, N. 2018. Empowering critical and creative thinking skills through REMAP STAD learning model. (In *Proceedings of the 2nd International Conference on Education and Multimedia Technology.* NY: ACM, pp. 75-79.) https://doi.org/10.1145/3206129.3239435

# Learning and teaching support materials in IT and CAT classes

**Elsa Mentz & Roxanne Bailey**

## OBJECTIVES

After completing this chapter, you should be able to:

- create your own learning and teaching support materials, which can assist teachers in the IT and CAT classes; and

- evaluate learning and teaching support materials according to the guidelines from this chapter.

## 9.1 INTRODUCTION

Learning and teaching support materials (LTSMs) are resources, media and tools that can be used for effective teaching and the enhancement of the learning experience for learners. This includes printed resources such as books, periodicals, newspapers and pamphlets; graphic resources such as pictures, posters, graphs, models, simulations and real objects; audiovisual resources such as videos, films, slides; and electronic resources such as computer software, multimedia, CDs, DVDs and the World Wide Web. Clearly, a broad variety of different resources exist that can be classified as LTSMs. In this chapter, we will not try to explain every type of resource and material that exists, but rather attempt to give some guidelines on how to effectively select and evaluate LTSM and how to use different LTSMs in IT and CAT classes. After studying this chapter, you need to be able to create your own LTSM, which can assist teachers in the IT and CAT classes, and evaluate them according to the guidelines from this chapter.

## 9.2 GUIDELINES FOR THE SELECTION AND EVALUATION OF LEARNING AND TEACHING SUPPORT MATERIAL

The selection of LTSM forms an integral part of lesson preparation and delivery. It is the responsibility of the IT and CAT teacher to ensure that the teaching and learning material used in every lesson is appropriate and relevant in order to achieve the objective set for the lesson. The selection of LTSM from the available resources therefore should take into account which resources are the best and most appropriate for the specific learning activity, and which would be the best in clarifying certain concepts, enhancing understanding and clarity and fostering the application of knowledge. The teachers must always assess the educational value within the context of the learning objectives that need to be achieved. In the selection or development of LTSM it must:

▶ play an integral role in the development of learners;

▶ help to achieve the learning objectives;

▶ help to expand learners' knowledge;

▶ be contemporary, relevant and accurate;

▶ be accessible to all learners;

▶ be on the correct level for learners; and

▶ be cost and time effective.

It is always important to evaluate LTSM as well as to carefully plan the presentation of the lesson using the specific LTSM. Although different LTSMs will not necessarily be evaluated by precisely the same criteria, the following guidelines for the evaluation, regardless of the type of LTSM, can be helpful:

▶ **It must be relevant in order to achieve the learning objective.**

▶ **The content must be appropriate and trustworthy:**
  – is the content accurate?
  – is the content up to date?

- is the content objective, that is, free from any bias?
- can the content be verified and supported by other sources?
- is the author's credentials acceptable and is he/she a specialist in the field?
- is the publisher known from pre-publication reviews?

▸ **The material should be suitable for the specific age group:**
  - is the language appropriate for the academic level of the learners?
  - will it be suitable for learners' level of cognitive development?
  - does it take into consideration the foreknowledge of learners?
  - is it suitable for learners' age and grade level?
  - will it be appealing and interesting to learners?
  - will it promote learner participation and involvement?
  - will it be easy for learners to use?
  - if applicable, are clear instructions and directions available?
  - are the required equipment available to fully utilise the material?
  - are the cost implications acceptable?
  - is the time required to use it acceptable?

Evaluation not only needs to take place during the selection of support material, but also while using or implementing the specific LTSM. Reflection on the selection, planning and implementation is also part of the evaluation process. Figure 9.1 explains the evaluation process before, during and after the use of LTSM.

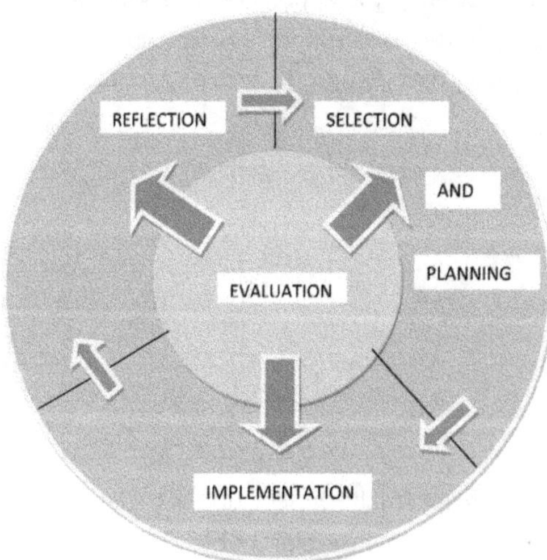


*Figure 9.1     The evaluation process*

There is an appropriate balance between different teaching methods and LTSM used. The best LTSM can be ineffective if the teacher does not plan correctly to incorporate it into the class situation. This implies not only the moment when it is introduced into the lesson, but also the way in which it is applied. For example, discipline in the class plays an important role. The best LTSM can be ineffective if the teacher is not able to control the class. After each class the teacher ought to evaluate whether the LTSM had the desired effect on the learning.

As most recent LTSMs are digital, it is worth referring to Bloom's taxonomy for digital learning. Churches (2008) indicated how Bloom's taxonomy can be addressed through the use of digital LTSM. Subsequently, a summary of Bloom's digital taxonomy where each level of Bloom's taxonomy is accompanied by its relevant digital LTSM:

- **Remember:** Social Networking, Googling, online quiz/flashcards, and/or Social bookmarking;
- **Understanding:** Blogging, Subscribing to relevant feeds and/or Advanced Boolean searches;
- **Applying:** Graphic tools, Mind map tools and/or Editing software;
- **Analysing:** Surveying tools, Graphic tools, Charting tools and/or Database software;
- **Evaluating:** Blogging (commenting on other blogs), Collaborating tools and/or Networking (social networking and email);
- **Creating:** Programming software, Filming/editing software, Podcasting and/or Painting.

The tools mentioned above give teachers the opportunity to utilise digital LTSM to address each level of Bloom's taxonomy as described in the IT and CAT CAPS.

In the following section, the LTSMs (digital and non-digital) which are used more frequently will be discussed in more detail because of the importance of evaluating these materials. These evaluation guidelines can also be applied to other LTSMs.

## 9.2.1 Textbooks

### 9.2.1.1 Evaluation of textbooks

General guidelines for the evaluation of textbooks most certainly also apply to the evaluation of IT or CAT textbooks. We will briefly discuss that first.

To evaluate any textbook, you need to look at the author and the publisher. To determine if the author can be trusted, look for the author's educational and professional background, or any available biographical information and try to determine whether the author is a well-known specialist in his/her field by searching for other books and articles by the same author. The publisher of a book can also indicate valuable information. If it is a well-known publisher, you can assume that the book went through a series of peer reviews and critical reading sessions. You can search for book reviews on the book, which can help you to decide on the appropriateness of the book for your purpose (University of South Florida 2008).

Content validity plays an important role in evaluating the appropriateness of the book. The University of South Florida (2008) offers a few pointers on their website on how the validity of the content can be determined:

- ▸ For what **purpose** is the book written? The purpose always determines the audience. Determine if the audience can well be your learners in terms of development and grade level. If the purpose is not for educational use, it will not be an appropriate IT or CAT textbook.

- ▸ **Verify the information** provided. The easiest way to verify information is to determine if the information given can also be found in other resources. Always try to answer the question: "How accurate is the information given to the reader?" If information is not accurate, it is not a suitable textbook to use.

- ▸ Check the list of **sources.** Does the author document the information by giving a source list or bibliography? Are all the references current? In IT and CAT, current sources are very important.

Language and style must be appropriate for learners to understand and master the content, without being offensive. The readability depends on the writing style of the author as well as the visual display of the text. A narrative writing style which is descriptive and uses vocabulary that is familiar and clearly defined is essential for school textbooks. Headings and subheadings, which are a clear indication of what will follow, are necessary. The text must be supported by visual presentations of the information, with colour illustrations, photographs and graphics, where appropriate.

Normally better textbooks have a separate manual for the teacher, a glossary with unfamiliar or specialised terms, as well as recommended reading and websites for further information.

The above points are not the only factors to consider when you need to decide on an IT or CAT textbook. Most certainly the textbook must also be interesting and appealing to the learners and it must be affordable. In the next few sections, we will discuss the guidelines for evaluation of an IT or CAT textbook.

Compare the learning objectives of the IT or CAT curriculum with the content of the book. You do not want to buy more than one textbook to achieve all the objectives. You also do not want to buy a textbook with only a few relevant chapters. Therefore, the content should focus on the objectives and should provide the teachers and the learner with a basic framework for instruction.

Good content alone does not make a good textbook. Teaching-learning guidelines, learning activities, assignments, evaluation and review are important factors in an IT or CAT textbook for learners. An interesting introduction in which common misconceptions are stated or where unknown terminology is defined, is valuable information for IT and CAT learners. There needs to be a logical flow of information and a consistent focus from the beginning to the end of each chapter and throughout the book. Materials should be presented in an order that makes sense for teaching and learning. The author needs to keep in mind that the reader does not have prior knowledge of the specific theme under discussion. Therefore, new material should be based on previously taught skills or information that has already been defined or discussed. Especially in teaching programming skills, new concepts should be built on knowledge of previous concepts and their limitations. Before beginning with a new theme, the necessary background information and links to previous knowledge gained must guide the learner to be able to understand the context of the new information. Therefore, the purpose of each new section must be clearly stated, as well as the objectives which the learners need to achieve and its relevance to previous knowledge.

Learner tasks and assignments should be on the learners' level, should be of interest to the learners, and should specifically keep in mind the work done in the previous sections or chapters. For teaching and learning of programming skills, enough practical examples and practical tasks need to be included. Learning activities should be at different levels of difficulty and provide a variety of learning experiences to develop critical thinking and problem-solving skills. Assignments should be challenging, encouraging learners to explore more about the topic and reach beyond mere memorisation of knowledge to application and evaluation of new knowledge. A variety of assignments (research projects, questions and answers, group work, etc.) is also important, because learners become bored with one type of assignment. Assignments should always focus on the learning objectives that the learners need to achieve. Questions in the assignments should be multi-level and provide ample practice for learners to achieve the objectives. Check if there is some form of feedback to learners, not only to validate their answers, but also to enable them to monitor their own progress and take remedial steps if necessary.

The criteria for selecting textbooks can be divided into four main categories:

- **Content**
  - Does the content reflect the latest trends in IT and CAT?
  - Does the textbook follow a thematic or scenario approach?
  - Does the textbook cover all the objectives stated for the subject?
- **Learning activities and assessment**
  - Do the learning activities and assessment tasks promote and generate creative thinking and problem-solving?
  - Does the textbook provide guidance in order to conduct practical assessment tasks?
- **Layout, design and overall quality**
  - Is the layout and design clear, simple and logical?
  - Did the author include graphical and visual representations?
- **Teacher guide**
  - Is a teacher guide included or is there any guidance available for the teacher on the internet or on a CD/DVD?

These guidelines will assist you in determining the suitability of the textbook for use in the IT or CAT class.

### 9.2.1.2 The use of textbooks in the IT and CAT classes

Textbooks play a central role in education in South Africa and are therefore one of the most important LTSMs for any teacher. The Department of Basic Education normally provides a list of suitable textbooks for different subjects. From those textbooks, the school or the IT/CAT teacher needs to select the most suitable textbook for their specific learners and environment. In general, schools only buy one of these textbooks, but it is preferable that teachers ask for more of these books on the list for the school library. It can be useful when preparing a lesson to compare different textbooks on a given topic. It can also assist learners in their research assignments. Learners can be sent to the library to fetch their own textbooks for additional information on a specific theme, which they can then share with the class.

The teacher needs to know how to use textbooks in an appropriate way to enhance the learning experience of the learners. If each learner has the same textbook, it can be used for referencing a specific chapter or part of a chapter. To read long passages from a prescribed textbook in class is not an effective way of teaching. Learners can read it themselves and any teacher who is well prepared can present the facts in a much more interesting way to learners than merely reading from a textbook. Then, learners can use the textbook at home to revise certain topics dealt with in class. Assignments from the textbooks can save the teacher time in creating his/her own assignments and duplicating them for each learner. In addition, the teacher can use additional textbooks for reference purposes or for assignments and test questions. Additional textbooks can also be made available to learners for research purposes or when they need to complete practical or theoretical assignments.

It is important that the teacher support learners in the evaluation of information found in textbooks. They need to support learners to compare information in different textbooks with each other and evaluate the given information critically. It is the responsibility of the teacher to encourage learners to supplement their textbooks with innovative material of their own. Since the information in IT changes rapidly, teachers must be aware that textbooks can be outdated and that learners must always check the information against more up-to-date information in newspapers or magazines, or on the internet.

# ACTIVITY 9.1

**Design criteria for the evaluation of IT or CAT textbooks and evaluate any Grade 10 IT or CAT textbook according to your criteria. Use the form provided to specify the textbook's title, the author, the publisher and the year published. Also write a motivation of 200 words maximum to clarify your responses.**

| Textbook evaluation | | | | | |
|---|---|---|---|---|---|
| Title of book | | | | | |
| Author(s) | | Year | | | |
| Publisher | | Place | | | |
| Criteria | | Rating | | | |
| | | Poor | Fair | Good | Excellent |
| | | 1 | 2 | 3 | 4 |
| | | 1 | 2 | 3 | 4 |

## 9.2.2 Magazines and newspapers

### 9.2.2.1 Evaluation of magazines and newspapers (digital or paper-based)

Newspaper articles aimed at the general public normally do not contain technical details and specific information, whereas IT magazines aimed at the more informed IT market will be more specific, and will contain more technical details. Keeping this in mind, it is still important to evaluate newspaper and magazine articles for accuracy and reliability. For example, a letter published in the letters column of a newspaper can be incorrect as it reflects the opinion of the person who wrote the letter. Always validate information found in magazines and newspapers with other sources on the internet or from an IT dealer. It is also the responsibility of the teacher to create the same critical awareness in learners when using magazine and newspaper articles in the IT or CAT class. When planning a lesson in which magazines and newspapers are incorporated, always determine if the specific article or articles help to achieve the objectives set for the lesson.

### 9.2.2.2 The use of magazines and newspapers in the IT and CAT classes

Magazines and newspapers should play an important role in IT and CAT classes because the information in recent magazines and newspapers can be more up to date than information in prescribed IT or CAT textbooks. Newspapers also form part of a learner's experience of daily life. Topics in newspapers and magazines are planned to be interesting and relevant to the readers and using these can enrich the learner experience, if planned correctly. This is true especially for the introduction of new technologies in the IT or CAT class as they can provide valuable information which would not be included in textbooks. Therefore, these can complement textbooks and supplement relevant information (Jarman and McClune 2002; Rao 2019).

Learners learn best when they are motivated. Newspapers and magazines provide some of the best motivational activities for learners if assignments are planned correctly. Newspaper and magazine articles can be used to introduce a lesson or a topic, they can form the focus for the core activity of a lesson or topic, or they can be used to conclude a lesson or topic (Jarman and McClune 2002). Newspapers or magazines may also be the basis of a homework exercise or a revision session. A diary or bulletin board on IT-related news stories can also be used in the class and act as motivation to learners to look for IT news. A timeline on technology development or specific product development can be an interesting assignment for learners. Challenging assignments can be given to learners to collect advertisements for products which were not available two or five years ago. Learners can also be asked to find information on new technologies in magazines and newspapers and explain it to the rest of the class. If recent newspapers or magazines are not available in class, old magazines and newspapers can also be used to describe the development in products since the time the advertisements were published. Feature articles in leading IT magazines can serve as additional enriching material and can also lead to a critical discussion on the theme. Assignments with newspaper and magazine articles can be done cooperatively to enhance the enjoyment factor and improve social skills. If magazines are used in class activities, the teacher needs to focus the learners' attention on a specific article, thus preventing aimless paging through magazines without any learning gain.

In planning lessons, assignments and activities with newspapers and magazines, the teacher should try to include as many types of newspapers and magazines as possible. The use of newspapers or magazines depends on the objectives that the learners must achieve. With complicated technical issues which learners will not easily relate to, it will be more difficult to use newspapers and magazines to enhance learning. It is preferable to select short articles with demonstrations, pictures, photographs or graphics, if possible. Remember to stay focused on the learning objectives you hope to achieve and structure the learning experience carefully.

# ACTIVITY 9.2

**Formulate one lesson objective where magazines or newspapers can be incorporated to enhance the learning experience and achieve the lesson objective. Find at least one newspaper or magazine suitable for the lesson objective and evaluate it according to your own preset criteria. Also specify clearly how you will utilise the magazine or newspaper articles in the specific IT or CAT lesson.**

## 9.2.3 Electronic presentation media

One of the most familiar and frequently used electronic presentation media is MS PowerPoint. Therefore, PowerPoint will be used in the discussion of this section. Any other electronic presentation media can be applied in the same way (PowerPoint 2002; Crispen 2006).

### 9.2.3.1 Evaluate electronic presentation media

PowerPoint is nothing new and has become part of the teaching-learning environment in most schools. However, when PowerPoint is used poorly or inappropriately, it may actually hinder the learning in the classroom. Therefore, it is important that all teachers who would like to use PowerPoint in their classes should know about the strengths and limitations of this tool. Good slide composition makes all the difference. Poor slide composition can distract learners from the objectives that they need to achieve. Therefore, PowerPoint presentations must be planned and evaluated carefully by thinking about what needs to be included in a presentation for learners to achieve the objectives, and how it needs to be presented.

In the discussion that follows, the guidelines for a good PowerPoint presentation will be provided. Thus, these guidelines can be followed, along with the general guidelines for evaluation of LTSM, to evaluate a presentation.

Consider the following guidelines when creating a PowerPoint presentation:

- keep track of the learning objective(s) the learners need to achieve;
- the main focus of any presentation must be on the content. Accuracy of content knowledge is imperative;
- avoid including too much detail on one slide. A slide should focus on one or two key concepts or ideas – the teacher needs to give the important extra information while displaying the slide;
- never use slides to copy long parts from a textbook. When a slide includes too much text, learners focus on reading the slide and neglect to listen to the teacher. Use keywords to present the background and key concepts of the lesson. Be careful not to be too cryptic with the bullet points – each must be understandable on its own and easy to follow and read;
- do not use too many bullet points on one slide and avoid using long sentences at each bullet point;
- try to illustrate concepts visually;
- a heavily animated presentation distracts the learners from the objectives you are trying to achieve. Keep animation simple and use only one or two basic animations and transitions for the whole presentation (CAT 2005);
- colour can be attractive on a screen, but certain colours are not visible when displayed on a big screen. Always use light text when using a dark background for increased readability. Keep the background simple. Be careful with background patterns because they usually make text more difficult to read. Use one background for the entire presentation;
- always try to develop PowerPoint slides in such a way that they invite interaction between the learners and yourself;
- use suitably descriptive headings that are short and to the point;
- use a big font size (18 to 24 points) that would be readable to all learners in the class. Sans-serif fonts, such as Arial or Verdana, are always a good choice. Do not use different fonts for each slide;
- use bold and italic with different colours or fancy animation if you occasionally want to emphasise a point;
- do not write everything in upper case;
- images must be relevant to the content. Well-known images on each slide have no purpose other than distraction;
- limit the use of sound. Transitions connected to sound must be avoided. If sound does not contribute to the learning experience of the learners, do not use it. It distracts learners from the actual learning objectives and it is makes it difficult to keep learners' attention and to maintain discipline;
- animate slide content at the right pace and only animate one bullet at a time;
- no slide ought to distract the attention from the actual objective of the lesson;
- plan the layout of each slide carefully. If it is too cluttered, the animation tiresome and the sound irritating, it detracts from what needs to be achieved; and
- always watch the entire presentation before presenting it. Proofread the slides for spelling and language errors, as well as for the visibility of each slide. Remember that a presentation on a big screen always looks different from on your computer screen (Clark 2002; University of Auckland 2004).

### 9.2.3.2  Using electronic presentation media in IT and CAT classes

One of the major advantages of PowerPoint is its capability to use animation, pictures, diagrams, tables, graphs, figures, images, photos, movies, sound, video clips and hyperlinks to web pages. The explanation of IT or CAT concepts can be difficult in a static world of transparencies and blackboards, but much more interesting and easier to explain if animation can be part of a lesson. Computer architecture, for example, can be explained and photos and schematic diagrams can be used to explain the flow of data. Recent websitescan also be used to show new technologies or demonstrate specific concepts.

PowerPoint presentations are not a shortcut for lesson preparation or an aid for the teacher to remember all the facts. Always apply the principles of active learning and do not use PowerPoint as a reason to lecture to a class. Plan the presentation carefully, according to the time you have to present it. It is confusing and frustrating when a teacher skips some slides or accelerates the pace through the slides at the end of a class in an effort to complete the slides in time. Do not read your slides aloud. When it is necessary to show text on a slide, give enough time for learners to read the slides themselves and sum up or clarify important facts on the slide in more detail afterwards. Do not race through the slides – give learners time to comprehend what they see. Avoid depending exclusively on the slides when presenting the lesson. Integrate PowerPoint presentations with other class activities such as exercises, own research, discussions, group activities, etc.

One advantage of using PowerPoint is the fact that it is not necessary for learners to take notes in class. They need only to concentrate on the objectives they need to achieve. If possible, make the slides available to learners at the beginning of the lesson. This will enable them to listen and concentrate without being concerned about copying everything down.

Always remember the words of Prof. Edward Tufte of Yale University: *"If your words or images are not on point, making them dance in color won't make them relevant"*. PowerPoint presentations are teacher centred at best and tend not to allow the learners to be actively involved in their own learning. Apply these presentations only when absolutely necessary.

## ACTIVITY 9.3

**Create your own PowerPoint presentation on any learning objective you prefer. In a separate document, clearly state your learning objective, lesson objective, time allocation, and grade, as well as the way in which you plan to incorporate the presentation into the lesson. Design criteria for evaluating PowerPoint presentations and evaluate your own presentation according to these criteria.**

## 9.2.4  The internet

### 9.2.4.1  Evaluation of the information found on the internet

Evaluating the information sourced from the internet is essential within a teaching-learning environment as anyone can set up an internet site and publish any information on it, without any approval of the content. There is no guarantee that the information is correct, up to date, reliable and useful. Therefore, it is important that the learners also know how to critically evaluate information found on the internet and distinguish between good and bad information (Schrock 1999).

Some guidelines which IT and CAT teachers and learners should apply will be discussed in this section.

- Always try to verify the author of the source and his/her credentials. Look at the author's qualifications and affiliation. It is riskier to trust James Nell, with no affiliation to any organisation, than to trust Prof. James Nell from a specific university or research institute. Check if the author documents the information, which was published on the internet, and whether the author provides a bibliography for the information. Be careful of any information where the author is unknown. Look for additional information on the author, if possible, as well as a contact person or address.

- Check the date of publication. Credible websites normally include the date that they were created and the date of last update. Recently published or updated sites could be more reliable than information published ten years ago. Some websites are not updated regularly and in the IT field this can be a problem as technology changes rapidly. Sometimes no indication of the time the site was last updated can be found on the website, but the currency of the sources used by the author could give an indication of how recent the information is.

- Check the accuracy of the information by cross-checking it with other information on the web. When quoting other authors, check if it is done correctly. Apply critical thinking skills, including previous knowledge and experience to validate information. Sometimes the author also states the purpose of the website, which can be an indication of reliability. Be careful of biased sites containing words that try to persuade or advertise, rather than inform. Data must be presented objectively, without any personal prejudice. Questions like this must be asked: Was some information left out and are both sides of an issue presented?

- The URL extension can also tell us something about the information. If it is .edu (higher education, college or university), .gov (government agency or organisation), or .org (non-profit organisation) it could be more reliable than extensions like .com. A tilde (~) after the type of domain usually indicates a personal web page.

- Check if information is copyright protected or if it is explicitly stated that it is in the public domain.

- Check if links to other sites are up to date (DataRecoveryLabs 2012; Harris 2007; National Teacher Training Institute 2006).

An IT or CAT teacher should follow the above guidelines, along with the general evaluation guidelines discussed in this chapter, to evaluate an internet website when preparing a lesson and should also assist learners to follow these guidelines when using the internet for assignments or projects.

### 9.2.4.2 Using the internet in IT and CAT classes

One of the most powerful instructional tools that a teacher can use in class is the internet. With the internet, you have all the latest information at hand that makes teaching exciting and new. Not only should the internet be used in class and incorporated into the lesson if the technology is available, but the internet should also be used when preparing a lesson. Learners should also be encouraged to assume responsibility for their own learning by accessing the internet in their quest for knowledge.

The use of the internet should always enhance the classroom practice. Use the internet, for example, to show learners images or photos,to obtain data such as the exchange rate or rainfall, to collect data for a database, to allow learners to explore a new topic or to do a research project, or when a learning objective is not well covered or current in your textbooks. In the IT or CAT class, the best place to find information on the latest computer technology is on the internet. In addition, the internet can be an excellent way to supplement and extend the learning experience of more advanced learners who often are finished earlier with assignments than the rest of the class.

All these activities using the internet should be carefully planned in such a way that learners are not distracted from the learning objectives that they aim to achieve. Do not assume that all learners know how to use the internet effectively. The information available on the internet can be overwhelming. Learners should be aware of the acceptable way to use the internet. Take time to show them how to search for a topic or fact and how to use the internet effectively. Always coordinate the use of the internet in class, e.g. by providing a curriculum page (or hotlist), which is a teacher-created document or web page that contains hyperlinks to teacher-selected and evaluated websites for specific learning activities. This will save learners a lot of time in aimless searching. Learners should search for specific information and not be allowed to surf the web uncontrolled. The teacher's involvement when learners access the Web during class is important. Computer monitors should be placed where they are easily visible for the teacher or the teacher could use administrative tools on his/her computer to track individual usage, if it is available. Always try to visit a site before the learners visit it or use a filtering service to block access to inappropriate sites. It is good practice to ask them to write down the URLs of each site that they use. Exposure to inappropriate material is always a risk; it is the teacher's responsibility to minimise the risk and assist learners to make appropriate decisions, in order to prepare them for the adult world.

One of the most important issues around the use of the internet is the evaluation of data, as discussed above. As an IT or CAT teacher, it is your responsibility to teach your learners to evaluate information that was found on the internet. Anyone can publish on the internet and the responsibility is on the user to evaluate the information (Norlund 2007).

Interesting websites for IT and CAT classes are the following:

▸ http://www.brainpop.com/ This website can be entered free for a trial version, but then you need to register. There are videos and other information on certain topics, including computer viruses, that learners can access.

▸ Blue Web is an online library of outstanding internet sites categorised by subject, grade level, and format (tools, references, lessons, hot lists, resources, tutorials, activities, projects). https://www.blueweb.co.za/

## ACTIVITY 9.4

**Find two interesting websites that can be used to achieve a specific lesson objective. Clearly specify the lesson objective(s) and how it can be incorporated into the lesson plan. Evaluate the site according to the guidelines given in section 9.2.4.1, as well as the general guidelines in section 9.2. In your evaluation you need to indicate if the website is suitable or not for use in the IT/CAT class. Also provide a motivation for you answer.**

### 9.2.5 Software programs, application packages, videos and other electronic/digital media

There are a number of software programs, application packages, videos and other electronic media that can assist the IT and CAT teacher to enhance the learning experience in the class. Some of these programs and videos are available on the internet. In all cases when using software programs, application packages, videos and other electronic/digital media, attempt as far as possible to make use of Open Educational Resources (OERs). OERs are LTSM in various forms which are legally bound by open licences so people may "reuse, revise, remix and redistribute" them as needed (Franco and Kommers 2019). These OERs give teachers the freedom to adapt the LTSM to better suit their classroom and can thus be made more relevant in the IT or CAT class. The success of OERs lay with individuals who are willing to share their work while knowing that they themselves benefit from others' work. Creating a network where teachers share OERs will not only benefit the teaching community, but will ensure that learners are exposed to a myriad of resources previously not available to them.

In this section, we do not attempt to list all possible types of software programs and application packages suitable for the IT or CAT class, but rather provide a general discussion of different electronic media.

#### 9.2.5.1 Evaluation of software programs, application packages, videos and other electronic/digital media

In evaluating software, the teacher needs to determine if it is worthwhile using the software to achieve the learning objective. Evaluation of software must look at the pedagogy used in its development, as well as design features such as help functions, accommodation of different abilities, and the ease of access to the components in the program. For pedagogical purpose, the developmental level of the learners should be kept in mind. Do not choose a software program for Grade 10 IT or CAT learners which is intended for Grade 7 IT literacy learners. The theme of any graphics, style of music, language and content should be appropriate for what specific learners are intended to gain from that specific software package. If you have to buy a specific software program, always consider the technical support and documentation that the package provides. It is always preferable that software packages provide tutorials where learners can learn to use the program. Do not choose the first program you can find, but rather compare different software packages to find a suitable one for the purpose you require it for. As in the case of the evaluation of textbooks and the internet, the teacher must be aware of the fact that current software, using the latest technology, needs to be used in IT and CAT classes. In an educational environment it is important that the program is easy to use, with clear instructions guiding learners through the use of the program. Always look at the entire video before displaying it to learners to determine if the video is suitable and aimed at the objectives that the learners need to achieve.

One of the most important aspects of software evaluation is the content. You need to determine if the content is valid and meets the standards that are required for the specific learners. Relate the content to the objectives that you want to achieve.

The following guidelines can be used to evaluate software programs and applications:

- download a trial version from the internet if applicable;
- use software evaluation rubrics which provide criteria according to which the content, documentation, technical support and quality, academic level, and ease of use can be evaluated. Some internet sites provide some of these evaluations for known software. You can also develop your own software evaluation rubric with specific criteria which fit your requirements;
- use bulletin boards and discussion groups to get the opinion of other users; and
- find reviews on the internet which could help you to decide on which software to choose.

The main question in evaluating any LTSM is always the same – does it contribute to the objectives that the learners must achieve? A substantial contribution to the objectives justifies the time and money put into specific LTSMs. Software programs for computer-assisted learning should also incorporate proper assessment methods and remedial work for learners.

### 9.2.5.2 *The use of software programs, application packages, videos and other electronic/ digital media*

Electronic simulations of videos can assist in the learners' understanding. In IT and CAT classes where computers are readily available, IT and CAT teachers should take advantage of this fact and use the software programs available to enhance the learning experience of learners. It must not be used only for interest's sake or to keep learners busy, but rather to clarify complicated terminology, simulate computer operations for better understanding, or to learn basic skills interactively. Always attempt to build in a discussion or evaluation of the specific LTSM that you have been using to ensure that all the learners gain optimum learning experience from it. In this regard, the teacher should also be actively involved in the class activity to ensure that all learners pay close attention. Learners often think it is time to relax when a video is shown.

## 9.2.6　Other LTSM

### 9.2.6.1　Real artifacts

The use of real computer components to demonstrate computer architecture, to build a computer, or to find the malfunctioning component is much more of a learning experience than to show pictures of components in a textbook. The use of component boards in computer architecture lessons is common practice. Real life situations are always a good learning experience. If possible,organise a visit to a computer vendor or computer exhibition/fair where real products can be seen and questions can be asked about their operation. Investigating such LTSM would usually be done outside normal class hours, aimed at enriching and stimulating learners and not for achieving formal objectives set for IT or CAT.

### 9.2.6.2　Interactive whiteboards

Other popular teaching tools are interactive whiteboards and data projectors. The great advantage of the interactive whiteboard is that you can press on its surface to access or control a computer application and write onto it. It can be saved, printed and handed out to the learners afterwards.

### 9.2.6.3　Social networks

A social network is a website that provides a virtual community in which people with a shared interest partake and communicate. It is a way to network with different people on the internet. Users with the same interest can communicate with each other. Within an education setting it can be used to bring together experts and knowledgeable people for a discussion on a certain topic. Information is freely available by simply asking. Social networks, however, should be used with caution as personal details can easily fall into the wrong hands. If a teacher decides to use a social networking site in a class situation, there should be strict control over the flow of information.

### 9.2.6.4　Learning management systems (LMS)

LMS are web-based software platforms which are used to ease administration, provide access to educational content and give learners the opportunity to interact with the content online (Turnbull, Chugh and Luck 2019). On its own, it is not a LTSM, but it can assist teachers when they need to distribute support materials to learners or communicate with learners about where to find specific materials or information.

## 9.3   CONCLUSION

No clear formula exists for the incorporation of LTSM in IT and CAT classes. The guidelines mentioned in this chapter, along with a great deal of creativity, should help the IT and CAT teacher to effectively incorporate LTSM into their classes in order to enhance the learning experience of learners.

## ASSIGNMENT 9

**9.1**   Go back to Chapter 3 where you designed lesson plans for IT or CAT. Evaluate the media that you planned to use according to the guidelines in this chapter.

**9.2**   Design a web evaluation rubric to evaluate the educational value of a website.

**9.3**   Find a reputable OER repository and share your web evaluation rubric (designed in 9.2) on the repository.

## REFERENCES

CAT (Centre for Academic Technology). 2005. General design guidelines when using PowerPoint. https://bit.ly/3jSUcHP

Churches, A. 2008. Bloom's digital taxonomy. https://bit.ly/3vqLaap

Clark, G.C. 2002. Design tips for effective use of PowerPoint in the classroom. https://bit.ly/3ryDWQz

Crispen, P.C. 2006. Guidelines for effective use of PowerPoint. http://www.netsquirrel.com/powerpoint

DataRecoveryLabs. 2012. 10 C's for evaluating Internet resources. https://bit.ly/3JOo2Yz

Franco, P. and Kommers, P. 2019. Guidebook on Open Educational Resources (OER). https://bit.ly/3JRPbtU

Harris, R. 2007. Evaluating Internet research sources. Virtual salt. http://www.virtualsalt.com/evalu8it.htm

Jarman, R. and McClune, B. 2002. Why use newspapers in the science classroom? https://bit.ly/3jMHHh3

National Teacher Training Institute. 2006. Why use Internet in the classroom? https://bit.ly/3OfEDYR

Norlund, A. 2007. "When anyone can publish anything" – How to evaluate source according to textbooks for different educational choices. *The Reading Matrix*, 7(1):85-98.

PowerPoint. 2002. Potential & Pitfalls. Using PowerPoint effectively in the classroom. https://bit.ly/3uPm8mt

Rao, P.S. 2019. The role of newspapers and magazines to teach English in the ESL/EFL classrooms in the digital era: A comprehensive study. *Journal of English Language and Literature*, 6(2):165-173.

Schrock, K. 1999. Teaching media literacy in the age of the internet. The ABC's of website evaluation. https://bit.ly/3xuZVMd

Turnbull, D., Chugh, R. and Luck, J. 2019. Learning Management Systems: An Overview. *Encyclopaedia of Education and Information Technologies*. https://bit.ly/3jNSac1

University of Auckland. 2004. Using PowerPoint in the classroom. https://bit.ly/3jMHKtf

University of South Florida. 2008. Evaluating sources. https://bit.ly/3rxdl0X

# CHAPTER 10

# The design and management of a computer laboratory

Ulza Wassermann & Elsa Mentz

## OBJECTIVES

**After completing this chapter, you should be able to:**

- explain the IT/CAT teacher's responsibilities in managing a school computer laboratory;

- suggest ways to create a vibrant and informative classroom environment;

- list and identify administrative tasks to be completed when teaching a subject using computers;

- explain what actions should be performed before a final, practical examination can be conducted; and

- discuss the aspects and importance of ergonomics in the IT and CAT laboratory

## 10.1   INTRODUCTION

Managing a computer laboratory requires a multi-skilled teacher. Fortunately, because learners are usually excited and enthusiastic to use a computer, teachers do not have much trouble in getting learners to do their work in the class. However, there are a number of challenges that could confront the IT/CAT teacher. For example, computers that break down or "freeze" while you are teaching, printers that "grab" more than one page at a time (or refuse to print any copies at all), and power failures at the most inconvenient times, such as ten minutes before the end of a practical examination. These are only a few events you will have to cope with daily – after a while you will consider it quite normal!

Due to the uniqueness of these two subjects you will probably have more interruptions and un-expected events than in a subject where you teach a theoretical lesson and you are able to control the flow of a lesson. Unexpected events for which you do not have solutions in place could lead to disciplinary problems and ultimately wasted time. Therefore, it is essential that the IT/CAT teacher is always one step ahead through proper planning.

In this chapter, we are going to discuss how a computer laboratory can be planned and managed effectively.

## 10.2   PLANNING AND DESIGN OF A COMPUTER LABORATORY

### 10.2.1   Ergonomics as main consideration

Computer ergonomics can be defined as the study of the interaction between humans and the elements of a computer in order to optimise human well-being and overall computer performance. It is concerned with design principles that optimise the performance and effectiveness of the people working on the computers without compromising their health, well-being or safety. In a computer laboratory it also includes the environment in which learners have to work. It is all about the effective, safe and productive use of computers in the laboratory.

Ergonomic concerns have become an increasingly significant health issue as a growing number of individuals frequently use computers for long periods of time. Borhany, Shahid, Siddique and Ali (2018) found that musculoskeletal symptoms are quite commonly associated with prolonged use of computers. Children are also gaining more and more access to computers on a regular basis and spend more and more time in front of a computer. Therefore, there are concerns about the short and long term physical effects that poor ergonomic workstation design and use of computers can have on children (Choudhary *et al.* 2020). When learners use computers for learning it is extremely important that the teacher should be aware of the ergonomic aspects that will promote a safe and healthy environment. Children do not have a natural awareness of correct ergonomic use of a computer and are therefore normally unaware of any health risks associated with working on a computer. The incorrect use of computers can cause musculoskeletal pain and discomfort or disorders amongst children and adolescents (Choudhary *et al.* 2020). Symptoms could at first only be an uncomfortable or stiff feeling, but could result in severe pain which could affect the back, neck, elbows, shoulders, legs, feet and joints. This could be caused by repetitive movement over a long period where the body is in an uncomfortable position and direct pressure on the soft tissue of the body occurs.

It is important that children learn the correct ergonomic use of a computer in order to carry it through to their home computer use and eventually through to their workplace. Teachers are in the best position to create awareness amongst learners about the importance of good posture and the health risks associated with the incorrect use of computers. Some requirements for a computer laboratory will be discussed in this chapter, always keeping ergonomics in mind.

## 10.2.2  Layout of computer laboratory

Even if there is an existing laboratory at the school you will be teaching at, it may happen that the computers need to be moved to a larger venue, or that you are fortunate enough to be involved in the design of a new laboratory, where you can specify how you want to arrange the tables and equipment. Therefore you need to investigate aspects that will influence the layout of a computer laboratory, possible ways computers can be arranged in a laboratory, and also what the advantages and disadvantages to each way may be.

The way the computers are arranged in the computer laboratory can depend on:

- the size of the laboratory;
- where doors and windows are placed;
- the preference of the teacher;
- the current infrastructure, for example, existing fixed tables in the laboratory;
- the use of a network, or wireless connection; and
- the money available to install the computers.

Other questions you can ask yourself to make decisions about the layout of the laboratory are the following:

- Will the theory and the practical components of the subject be taught in the same room? Some computer laboratories are big enough to have separate tables installed for use during theory lessons. It is advisable to use separate desks if possible, as learners tend to work on their computers during theory lessons and do not give their full attention if the computers are on their desks during a theory lesson.

- How will learners be prevented from looking at one another's screens when writing practical tests and exams? Keep in mind that it might be necessary to plan a removable divider as learners need to work comfortably when doing pair programming on one computer (see Chapter 6).

- Where will the tables be situated, taking into account the position of the windows? Keep in mind the position of the sun at all times of the day. Consider having blinds or curtains installed if computers cannot be placed out of the way of direct sunlight.

- Will a number of computers be accessible to students with disabilities such as those who have to make use of a wheelchair?

- How many printers will be installed? Place the printers in a place where it will be easy for learners to fetch their printouts.
- Where are the USB ports situated on the computer cases? Will the position of the cases allow learners to plug in their memory sticks without having to walk around the tables to the back of the computer? (You can always consider installing additional USB cables.)
- How will the network cables be fitted and protected so that no-one will trip over the cables?
- Where should the network switches be installed in order to minimise the length of the network cables?
- How many electrical outlets will be needed and where should they be placed? Always plan for more to avoid overloading when you need to extend or add other computer equipment to the laboratory at a later stage.
- How many air conditioners need to be installed to sufficiently cool the laboratory and where should they be installed? Remember that computers can overheat if a large number of computers are installed in a room. Ensure that there is adequate ventilation.
- What kind of overhead projector, interactive white board or normal white board will be suitable for the computer laboratory? (The dust of normal chalk is not suitable in a computer laboratory. If possible, cover computers every night to protect them against dust.)
- Where will the cupboards be placed to be accessible to the teacher during class? Have enough cupboards built in to store consumables such as paper, printer cartridges and other equipment.

The lighting in a computer room is also an important ergonomic requirement. Monitor glare should be eliminated either by dimming the lights, using alternative bulbs, or covering windows. Dimming of lights should, however, still provide enough light for learners to read in textbooks. Do not place computers in front of windows. If the computer faces towards the window or away from the window it will be difficult to read on the screen if the windows are not covered with curtains or blinds.

The most popular methods to arrange computers in a computer laboratory are shown in Diagrams 10.1 to 10.4. Note that the drawings are not to scale and are just an indication to demonstrate the way equipment can be arranged. Furthermore, you might not use a network server anymore and only connect each computer to Wifi. Wifi routers might not even be in the classroom but at a central place in the school. In that case, no UTP network cables, port switches or servers will be necessary Always keep in mind that there should be enough space available to allow for safe movement between computers.

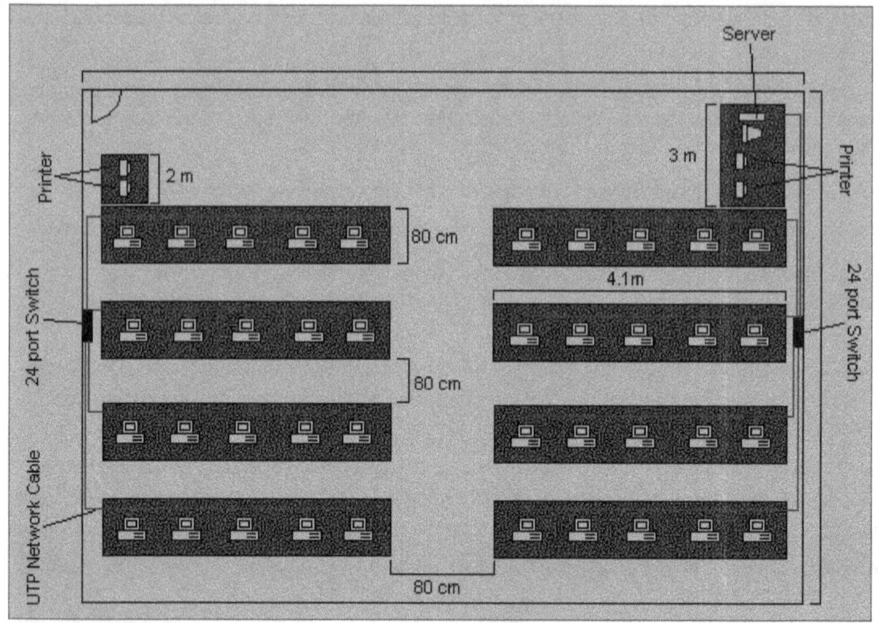


Diagram 10.1    Tables in rows

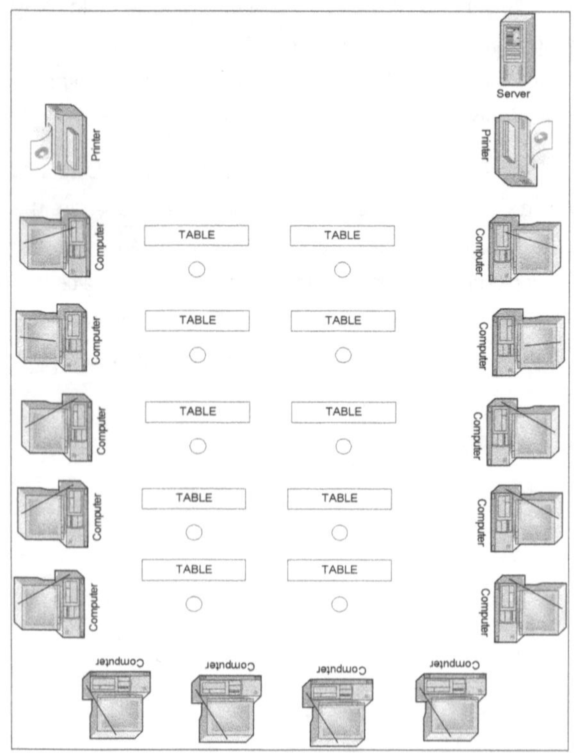


Diagram 10.2    U-layout with tables in rows

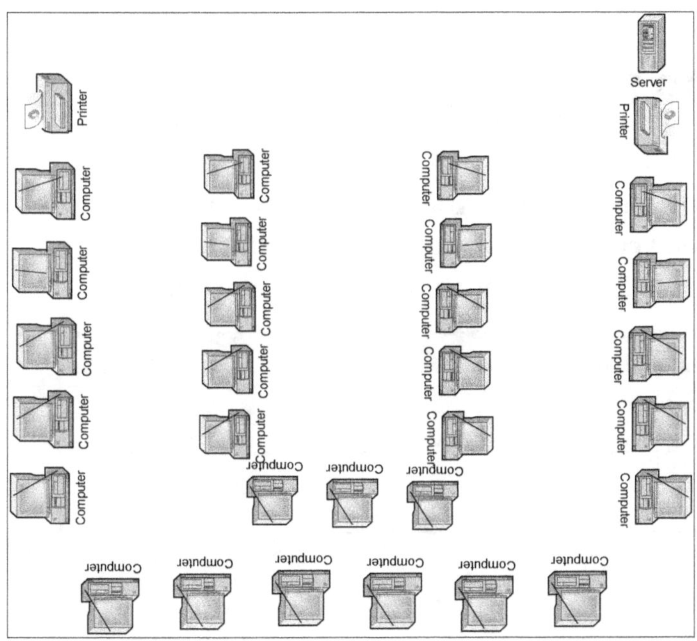


Diagram 10.3    Double U layout

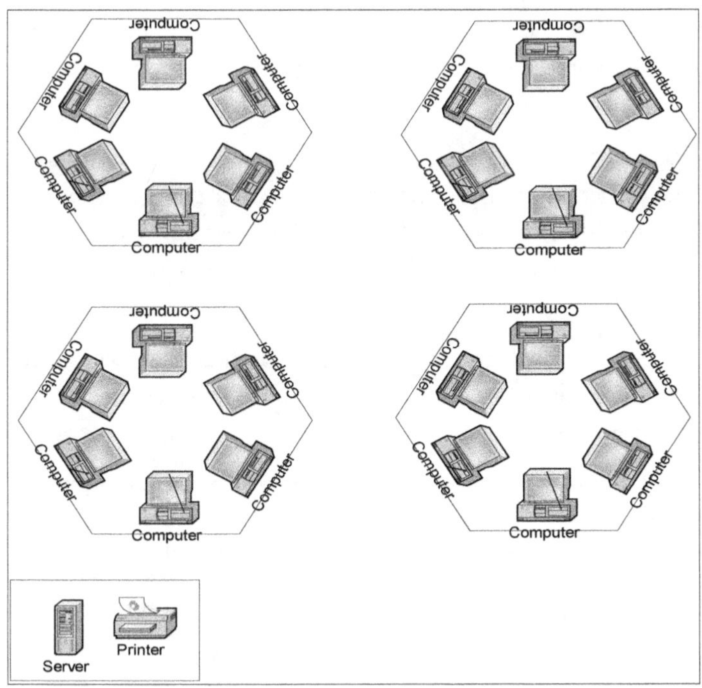


Diagram 10.4    Clusters

# ACTIVITY 10.1

**Study diagrams 10.1 to 10.4 and name some advantages and disadvantages you can think of if you consider each of the configurations for a computer laboratory as illustrated in the diagrams. Use the following table to complete this activity:**

| Layout | Advantages | Disadvantages |
| --- | --- | --- |
| Tables in rows | | |
| U-layout with tables | | |
| Double U-layout | | |
| Clusters | | |

## 10.2.3  Safety and security requirements

Although only a few aspects concerning the equipment of an ergonomically correct computer laboratory are discussed in this chapter, the teacher should always be on the lookout for any situation that could be harmful to the learners and should have safety precautions in place to address these concerns.

Any potentially dangerous situation should immediately be attended to by the teacher, for instance, loose cables or tiles on the floor, dangerous electrical connections or electrical cables underneath a carpet, near water, or where learners need to walk across them. Electrical cabling should be secured and mounted inside cable lining, out of the walkway. Fire distinguishers should be in working order and mounted inside the computer classroom.

Security issues in a computer laboratory include security regarding the physical equipment, as well as all the software and data on the computers. Therefore, a teacher should also pay attention to the following when taking charge of a laboratory:

- What are the requirements of the school's insurance company with regard to burglar bars, safety gates and alarm systems? What type of antitheft devices will be installed?
- How will provision be made for power failures and power surges to prevent damage to the computers and loss of data?
- What type of backup devices will be used?

## 10.2.4   Equipment and services

The minimum requirement for a school to present IT or CAT as subjects is that each learner taking the subject must have a computer to work on during class sessions, and that there should be at least two printers in the laboratory. However, there are many other devices you can have installed that will contribute to the effective use of the computer laboratory. Some of the devices you may consider are the following:

- **Scanner:** The use of pictures from books and magazines in assignments by learners is not an infringement of copyright. Therefore it is useful to have a scanner in class for learners to scan pictures or diagrams.

- **Data projector:** The data projector can be a powerful teaching tool in IT or CAT. You can create presentations to be used in presenting a lesson, or display your computer's screen while you demonstrate new skills in the use of an application or writing a program.

- **Uninterrupted Power Supply (UPS) or inverters:** Frequent power failures and unusual power surges ("spikes") can damage electronic equipment. Many schools invest in UPS units or inverters, or even replace PCs with laptops to prevent damage.

- **Interactive electronic whiteboard:** An interactive whiteboard is a large interactive display that connects to a computer and projector. A projector projects the computer's desktop onto the board's surface, where users control the computer using a pen or other device. The board is typically mounted to a wall or on a floor stand. The interactive whiteboard can be used to involve learners more in lessons, since it is easier for them to touch the board to interact with the software, than to take control of the computer connected to the data projector.

- **Internet connection:** No IT or CAT computer laboratory can be without an internet connection because the teacher needs to download updates for software, learners should find information for research assignments (for example the PAT) and communicate via email.

Part of your responsibilities as IT/CAT teacher will be to advise the principal or governing body on equipment to buy for the computer laboratory. This can happen either when developing a new laboratory, or as part of the maintenance of an existing laboratory. Since technology is continually evolving, it can be a daunting task for you as teacher to keep up to date with the latest developments. Therefore you should involve experts when purchasing equipment, and ensure that you obtain quotations from more than one vendor for every component of the laboratory.

Complete the following activity keeping in mind the above-mentioned guidelines.

# ACTIVITY 10.2

1.  As an IT/CAT teacher you will be expected to advise the school
    on new equipment for the computer laboratory, as well as to
    create a budget for the new financial year. Create and complete
    the following table using the headings as indicated. Attach
    a copy of any quotations you have received from dealers or
    advertisements you have used to obtain prices.

| Description of equipment | Price | Contact details of dealer |
| --- | --- | --- |
| Computers | | |
| *<Include full detail of computer, e.g make, processor speed, amount of memory, hard disk size, CD-ROM included, USB ports available, software included>* | | |
| | | |
| Printers * | | |
| Laser printer<br>*<Make and model of printer>* | | |
| Ink cartridge refill | | |
| Ink cartridge replacement | | |
| Service of printer | | |
| | | |
| Colour printer<br><Make and model of printer> | | |
| Ink cartridge refill | | |
| Ink cartridge replacement | | |
| Service of printer | | |
| | | |
| Scanner | | |
| Internet access ** | | |
| Additional equipment | | |
| Installation fees | | |
| Monthly fee for connection | | |
| Fee to download data | | |
| Monthly fee for email | | |
| Monthly fee for ISP | | |
| Additional cost for large downloads | | |

| Description of equipment | Price | Contact details of dealer |
|---|---|---|
| Number of people who can connect at a time | | |
| Additional cost for website hosting | | |
| Cost for estimated number of hours to be spent using the internet per month if applicable | | |
| Any other equipment needed | | |

IMPORTANT

* Complete the information for printers for more than one supplier, for example HP, Samsung and Canon. Remember that some cartridges cannot be refilled, while others are more expensive to refill. It is worthwhile to spend time to do the research; you will save a considerable amount of money this way!

** You will have to investigate the cost for more than one method of connecting to the internet. Read the note below for more detail.

*NOTE: At the time of writing this chapter, the most popular ways of connecting to the internet for a number of people at the same time was through fibre, ADSL, ISDN lines or wireless connections. However, there may be new technology available by the time you do this activity. What is important is that you obtain prices for more than one way of connecting, that you are aware of the latest trends, and that you are aware of the different ways that the costing is structured. For example, you have to make sure if the price listed includes the fee for an Internet Service Provider (ISP) and email. In some cases, access to the internet is provided, but you have to pay an additional fee for another service provider for an email account. Sometimes the monthly fee looks very reasonable, but if you read the fine print you realise that you pay extra if more than a specified amount of data is downloaded. Therefore, you need to do thorough research, investigating more than one option, to make sure you are aware of all possible hidden costs, so that you can compare the costing for the final option you will use in your computer laboratory.*

## ACTIVITY 10.2 *(continued)*

2.  **Use a spreadsheet application such as Excel to create an annual budget for a computer laboratory. Use imaginary numbers and figures for equipment such as the number of ink cartridges to replace or new equipment to buy, but obtain real figures for consumables and repairs such as the price of paper, textbooks and maintenance of equipment.**

## 10.2.5  Layout and dimensions for workstations

The awareness of the importance of an ergonomic, well-equipped computer laboratory and the impact thereof on children's health is the first step in creating a safe environment that is conducive to learning. In this section, we are going to review a few aspects to take into consideration and also some questions you can ask to ensure an environment based on sound ergonomic principles. We will also provide innovative suggestions to assist learners to take responsibility for their own health while working with computers.

### 10.2.5.1   Computer desks

The following are practical and ergonomic considerations you can take into account when choosing computer desks:

- Will keyboards be placed on the tables or will there be a pull-out keyboard drawer? When working on a keyboard, the learners' shoulders should be relaxed with their upper arms hanging freely at the side and their forearms more or less horizontal with the wrists in a neutral position (Middlesworth 2021). Be on the lookout for bent wrists, hunched shoulders and winged out arms as a result of inappropriate height of the keyboard. It could result in neck, back, shoulder and wrist injuries.

- The desk or work surface should be wide and deep enough to accommodate the computer equipment. The neck should be in a neutral position most of the time, therefore a document holder should be in place next to the computer, positioning the reference material as close to the screen as possible (Harisinghani *et al.* 2004). This could help reduce the risk of poor neck posture, body discomfort, back pain, eye fatigue and musculoskeletal problems (Mayo Clinic 2021).

- A monitor should be adjustable to suit the unique needs of different learners. The monitor should be an arm's length away with the top of the screen just below eye level (Mayo Clinic 2021). If the viewing angle of the monitor is too high or too low, learners will have to look too far up or too far down which may result in neck spasms.

- There should also be enough space underneath the table for the learner to sit comfortably within reaching distance of the keyboard. The chairs should allow them to place their feet on the ground and support their upper and lower back.


### 10.2.5.2   Innovation in applying ergonomic principles

In a school situation it could be quite expensive to install all the right furniture and equipment, and in some cases it can be difficult to adjust the furniture according to the size of the learner. It is also not possible to throw out all equipment that is not ergonomically correct. However, a teacher can encourage the learners to address these problems themselves by sitting on a cushion, putting the keyboard or monitor on a book or box, using a bean bag in front of the keyboard or mouse, putting their feet on a box, etc. The teacher should inform learners about adjusting their workstations and taking responsibility for their own health. Teachers should give learners regular reminders to take breaks and stretch, to focus on something else, or to relax their shoulders and maintain a good posture. Pop-up reminders on the screen can also assist teachers with learners' postural training. This is essential so that learners can get into the habit of doing so at home and in the world of work as well.

# ACTIVITY 10.3

1. **Evaluate any computer laboratory you visited during your practical teaching period in terms of the ergonomic and other guidelines in this chapter. Identify any health or safety risks and provide guidelines to the teacher in terms of ways to improve the computer laboratory and/or workstation layout with the minimum money spent.**

2. **Use the knowledge you have gained in this chapter, as well as your own practical experience, and draw a diagram of the way you would prefer the layout of a computer laboratory for at least 30 computers.**

   (a) **Indicate all the equipment you would like to have, as well as where you would like to place it in the laboratory. Include safety devices such as fire extinguishers.**

   (b) **Explain why you would like the computer laboratory to look this way and what you consider to be the advantages and disadvantages of this layout.**

   (c) **Give an indication of the size of the room needed for all the equipment.**

## 10.3 MANAGEMENT AND ADMINISTRATION OF A COMPUTER LABORATORY

### 10.3.1 Create a vibrant classroom conducive to learning

#### 10.3.1.1 Classroom decoration

The decorations used in a classroom form part of the teaching and learning process. The teacher and learners should be proud of their classroom (or computer laboratory). Learners should be involved in the decoration of the computer laboratory, since that will also give them a sense of ownership and will prevent them from damaging the equipment and decorations.

## ACTIVITY 10.4

**Write down how you plan to create a classroom where classroom decorations will contribute to learning.**

### 10.3.1.2    Code of conduct

Many problems with hardware and software failure in a computer laboratory are the result of learners misusing or tampering with equipment. Computer programs are available that prevent any changes made to the system to take effect, but most of these programs are quite expensive. The best way to prevent damages is to have learners realise that they are not doing themselves a favour by damaging equipment, since it will prevent them from acquiring new skills and may even result in having to pay more school fees to repair equipment. One way to have them realise that they have to accept responsibility for their actions is to draw up a code of conduct – with their help – to describe the acceptable behaviour of an IT/CAT learner and to specify what will happen if they misbehave. Remember, it is important that you spend time to allow learners to take part in the formulation of the code of conduct. If learners feel they took part in the design of the rules, they will be more willing to follow the rules.

## ACTIVITY 10.5

**Download and study different codes of conduct (rules to be applied in a classroom or a list of acceptable behaviour) for computer laboratories which are available on the web. Use these examples to compile a code of conduct suitable for use in South African schools.**

### 10.3.1.3    Seating plan

Learners should learn to accept responsibility for their actions. If possible, assign learners to a specific computer at the beginning of the year. Use a seating plan to keep record of each learner's workstation. If a computer is damaged, all the learners who use the computer can be investigated. Learners are exceptionally good at networking. There is always someone who knows who the culprit is, and who is willing to provide information, especially the ones who sit at the damaged computer and who did not cause any damage – they will be very eager to find the real culprit to clear their own names!

However, the bottom line is that disciplinary problems usually occur in classes where the teacher is not prepared for lessons and where learners are not engaged in useful activities.

## 10.3.2   Maintain the environment

### 10.3.2.1   Consumables

Printers usually are the equipment on which the most time and money is spent. Depending on the ratio of learners to printers in most laboratories, an ink cartridge is replaced twice a year. The following may also help to decrease the number of problems you may experience:

▸ Buy quality paper – avoid "specials" at the local supermarket. Low quality paper creates paper residue that sticks to the drum and gears of the printer – this means that the printer needs to be cleaned by a technician and most probably will also need to have some parts replaced.

▸ Teach learners how to arrange paper before feeding it into the printer. Most printers are quite sensitive. If the pages are skew and untidy in the feed tray, they jam inside the printer. Usually someone pulls out the paper forcefully, resulting in damage to parts inside the printer. Educating learners on the use of a printer will save you a lot of time and trouble – and save the school money as well!

### 10.3.2.2   Upgrading

In the corporate world computers are often replaced every three to four years, but schools do not have the luxury of replacing equipment just because there is better technology available. However, because new software – both operating systems and applications – often require more resources such as memory and hard disk space, it becomes necessary to upgrade all the computers after a number of years. You need to keep up to date with the latest trends in computer hardware and software, and the specifications provided by the Department of Basic Education with regards to the type of software to be used in teaching IT or CAT, so you can warn school management in advance about the need to upgrade the computer laboratory.

It is often not necessary to replace the complete system unit of the PC. You may be able to purchase more RAM and/or bigger hard disks. Obtain quotes from more than one supplier and ask advice from technicians recommended by other satisfied customers before you purchase any components.

### 10.3.2.3   Troubleshooting

Some learners are very eager to display their knowledge of computers, but unfortunately they use this knowledge to prevent other learners from working. Here are some of the ways learners make changes to the computers which can take quite some time to fix if you have to figure it out for the first time:

▸ Unplug a mouse or keyboard at the back of the keyboard – it then seems as if the computer "freezes" and some learners reset the computer which wastes a lot of time and does not solve the problem.

▸ Stick a piece of paper to the bottom of an optical mouse. The mouse cannot detect motion and the cursor cannot be moved on the screen.

- Remove the rubber ball inside a mouse.

- Create a screen shot of a program that gave an error message. .

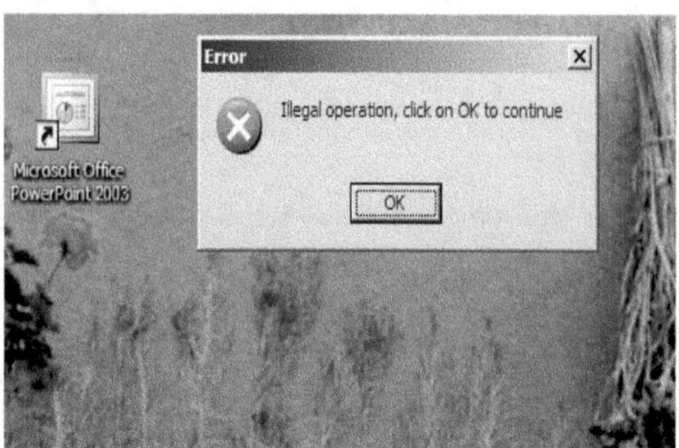


They use this screen shot to create a background and also hide the taskbar of the desktop. When the next learner arrives at the computer, they click on the error message but will not receive any response. The solution is to move the mouse to the bottom of the screen so the **Start** button can become visible, and change the background to one of the standard backgrounds provided

- Some of the learners in the class may be reasonably computer literate. Unfortunately, some of them do not use their knowledge to the benefit of others, but rather to amuse them and try to outwit the teacher. One favourite trick is to change the CMOS settings and then set a password on the CMOS setup utility so that nobody can change the settings back to what it should be. Therefore, it is a good idea to set a password on the CMOS. Just make sure you write the password down, store it in a safe place, and give a copy to a reliable person in case you are not available when the password is needed.

### 10.3.2.4   Maintenance contract

To maintain a computer laboratory can be a time-consuming and complicated task. Very few schools have the means to afford a full-time person on site to configure and repair all computers. Therefore most schools enter into a contract with a maintenance company. There are many different ways in which companies will construct such a contract. You need to contact more than one company, and make sure that they supply references so that you can talk to their current customers to determine if they are satisfied with the service the company renders.

There are some questions you should ask a maintenance company and pitfalls that you need to look out for. We mention only a few:

- Usually a monthly or annual fee must be paid. Determine what products and services are included in this fee. Will there be additional costs for labour per hour or components to be replaced?

- Will the school be able to buy components from other companies or vendors, or will it be limited to buy only from the company with whom the contract has been signed?

- What does the Service Level Agreement (SLA) entail – for example, must the technician be available within a certain number of hours, must the school transport broken equipment to the company, or will they fetch it from the school?

- Will equipment belong to the school or does the school only rent it from the company?

- Will they assist to set up backup procedures and devices?

- Will they only set up the hardware, or will they also configure the network operating system? Especially when preparing the laboratory for a final examination, it is advisable to have the services of an expert who can clean the system of viruses and previous work of the learners, create new login accounts to be used for examination purposes only, and ensure that learners cannot have access to each other's work.

- Will the company assist in installing new software, patches and service packs? How will these services be charged for?

### 10.3.2.5   Documentation to be maintained

You will be expected to handle the following in the computer laboratory:

- Stock control for insurance purposes. Make an inventory of all the equipment in the laboratory. Include specifications such as the make, model and serial number of equipment. Keep all invoices and receipts in one file.

- Annual budget for stationery such as white board markers, paper, ink cartridges, books (if the school supplies textbooks to the learners), flashdisks and running costs such as Internet Service Provider (ISP) fees, telephone bills, replacement of equipment, and new equipment to be bought (such as keyboards, mouse devices and power supplies). You need to keep record of all repairs done, all equipment bought and stationery used to give you an indication of the money you will need for the next financial year.

- Budget for upgrading of computers and software.

- Provide proof of licences for all software such as the Microsoft Office suite, Adobe Photo Shop and PageMaker.

- An exciting option that is investigated by more and more schools in South Africa is to make use of Open Source software.

- Ensure that antivirus software is installed and kept up to date.

### 10.3.2.6   Configuration for data access

Depending on whether the computer laboratory you use has a file server or is a peer-to-peer network, you will have to provide for the following:

- Hard disk space or network disk space for learners to save their class work and assignments. The ideal is for every learner to have a user account and to save their work on the network. If you use the hard disk of the computer for learners to save their work, there is the risk that work could be lost because someone may delete work, either by accident or deliberately.

- During an examination, learners must not have access to each other's work or to work they have done previously. If learners have a user account, it is usually not difficult to prevent access to certain folders; learners can be provided access to their previous work once the examination has been completed. It is always advisable to let learners make backup copies of their work on a regular basis. You have to prevent learners from having access to their normal files during an examination to prevent learners from trying to use old documents as reference during the examination.

### 10.3.3  Planning and running a final practical examination

The Department of Basic Education provides a policy document containing instructions on the measures to be taken before and during the final, practical examination for IT and CAT. See to it that you follow the instructions carefully.

There are two phases to these measures one should be aware of:

1.  Computer laboratory certification
2.  Invigilation during examination

It is of the utmost importance that an IT or CAT teacher prepares the computer laboratory for the examination properly. The teacher and the learners are under immense pressure during examinations since there are so many things that can go wrong, for example failure of equipment or power. Proper planning (which includes knowing what the procedures to follow in case of an event such as a power failure) will help the teacher to make informed decisions and prevent added stress. Teachers should study the DBE's policy document thoroughly, and talk to other, more experienced teachers who have already conducted an examination since they will be able to provide useful guidelines and advice.

## ACTIVITY 10.6

**Create a checklist for each of the phases of preparing for the final examination that can be used by an IT or CAT teacher to ensure that all the requirements for preparing and conducting the final, practical examination are met. Group the checklist activities according to a timeline, for example tasks to be completed in January/February of the year the examination takes place, three months before the time, two weeks before the time, two days before the time, etc. You need to decide on the time intervals yourself, based on the tasks as specified in the policy document.**

## 10.4  CONCLUSION

In this chapter, some advice was provided on ergonomic and practical aspects to take into consideration when creating a computer laboratory, the maintenance of a computer laboratory, as well as ways to create a professional classroom atmosphere. You will find that a well-maintained computer laboratory, where learners take part in the creation of the classroom atmosphere, contributes to a culture of learning.

# ASSIGNMENT 10

**Conduct an interview with a teacher currently teaching IT or CAT at a school. Create a report that includes the following:**

**10.1** Name, contact details and signature of the teacher.

**Computer laboratory layout**

**10.2** A diagram of the layout of the computer laboratory.

**10.3** What are the advantages and disadvantages of this layout, according to you and according to the teacher?

**10.4** The hardware they use, for example, the type of computer, colour printer, scanner, etc.

**10.5** The software they have installed, for example, operating software, application software etc.

**10.6** What would the teacher want to change in the computer laboratory (this can include the layout, additional equipment, upgraded computers, etc.).

**Management of the computer laboratory**

**10.7** What tasks does the teacher need to perform to manage and maintain equipment in the computer laboratory? What types of licencing agreements are relevant to the software used in the computer laboratory (e.g. open source, special agreements for education, software the school obtained, etc.)?

**Management of a PAT**

**10.8** Summarise the management of the Practical Assessment Tasks (PAT) of the learners. The summary should include a description of the purpose of the PAT, as well as the way it should be managed and assessed. Attach all official documentation teachers should hand out to learners, as well as all rubrics used for assessment.

# ASSIGNMENT 10 *(continued)*

**Conduct an interview with a teacher currently teaching IT or CAT at a school. Create a report that includes the following:**

**Management of the final practical examination for Grade 12 learners**

**10.9** What does the teacher need to do (hardware and software) to prepare for the final practical examination?

**10.10** Provide a description of the way the examination is conducted. What do the learners receive, do they make printouts, what will be used to assess the learners, etc.

**10.11** Obtain copies of official documentation provided by the provincial department regarding the preparation and conduct of the practical examination.

**10.12** What measures does the teacher take to prevent learners from copying one another's work during the final practical examination?

**10.13** If the number of students who need to sit for the examination is more than the number of computers available, they need to write during two sessions. How does the teacher ensure that the learners writing in the second group cannot gain access to the files of the first group?

## REFERENCES

Borhany, T., Shahid, E., Siddique, W.A. and Ali, H. 2018. Musculoskeletal problems in frequent computer and internet users. *Journal of Family Medicine and Primary Care*, 7(2):337-339. https://doi.org/10.4103/jfmpc.jfmpc_326_17

Choudhary, M.S.B., Choudary, A.B., Jamal, S., Kumar, R. and Jamal, S. 2020. The impact of ergonomics on children studying online during COVID-10 Lockdown. *Journal of Advances in Sports and Physical Education*, 3(8):117-120. https://doi.org/10.36348/jaspe.2020.v03i08.001 (Accessed: 25 November 2021).

Harisinghani, M.G., Blake, M.A., Saksen, M., Hahn, P.F., Gervais, D., Zalis, M., Da Silva Dias Fernandes, L. and Mueller, P.R. 2004. Importance and effects of altered workplace ergonomics in modern radiology suites. *Radiographics*, 24:615-627. https://doi.org/10.1148/rg.242035089

Mayo Clinic, 2021. Office ergonomics: Your how-to guide. Healthy Lifestyle Adult health. https://mayocl.in/37XVTRz (Accessed: 29 November 2021).

Middlesworth, M. 2021. Office Ergonomics: How to select an duse and ergonomic keyboard. ErgoPlus. https://bit.ly/3OeZ48i

# CHAPTER 11

# Teaching of keyboarding in the IT/CAT laboratory

## Elsie Lubbe

# OBJECTIVES

**After completing this chapter, you will be able to:**

- *explain the value of keyboarding to IT/CAT learners;*

- *evaluate the different approaches and methods that could be followed in teaching touch-typing;*

- *explain the value of the correct posture in front of the computer, the hand position on the keyboard, and proper keyboarding technique during the mastering of touch-typing;*

- *complete a list of guidelines the teacher should keep in mind while teaching keyboarding skills;*

- *compare direct keyboarding instruction with the use of keyboard software to teach keyboarding; and*

- *state your own opinion on the future of keyboarding.*

## 11.1   INTRODUCTION

Many individuals use a computer-like keyboard to key in data and therefore keyboarding can be seen as the penmanship of the 21st century. Keyboarding is an enabling skill that makes it possible for computer users to use the computer more efficiently. In practice, various typing techniques are used to key in data. The most frequently-used techniques are touch-typing, hunt-and-peck, buffering and thumbing. Thumbing is mostly used to key in data on cellular telephones. Although various techniques could be used, the most appropriate technique recommended is touch-typing.

Touch-typing implies the memorisation of the location of the 26 alphabet letters on the keyboard, the placing of the hands on the home row (left hand = **asdf**, and right hand = **jkl;**) and the typing of data without looking down on the hands to locate the keys. This is possible because the location of the alphabet keys and the distance from the home row keys to the top and bottom row keys are memorised in the muscle memory (Işeri and Ekşioğlu 2015:127). This technique, also referred to as the all-fingers-no-eyes technique (Russon and Wanous 1973:13), was already used since 1878 by Frank McGurren (Russon and Wanous 1973:10). The hunt-and-peck method, on the other hand, is a typing method by which computer users visually search for the letter on the keyboard while they are typing text. Most of the time, one or two fingers are used to type the letters on the keyboard. This occurs because there was no kinesthetic learning of the location of the alphabet keys on the keyboard. The hunt-and-peck and buffering methods result in slow keyboarding speeds, because it requires conscious attention to what the fingers are doing. The use of these techniques have a negative influence on the productivity of computer users.

The learning of keyboarding is often neglected in South Africa even though the use of technology is on the increase and most office workers use computers on a daily basis at office or at home. This statement is supported by the fact that only limited time is scheduled in the South African education policy documents for the teaching of keyboarding skills (Department of Education [DOE] 2011:19). The IT/CAT teacher has a role to play in the promotion of keyboarding for learners and future money earners in South Africa. In order to use this time efficiently, it is essential that the IT/CAT teacher knows exactly how to assist learners in the acquisition of the correct keyboarding skills. The focus of this chapter is on ensuring that future teachers know what it entails to teach touch-typing to computer users so that the learners will be able to apply this skill in the world of work.

## 11.2   KEYBOARDING SKILLS AS FINE MOTOR AND ENABLING SKILL FOR IT/CAT LEARNERS

In the literature, there are various perceptions of keyboarding as a skill. Keyboarding, with specific reference to the touch-typing technique, is considered a fine motor skill. A fine motor skill is seen as a skill where smaller muscle movements are responsible for holding and manipulating small objects using hands and fingers (Choi, Leech, Tager-Flusberg and Nelson 2018) or which require close eye-hand coordination (Nayak 2015). Since fingers and hands are involved in entering text, keyboarding can first be considered a fine motor skill. According to Gaul and Issartel (2016), poor mastering of fine motor skills can cause increased anxiety, distress in academic achievement and poor self-esteem. It is, therefore, important to make sure that learners reach a certain proficiency level before this skill is used as a writing tool. In practice, the touch-typing technique as a keyboarding skill can be used to type text from a manuscript, or it can be used to compile a report. In this context, keyboarding can also be referred to as (a) a sensory-motor skill (Russon and Wanous 1973:120), and (b) a perceptual-motor skill. Keyboarding as a sensory-motor skill (feel and do) is linked to copy typing, because the learners just use the keyboard to re-type the text they are reading (Russon and Wanous 1973:69, 120). Keyboarding is also a perceptual-motor skill because the learner has to formulate sentences (think and do) when they have to type a report (Russon and Wanous 1973:120).

The mastery of the touch-typing technique has certain advantages for the IT and the CAT learner. Learners who have IT as a school subject use a typewriter-like keyboard, namely the QWERTY keyboard, to input information as they write programs in Delphi or Java. When IT learners have mastered keyboarding, they will be able to concentrate on programming rather than on looking for the alphabet keys when they are programming. CAT learners, on the other hand, also need the skill to use MS Word and the other MS Office packages efficiently. Proper keyboarding allows learners to concentrate on the task (creating a table/typing a paragraph), rather than on the process of locating letters on the keyboard. When CAT learners have mastered the touch-typing technique, they will be able to concentrate on applying different functions of application packages during the creation of documents, rather than on the task of entering data. This skill not only has value for the IT and CAT learner at school, but also has further value for those who enter the world of work after the completion of Grade 12, because in the world of work you need advanced typing skills (at least 60 wpm and higher) to be hired for office positions (Ober 2011). It is, therefore, important that learners master this skill as soon as possible.

## 11.3   SKILL MASTERING STAGES

In the literature, there are various opinions about how many stages are involved in skill mastering. In this chapter, the focus will be on the phases identified by Gillmon (1991:10). The three stages identified are the cognitive stage, the associative stage, and the autonomous stage. These stages relate to the attentional demands when learning a skill and the amount of time one needs to practise the skill in order to become skilful (Shaw 2021). It is important to keep in mind that these three stages must not be seen as separate stages when teaching keyboarding. There should be a continuous flow of mastering from one stage to the next.

In the **cognitive stage**, the focus is on what must be done in order to master the touch-typing technique. In this stage, self-talk plays an important role (Shaw 2021). Typical questions the learners should ask in this stage are: How must I sit in front of the computer keyboard? On which keys must I place my fingers before I start to type? Which finger must I use to type which alphabet letter? During this stage, the learner will sometimes look at their hands to just make sure about the location of the alphabet letter on the keyboard. The execution of the skill is slow and the learners are typing letter-for-letter.

Next is the **associative stage**. Here, the focus moves from the *what* to do knowledge (declarative knowledge) to the *how* to do (procedural knowledge) knowledge (Shaw 2021). Practically, this means that in the cognitive phase the learner has to memorise the location of the alphabet letters on the keyboard and which finger to use to type which alphabet key. The movement from one key to another should deliberately be practised in the cognitive phase to save the distance from one to the other key in the muscle memory. In the associative phase, the drilling of the location and correct posture take place to gradually reduce the thinking time required between locating and striking individual keys, and to make technique errors due to the wrong sitting position. In the associative phase, the learner should be able to type words more fluently than in the cognitive phase.

In the final, **autonomous stage**, the skill is almost mastered and typing of the alphabet should be done without thinking. The learners should be able to type words, sentences and paragraphs while doing copy typing or conceptual typing, without looking at their hands.

## 11.4  HOW TO TEACH KEYBOARDING SKILLS

The expected outcome of teaching keyboarding skills is to develop a touch-typing skill which will enable an individual to enter alphabetical, numerical and other information at a speed that is faster than handwriting. It is essential that a teacher who is teaching keyboarding skills must know how to type, must know how the learning of a skill takes place, and must be able to share his/her knowledge.

There are various approaches (Russon and Wanous 1973:151) a teacher could follow while teaching keyboarding to learners. The approach the teacher follows has an influence on the keyboarding pedagogy because it reflects the mindset of the teacher about the role of accuracy, speed and technique as criteria for skill mastering. After the teacher has decided on an approach, the teacher must also decide on a method that will be used to select the sequence in which the alphabet keys will be learned in every lesson. The next section discusses the different approaches.

### 11.4.1  Different approaches

There are three approaches to teach keyboarding skills, namely the accuracy-first, the speed-first, and the technique-with-appropriate-speed approach (DOE 2005; Russon and Wanous 1973). Teachers who follow the accuracy-first approach for the teaching of keyboarding have an accuracy mindset. An accuracy mindset means that the teacher believes that if the learner takes care of accuracy, speed will take care of itself. This approach is not recommended, because if accuracy is emphasised at the beginning of keyboarding lessons, students will use a "stop-and-look" approach when memorising the keyboard, rather than a fluent approach to master the keyboard.

Teachers using the speed-first approach pay less attention to accuracy during the teaching of keyboarding skills, and incorporate systematic drills for speed improvement during keyboarding instruction (DOE 2005; Russon and Wanous 1973:154). One of the limitations of this approach is that it limits relaxation and building of good technique. Although the goal of keyboarding instruction is to deliver fast and accurate keyboarders, the end goal must not become the end itself. Another problem with this approach is that teachers emphasise speed too soon. As a result, technique does not develop well enough to accomplish the end goal of keyboarding (DOE 2005).

In conclusion, both the accuracy-first approach and the speed-first approach have limitations when teaching keyboarding skills. Accuracy and speed are essential to deliver "perfect" copy, but in order to achieve that the keyboard instructor first has to focus on technique (DOE 2005).

The technique-with-appropriate-speed approach is the best approach to follow for the following reasons. This approach focuses on the correct sitting position in front of the computer, the placement of the hands on the keyboard, the allocation of certain keys to certain fingers, and quick, sharp, rhythmic keystroking. All the above-mentioned factors contribute to a higher typing speed and better control of the keyboard. The focus of this approach is to learn the correct finger movement first and to develop a feel for keying data. The errors made during the beginning phase of keyboard mastering are of secondary importance. The only errors that should receive attention are the errors that could be linked to improper technique, such as the exchange of letters typed with the same finger of opposite hands, improper use of the ENTER key or Space bar, or improper keystrokes to the top or bottom row of the keyboard.

To improve learners' touch-typing technique, the teacher can use a technique evaluation rubric to evaluate individual learner's progress and give feedback to them. See Table 11.1.

*Table 11.1   Technique evaluation rubric*

| CRITERIA | DATE | YES | NO |
|---|---|---|---|
| Position of the keyboard on the table | | | |
| Keyboard level with the front of the table | | | |
| Maintain proper distance from the keyboard | | | |
| Sitting position in front of the keyboard | | | |
| Body centred in front of the keyboard (Belly button in line with the 'b'-key) | | | |
| Body erect and relaxed | | | |
| Eyes focused on the book or screen | | | |
| Elbows hanging naturally near the sides of the body (touching the body slightly) | | | |
| Forearms almost parallel with the slant of the keyboard | | | |
| Wrists low, just above the frame of the keyboard | | | |
| Feet flat on the ground (together or one in front of the other) | | | |
| Back straight and supported by the chair | | | |
| Stroking | | | |
| Fingers curved and upright lightly on the home keys | | | |
| Quick, sharp, even keystrokes (ballistic movement) | | | |
| Quick reaches to the top and bottom row keys | | | |
| Minimal hand movement while typing | | | |

| CRITERIA | DATE | YES | NO |
|---|---|---|---|
| Always use the little fingers or index fingers as placeholders | | | |
| Keep right hand index finger on the 'j'-key when striking the ENTER key | | | |
| Mindset | | | |
| Is enthusiastic about mastering the skill | | | |
| Has a positive attitude about advice, which could lead to improvement | | | |
| Is alert but shows no evidence of tenseness in shoulders, arms and hands | | | |

(Department of Education 2005:31; Eksteen and Allen 1982)

With the technique-with-appropriate-speed approach, relative speed of keystroking is part of the technique, and errors are of secondary importance because it is believed that most of the errors made during the first keyboarding lessons would disappear due to the development of proper technique (DOE 2005). The technique-with-appropriate-speed approach is the most appropriate when teaching keyboarding because it focuses firstly on technique, which is seen as the key to successful keyboarding.

# ACTIVITY 11.1

1.  **Design a poster for use in your IT/CAT laboratory on which you display the proper sitting position in front of a computer.**

2.  **Design a chart which the learners could use to familiarise them with which fingers need to type which keys.**

## 11.4.2    Methods for introducing the keyboard

Keyboarding is a complex skill. When teaching keyboarding, the IT/CAT teacher must remember that the correct keystroke consists of many participatory skills, for example, selecting the correct finger to type the key, moving the finger in the right direction to strike the key at a certain speed, releasing the key, moving to the next key, or moving back to the home row. Therefore, learners cannot be expected to master the skill on their own without proper guidelines and knowledge of what this skill mastering entails. Teachers need to motivate learners to improve their keyboarding technique and speed, and also to constantly monitor if they are using the correct technique. Teachers can use various methods to teach learners keyboarding skills, for example, the key-banks, the first-finger-first, and the skip-around method (Abdullahi 2010; Preminger, Weiss and Weintraub 2004). These methods are linked to the sequence of the alphabet letters presented to the learners in each lesson. These three methods will be discussed in the following sections.

### 11.4.2.1 Home row/key-banks method

Teachers who use this method first teach the home row (**asdf jkl;**), then the third row/top row (**qwertyuiop**), followed by the first/bottom row (**zxcvbnm**). The greatest limitation of this method is that there is only one vowel in the home row, making it difficult to practise words and sentences with only the keys in the home row. Typing words and sentences motivates learners and allows for interesting exercises (Abdullahi 2010; Russon and Wanous 1973) and, therefore, it is important that vowels form part of the very first lessons.

### 11.4.2.2 Strong/first-finger-first method

The strong/first-finger-first method or vertical method implies that all the keys allocated to the strong fingers (index fingers and middle fingers) are presented first (Abdullahi 2010; DOE 2005). Although this method sounds like a good idea, learners who were taught keyboarding with this method sometimes type an 'f'-key instead of a 'j'-key, or a 'g'-key instead of an 'h'-key. This is because these keys are all typed with strong fingers and therefore, according to this method, they are learned in the same keyboarding session, causing learners to become confused (Russon and Wanous 1973:170) about the location of the keys.

Another limitation of this method is that the stronger fingers get more exercise than the other fingers, because the keys of the first lessons are allocated to the strong fingers and too little time is spent on the weaker fingers that actually need more exercise. Due to its limitations, this method is not strongly recommended for the instruction of keyboarding (Russon and Wanous 1973).

### 11.4.2.3 Skip-around method

The skip-around method is a combination of the home row method and the first-finger-first method (Russon and Wanous 1973:171). This method is recommended most often to use for the teaching of keyboarding.

In a typical first keyboarding lesson, using the skip-around method, the teacher would first focus the attention of the learners on the correct posture in front of the keyboard. Secondly, the teacher would show the learners a diagram of the QWERTY keyboard on which the home row (left hand = **asdf**, and right hand = **jkl;**) is indicated. Thirdly, the teacher would either show the learners a picture of correct placement of the left and right hand on the keyboard or demonstrate the hand placement. Fourthly, the teacher would demonstrate proper keystroking of the keys. The teacher may also use a video to show the learners what is meant by proper keystroking. The reason learners look on their hands while typing is because they are not sure of the location of the keys. Therefore, let the learners look at the keyboard the first time a new key is introduced to them. Tell them to softly say the name of the key while they execute the keystroke. When they know the location of the key on the keyboard they will not look at their hands after they have typed the key a few times during the lesson. During the first lessons using the skip-around method, a lot of time is also allocated to the home row. The time spent on these lessons depends on the progress of the learners. After the learners are able to type the letters of the home row without thinking (automaticity- final stage of skill mastering), the other keys of the alphabet are presented randomly but according to the frequency they are used in a specific language. This method also starts by teaching the home row first. As with the key-banks method, this method has the advantage that the teacher can decide in which sequence the letters of the rest of the alphabet must be taught. The following guidelines are applicable to the skip-around method for the introduction of the rest of the keys on the keyboard:

- Every lesson (except for the lesson about the home row) should start with a warm-up. The warm-up is normally a revision of the keys learned in the previous lesson. Spend between three and five minutes on this.

- The second part of the lesson should focus on the new keys. A maximum of three keys should be presented in a lesson, except for the first lesson in which the home row is learned. Always focus the attention of the learner on the association stretching which is linked to a home row key. For example, if the new key is the letter 'e' then the association stretching is '**ded**'. The didactical principle applied here is to always work from the known to the unknown. Spend between three and five minutes on this.

- The third part of the lesson should be a drill exercise. In this part of the lesson, the learners should be given time to practise the new keys, together with the keys of the previous lessons. Spend between three and five minutes on this.

- The fourth part of the lesson should be used for typing words which are built with all the keys the learners have already learned. Spend between five and eight minutes on this.

- The fifth part of the lesson should be used for the typing of short sentences, only using the letters the learners have already learned.

- Remember, alphabet keys which should be typed with the same finger but with different hands (for example, left hand point finger ['t'-key] and right hand point finger ['y'-key]), should not be presented in one lesson. This rule does not apply to learning the home row because according to this method keyboarding instruction must start at the home row; thereafter the teacher must randomly select keys from the top and bottom row after the learners have learned the location of the various keys in the home row.

The above-mentioned guidelines could be used for all the keyboarding lessons until the learners have learned all the alphabet keys.

To learn the numerical keys, the teacher could use the same didactical principles or the learners could use the numerical pad on the right hand side of the keyboard to type the numbers.

The skip-around method is the most recommended method for teaching keyboarding, because it permits the typing of short words and phrases in the first few lessons. The fact that learners can type words and sentences in the initial phase of mastering the skill motivates them. Another great advantage of this method is the fact that it avoids certain common error traps like typing an 'e' instead of an 'i' (Russon and Wanous 1973:171). The last advantage is that the teacher can decide which keys to teach first. Therefore, the sequence of letter presentation for English- and Afrikaans-speaking learners could differ because the most frequent letters used in English are not the same as those in Afrikaans. The sequence of letter integration in the various lessons determines at which stage the learners will be able to type words and sentences.

## 11.4.3   Guidelines for teachers

The IT/CAT teacher should keep the following guidelines in mind during the planning of keyboarding exercises.

- Always make sure that the learners have mastered the keys of the previous lesson before you move on to the next lesson. Keyboarding is a cumulative skill and therefore skills mastered in previous lessons are essential for success in the next lesson.

- Make sure that the combination of keys in exercises is meaningful to the learner. Typing rows of '**fff**' is boring for the learners and does not stimulate them to concentrate while they are learning the new key. Rather use exercises with different combinations of '**f**'-keys", for example '**ff fff f ff fff f**', which is more meaningful because the learners must concentrate to type the correct sequence. It helps with the development of the Space bar technique, and it promotes rhythm while typing the keys.

- Do not aim to let learners master the whole alphabet in one or two class sessions. To master a skill takes time. Distribute the practice sessions so that learners have time to master each key before they learn new keys.

- Always set attainable goals for the learners. Make sure that most of the learners are able to complete the keyboarding exercise in class time by limiting the number of repetitions of each line to a manageable number per session.

- Create a positive learning climate by displaying subject-related posters on the walls of the laboratory.

- Never over-penalise learners for technique errors they make in the class while mastering keyboarding.

- Do your planning in such a way that there is enough time for practising, reviewing and relearning of keys.

- Use modelling to demonstrate how to sit in front of the computer, how to hold the hands, how to curve the fingers on the keyboard, and how to strike the different keys during keyboard lessons. Learners use imitation to learn skills. Make sure the demonstrations are perfect.

- The only way the IT/CAT teacher can evaluate the technique and sitting position of the learners is by walking through the class while the learners are typing. During these sessions, technique evaluation rubrics could be completed and given to learners for them to see which aspect of their technique or sitting position needs refining.

- Keep criticism to a minimum and try to limit learner self-criticism because the free-flowing smoothness of performing a skill (automaticity – typing without thinking about the location of the key) does not develop in a stressful atmosphere.

# ACTIVITY 11.2

1. There are various methods a teacher could use when teaching touch-typing. Critically evaluate the use of the Diana King and Almena methods in the CAT classroom. Motivate why you would use or not use these methods when teaching keyboarding skills.

2. Compile a list in which you indicate all the association stretches of each finger from the home row to the top row and the bottom row, for example 'ftf', 'dcd' etcetera.

3. Compile a lesson plan for the first keyboarding lesson. Indicate clearly what you are going to do in each of the three lesson phases (introduction, teaching, consolidating).

4. Design a slideshow that you can use in your first keyboarding lesson. Use the following guidelines for the slideshow:

| | |
|---|---|
| Slide 1 | Lesson theme |
| Slide 2 | Lesson objectives |
| Slide 3 | Correct posture in front of the computer and key stroking |
| Slide 4 | Layout of the QWERTY keyboard and division of keys between the left and right hands |
| Slide 5 | The home row |

## 11.5 THE ROLE OF KEYBOARD SOFTWARE

There are different opinions on the use of software to instruct keyboarding (Fleming 2002). Some individuals are of opinion that direct instruction has proven to be the most effective way to introduce the keyboard and teach correct typing techniques, while other individuals are in favour of the use of software packages to learn keyboarding.

The use of computer software to complement instruction given by a teacher or facilitator may seem like a good idea, but self-teaching packages or packages that emphasise game techniques are not recommended for instruction of touch techniques (DOE 2005; Fleming 2002). The main reason is that these programs can contribute to poor keyboarding skills because typing tutorials cannot comment on the incorrect sitting position in front of the computer or improper techniques and could violate psychomotor skill development (Erthal 2004).

When a teacher decides to buy software packages to teach keyboarding instead of using one of the above methods, he/she has to take a number of aspects into consideration before the school spends money on keyboarding software, for example:

▸ Does the sequence in which the software package introduces the keys on the keyboard and the compilation of the exercises conform to the psychological principles of keyboarding mastering, the learning approach of the teacher, and available textbooks on the market?

▸ Is there any visual material included in the package, which demonstrates the correct posture, fingering and technique?

▸ Does the software check errors according to the application of correct technique or does it only compare it with the text the learner should type – thus, focusing on accuracy rather than on technique.

When deciding to rather make use of keyboarding software instead of the traditional keyboarding instruction method, one has to bear in mind that most of the software packages are based on a behaviourist approach, meaning that, in order to move on to the next level in the program, the learner is required to demonstrate accuracy. Acquiring accuracy (text without errors) and speed as a requirement to move on to the next lesson is in contradiction with the technique-with-appropriate-speed-approach used for teaching keyboarding (Fleming 2002).

## 11.6   THE FUTURE OF THE QWERTY KEYBOARD AND TOUCH-TYPING

Effective typing speed is a prerequisite for many jobs. Average writing speed is approximately 12 to 22 words per minute (wpm). According to Rohs (2010/2011), effective typing speed should be at least three to four times your handwriting speed. According to Kumar, Tewari, Horrigan, Kam, Metze and Canny (2011), speech is the easiest and most common way for people to communicate. It is faster than typing on a keypad and more expressive than clicking on a menu item. Due to speech recognition software packages' inability to accurately recognise text in noisy environments (such as open-plan offices) and other limitations, speech recognition has not yet succeeded in dethroning the QWERTY keyboard. Therefore, touch-typing remains the most general input method. It is the privilege of each computer user to decide if he/she thinks that voice recognition is going to dethrone the QWERTY keyboard and make touch-typing an unnecessary skill in future.

Other technological developments such as the stylus or digital pen and the Kitty Keyboard-Independent Touch-Typing glove are input devices that can also be used by computer users instead of the keyboard. However, just as speech recognition packages have limitations, these input devices also have disadvantages, making the keyboard a more popular choice for input. Looking at the developments in virtual QWERTY keyboards (Kim, Dai, Cao, Picciotto, Tan and Tan 2012; Findlater and Wobbrock 2012), and despite spectacular advances in technology, it is the opinion of the author that the QWERTY keyboard and touch-typing are going to be with us for a while yet.

## 11.7   CONCLUSION

Keyboarding is one of the single most important "computer" skills a child could learn at school. To be able to use the computer keyboard effectively and efficiently, one has to learn the proper technique. Proper technique includes good posture in front of the computer, correct hand placement, and proper keystroking (Quackenbush 2012; Abdullahi 2010). Various approaches and methods could be followed for keyboarding instruction. Although some are more preferable than others, it remains the choice of the teacher. It is advisable that the opportunity is created that learners master the touch-typing skill as soon as they start to use a keyboard to key in data for formal documents, because it might be difficult to unlearn (Giulioni 2018) the hunt-and-peck method or other keyboarding techniques which do not contribute to higher productivity when a keyboard is used as a writing tool.

# ASSIGNMENT 11

**Apply the knowledge you have gained in this chapter to compile a manual teachers could use to teach learners touch-typing on the QWERTY keyboard. It must consist of 15 lessons. Three of the lessons must be revision lessons. Be creative and compile your own exercises.**

**11.1**   Design a front page. You are the author.

**11.2**   Remember to type a table of contents and list of references.

**11.3**   Attach a chart of the QWERTY keyboard layout.

**11.4**   Attach a list of self-teaching keyboarding programs/keyboarding software packages.

**11.5**   Font type – Arial, font size 14

**11.6**   Line spacing: 1.5; Margins: 3.17 left, right, justified.

**11.7**   Provide each lesson with suitable headings.

## REFERENCES

Abdullahi, I. 2010. An approach to keyboarding skills: A panacea for speed and accuracy. *Wilolud Journals. Continental Journal of Arts and Humanities*, 2:1-6. https://bit.ly/3uKKYE2 (Accessed: 25 November 2021).

Choi, C., Leech, K.A., Tager-Flusberg, H. and Nelson, C.A. 2018. Development of fine motor skills is associated with expressive language outcomes in infants at high and low risk for autism spectrum disorder. *Journal of Neurodevelopmental Disorders*, 10(1):14. https://doi.org/10.1186/s11689-018-9231-3

DOE (Department of Education) see South Africa. Department of Education.

Eksteen, F.R.L.N. and Allen, V.L. 1982. *Tik vir beginners. Standerd 7.* Goodwood: Nasou Beperk.

Erthal, M. 2004. Who should teach keyboarding and when should it be taught? https://bit.ly/380agFm (Accessed: 29 November 2021).

Findlater, L. and Wobbrock, J.O. 2012. Personalized input: Improving ten-finger touchscreen typing through automatic adaption. *Proceedings of the SIGCHI Conference on Human Factors in Computing Systems*, 5-10 May, Austin, Texas. https://bit.ly/36oNcj6 (Accessed: 25 November 2021). https://doi.org/10.1145/2207676.2208520

Fleming, S. 2002. When and how should keyboarding be taught in elementary school? https://bit.ly/3vjTFnW (Accessed: 24 November 2021).

Gaul, D. and Issartel, I. 2016. Fine motor skill proficiency in typically developing children: On or off the maturation track? *Human Movement Science*, 46:78-85. https://bit.ly/3xtFpLN (Accessed: 24 November 2021). https://doi.org/10.1016/j.humov.2015.12.011

Gillmon, E. 1991. Keyboard proficiency: An essential skill in a technological age. https://bit.ly/3jHGabZ (Accessed: 16 November 2021).

Giulioni, J.W. 2018. Unlearning: The other side of skills/knowledge acquisition. https://bit.ly/3OfP9PR (Accesssed: 29 November 2021).

Işeri, A. and Eksioğlu, M. 2015. Estimation of digraph costs for keyboard layout optimization. *International Journal of Industrial Ergonomics*, 48:127-138. https://doi.org/10.1016/j.ergon.2015.04.006 (Accessed: 15 November 2021).

Kim, J.R., Dai, X., Cao, X., Picciotto, C., Tan, D. and Tan, H.Z. 2012. A masking study of key-click feedback signals on a virtual keyboard. (In P. Isokosk and J. Springare, eds. *Haptics: Perception, Devices, Mobility, and Communication.* EuroHaptics 2012. Lecture Notes in Computer Science, vol 7282. Springer, Berlin, Heidelberg.) https://doi.org/10.1007/978-3-642-31401-8_23 (Accessed: 25 November 2021).

Kumar, A., Tewari, A., Horrigan, S., Kam, M., Metze, F. and Canny, F. 2011. Rethinking speech recognition on mobile devices. (In *IUI4DR: Proceedings of the 2011 International Conference on Intelligent User Interfaces*, 13 February, California, USA.) https://bit.ly/3jN31TL (Accessed: 25 November 2021).

Nayak, A.K. 2015. Effect of hand-eye coordination on motor coordinative ability of tribal adolescents. *International Journal of Physical Education, Sports and Health*, 2(2):328-330. https://bit.ly/3jQ4pVr (Accessed: 24 November 2021).

Ober, S. 2011. Typing speed requirements for administrative positions. An action-research project. https://bit.ly/3xxIDhE (Accessed: 25 November 2021).

Preminger, F., Weiss, P.L. and Weintraub, N. 2004. Ph.D. dissertation, *Hadassah and The American Journal of Occupational Therapy*, 58(2). https://doi.org/10.5014/ajot.58.2.193

Quackenbush, G. n.d. Computer devices leaving art of touch typing behind. https://bit.ly/3jLMO1c

Rohs, M. 2010/2011. Mobile input and output technologies. Mensch-Maschine-Interaktion 2, WS 2010/2011. https://bit.ly/3jHM5xJ (Accessed: 27 November 2021).

Russon, A.R. and Wanous, S.J. 1973. *Philosohy and pshycology of teaching type writing.* Cincinnati, OH: South-Western Publishing Co.

Shaw, W. 2021. The three stages of learning – cognitive, associative and autonomous. https://bit.ly/380i61K (Accessed: 11 November 2021).

South Africa. Department of Education. 2011. Curriculum assessment policy statement. http://www.education.gov.za (Accessed: 16 November 2021).

Virginia Department of Education. 2005. *Keyboarding Methodology Instructional Guide for Teachers and Administrators.* Developed by Business Education Centre, California State Polytechnic University and the CTE Resource Centre for Office of Career and Technical Education Services. Richmond, VA: Department of Education.

## Roxanne Bailey

Dr Roxanne Bailey is a senior lecturer in the Computer Science Education subject group at the Faculty of Education, North-West University. She is also the leader of the subarea 'Cooperative learning to enhance Self-Directed Learning', within the Research Unit Self-Directed Learning. Her main research focus is on the promotion of self-directed learning through the implementation of cooperative learning. She has received several research grants and is currently involved in three research projects set at investigating technology-supported cooperative learning. Roxanne was also selected as one of three research fellows to complete a 4-month fellowship under the guidance of the UNESCO Chair for Personalised and Adaptive Distance Education. She has published at national and international levels, and acts as a supervisor for postgraduate students.


ORCID: 0000-0001-5326-274X                    Email: roxanne.bailey@nwu.ac.za

## Betty Breed

Prof Betty Breed was an associate professor in the subject group Computer Science Education in the Faculty of Education at the Potchefstroom Campus of the North-West University (NWU). Prior to her involvement at NWU, she was a teacher in Computer Studies/Information Technology at secondary school level. Since 2001, she has been involved in the training of IT/CAT teachers, specialising in Information Technology methodology. Her main research focus is the effective use of cooperative learning and metacognitive strategies in the teaching and learning of Information Technology and Computer Applications Technology to promote self-directed learning among students and scholars, and to empower teachers in these subjects.


ORCID: 0000-0002-1127-4985                    Email: bettybreed25@gmail.com

## Leila Goosen

Prof Leila Goosen is a professor in the Department of Science and Technology Education at the Muckleneuk Campus (Pretoria) of the University of South Africa (UNISA). Prior to that, she was an associate professor in the School of Computing, College for Science, Engineering and Technology (CSET), also at UNISA. She has successfully completed supervision of more than 70 students at postgraduate level. Previously, she was a Deputy Director at the South African National Department of (Basic) Education. She has also been a lecturer of Information Technology (IT) and Computer Applications Technology (CAT) in the Department for Science, Mathematics and Technology Education in the Faculty of Education of the University of Pretoria. Her research interests include cooperative work in IT, effective teaching and learning of programming and teacher professional development.


ORCID: 0000-0003-4948-2699                    Email: goosel@unisa.ac.za

## Marietjie Havenga


Prof Marietjie Havenga is a professor in the School of Mathematics, Science and Technology Education in the Faculty of Education at North-West University. She is involved in lecturing courses to pre-service teachers at undergraduate level and the supervision of postgraduate students. She has published various articles, conference papers and chapters in research books. Her research interests are problem-based learning to enhance self-directed learning with specific reference to computer science education, engineering education and educational robotics.

ORCID: 0000-0003-1638-9834                    Email: marietjie.havenga@nwu.ac.za

## Elsie Lubbe


Dr Elsie Lubbe is a lecturer in the subject group Computer Science Education in the Faculty of Education at the Potchefstroom Campus of the North-West University. She has been involved in the training of CAT teachers, has published articles in various academic journals, presented papers at international conferences and has published numerous chapters in academic books. Her research interests include the role self-directed learning plays in teaching and learning in the Computer Applications Technology classroom, and in learning, unlearning and relearning keyboarding techniques related to the use of the QWERTY keyboard.

ORCID: 0000-0002-8614-9038                    Email: elsie.lubbe@nwu.ac.za

## Elsa Mentz


Prof Elsa Mentz is Research Director for the Research Unit Self-Directed Learning at the Faculty of Education of the North-West University. She is also a professor in Computer Science Education and her main research focus is the promotion of Self-Directed Learning through the implementation of cooperative learning. She is a National Research Foundation (NRF) C1-rated researcher and editor of several book publications. She received several research awards, including the 2020 Malcolm Knowles award for significant lifetime contributions to self-directed learning, and the 2020 Research medal of the Education Association of South Africa. She completed a number of funded research projects and has published at national and international levels. She also acts as supervisor for postgraduate students.

ORCID: 0000-0002-7267-080X                    Email: elsa.mentz@nwu.ac.za

## Carl Serfontein


Dr Carl Serfontein retired as a senior lecturer at the University of South Africa at the end of 2011. He has eight years' experience in training Information Technology and Computer Applications Technology teachers. His research focused on computer-integrated education, the application of learning theories and instructional principles in designing and developing IT and CAT learning events and the IT requirements of South Africa's national school curriculum.

Email: carl.serfontein@vodamail.co.za

## Sukie van Zyl

Dr Sukie van Zyl holds a PhD in Computer Science Education and joined the North-West University's Potchefstroom Campus in 2012. She is currently a senior lecturer in Computer Science Education and is mainly involved in research and training of Information Technology and Computer Applications Technology teachers. Her research is focused on applying cooperative learning to develop deeper self-directed learning in Computer Science Education. She initially completed a BSc (Hons) in Computer Science and worked in the programming industry before pursuing a career in education. She was an Information Technology teacher for 20 years and was also chief marker and moderator for the Grade 12 Information Technology question paper for most of her teaching career. She was also involved in writing text books for the subject Information Technology.

ORCID: 0000-0001-7070-2719                    Email: sukie.vanzyl@nwu.ac.za

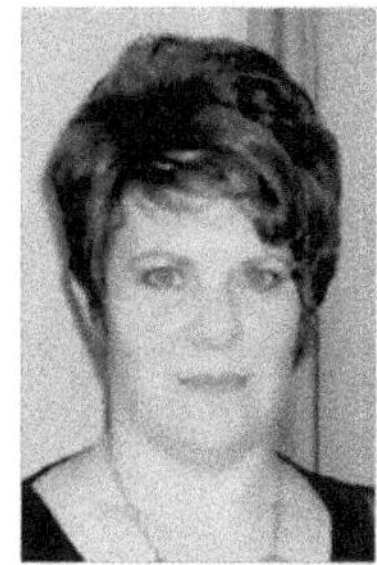

## Ulza Wassermann

Ulza Wassermann worked at the Tshwane University of Technology (TUT) for more than 16 years, teaching basic JAVA principles as part of the ICT extended programme. She has a special interest in developing lessons where students can apply their mathematical knowledge using computer applications and programming languages. Before joining the ICT Faculty, she was involved in the training of teachers for 12 years. She completed a BEd (Hons) degree in Computer-integrated Education at UP and an M(IT) degree at Nelson Mandela University on guidelines for and evaluation of the design of technology-supported lessons to teach basic programming principles to deaf and hard-of-hearing learners.

Email: ulza@telkomsa.net